1952

The Determinants
of Educational
Outcomes

The Determinants of Educational Outcomes

The Impact of Families, Peers, Teachers, and Schools

R. Gary Bridge
Charles M. Judd
Peter R. Moock

Ballinger Publishing Company • Cambridge, Massachusetts
A Subsidiary of Harper & Row, Publishers, Inc.

This book is printed on recycled paper.

International Standard Book Number: 0−88410−182−7

Library of Congress Catalog Card Number: 78−26467

Printed in the United States of America

Library of Congress Cataloging in Publication Data

Bridge, R   Gary.
  The determinants of educational outcomes.

  Bibliography: p.
  Includes index.
  1. School management and organization. 2. Education—
Economic aspects. 3. Intelligence levels. 4. Regression
analysis. 5. System analysis. I. Judd, Charles M., joint author.
II. Moock, Peter R., joint author. III. Title.
LB2806.B732   379′.15   78−26467
ISBN 0−88410−182−7

To Our Children—
Alastair, David, Jean, and Jennifer

Contents

List of Figures

List of Tables

List of Boxes

Preface

This book attempts to synthesize the findings of over fifteen years of input-output research in education. The literature in this area is growing rapidly and is improving in statistical precision, theoretical relevance, and practical value. Yet the literature on educational production is fragmented and often contradictory. Moreover, significant research in one discipline is often unknown to researchers in other disciplines. This situation is due, at least in part, to the way different disciplines phrase research questions, the variables that are assumed to be of interest, and the preferred statistical methods various disciplines bring to the study of educational achievement.

Our aim is to identify the inputs that seem to make a difference in educational achievement. We approach this task from the markedly different perspectives of economics, psychology, and sociology. The views presented in this book were forged in months of intense debate, and the final product represents consensus among the three authors. Hopefully, readers from the various disciplines will see in our synthesis an accurate representation of their discipline's viewpoint and will at the same time be enriched by alternative points of view.

This book was written with three groups of readers in mind: (a) school policymakers, at the local, state and federal levels, (b) students in courses that deal with the impact of schooling, and (c) researchers who use the input-output approach. We anticipated that the reading audience would have diverse interests and research training, and hence two strategies were followed in organizing the material. First, we began the book simply and with a minimum of statistical detail. It is hoped that the pace we maintained in this incremental strategy will be appropriate for most readers. Second, we provided opportunities at several points in the text for advanced readers to skip over introductory material such as basic statistics. No mathematical training other than elementary algebra is required, although readers with training in statistics and calculus will be at some advantage.

We are indebted to a number of people and organizations. Financial support for this project was provided in part by separate Young Faculty Awards from the Spencer Foundation to Bridge and Moock, and in part by the Board of Cooperative Educational Services (BOCES) of Westchester and Putman counties (New York). The latter support was particularly significant and timely, and we gratefully acknowledge the guidance, encouragement, and support of BOCES's Bruce Bothwell. We are also indebted, individually and collectively, to Morton Deutsch, David Kenny, Victor Levine, George W. Mayeske, Harold Noah, Tetsuo Okada, Daniel L. Rourke, Robert Shakotko, Charles Skoro, Robert L. Thorndike, and Richard Wolf. Their comments have surely improved the manuscript, but of course none of these people can be held responsible for any defects in the final product.

New York City	**R. Gary Bridge**
New York City	**Peter R. Moock**
Cambridge	**Charles M. Judd**

✳️ *Chapter 1*

Introduction

- Everyone "knows" that small classes are beneficial to children's learning, but exactly how much benefit do small classes provide? Is there a difference between twenty and twenty-five students? Twenty-five and thirty? Thirty and thirty-five? Exactly what is the optimal pupil-teacher ratio, and is it the same for all kinds of children? Do some kinds of children suffer more from large classes?

- What is it that makes teachers effective? Are teachers with graduate degrees more effective than teachers with only bachelors degrees? Are teachers with B.A.s really more effective than "paraprofessionals?"

- How much supervision should teachers receive? Is there an optimal ratio of administrators to teachers?

- How much impact does per pupil expenditure have on student achievement? The money that schools spend on children varies widely from district to district because school expenditures are tied to the wealth of the local tax district. Since the Serrano decision,[1] there has been a clamor for legislation to equalize the expenditures of rich and poor school districts. Is there conclusive

1. In this California case (*Serrano* v. *Priest*, 1971), the courts held that the public school finance system, which relies heavily upon local taxes, was unconstitutional because wide variations in local tax bases led to wide variations in the amounts spent on children's schooling in different districts. See Pincus (1977) for a summary of the history of this case and resulting changes in California public school finance.

evidence, however, that the amount schools spend really makes a difference in student performance?

- When should children begin school? Does kindergarten make a difference in how much children learn in the long run, or can it be eliminated as has been proposed in some districts?

- How much can schools by themselves do to raise achievement, particularly when school achievement may not be reinforced in the home. Clearly children begin school showing large and predictable differences in initial learning, and they finish their formal schooling showing even larger differences in achievement. How much of these differences is due to family background? How much is due to the schools? How much is due to the influence of peers?

In the last decade, questions like these have been addressed in a number of empirical studies of schooling effectiveness, and the results of these studies have had a discernible impact on American schools. Simply stated, the idea of these studies is to identify what makes a difference in education, and then apply cost information in order to decide the best way to spend scarce schooling dollars.

Allocation decisions of this kind are made every day in an intuitive manner by school leaders and legislators at every level of the hierarchy from Congress (Should we continue to put millions of dollars into Head Start and similar preschool programs?) to the school principal (Should I hire one teacher or two paraprofessionals?) and the classroom teacher (How much time should I spend teaching arithmetic as opposed to reading?). School decisionmakers at the local, state, and federal levels are charged with responsibility for combining the available resources in such a way as to produce the "best" schooling for children.

At the moment, most schooling decisions are based on commonsense hunches about what makes a difference in schooling outcomes; however, there is substantial sentiment that in using this approach schools have failed to produce what the public wants them to produce. But, of course, one cannot blame schools for failing to solve certain social problems (e.g., the intergenerational transmission of poverty) because to some extent their hands are tied. Some determinants of educational outcomes are under their control (e.g., the qualifications of the teachers they hire), but others are beyond their control (e.g., students' socioeconomic background, the initial ability levels of children entering the schools). Before we can say how well schools are doing we must be able to say what they should be able to produce, given the characteristics of their student bodies and the resources available.

In short, we need answers to the question, "What makes a difference in educational outcomes?" This is the general question we will address in this book. The issue, however, is not simply *what* makes a difference in educational outputs but also *how much* of a difference does it make and *why?*

One way to learn what makes a difference and how much of a difference it makes is to measure schooling *outputs* (e.g., achievement test scores) in a large number of settings that vary in terms of the characteristics or *inputs* that are thought to make a difference. Examples of inputs include characteristics of the *child* (e.g., sex), characteristics of the *family*, (e.g., two-parent vs. single-parent households, income, family size, parents' educational background), characteristics of the *student body*, (e.g., percent white, age span, college aspirations), characteristics of the *teachers* (e.g., degrees, years of experience), and characteristics of the *schools* (e.g., per pupil expenditures, administrative organization, physical plant and library facilities). To discover the relative importance of each input, a statistical technique—multiple regression analysis—has been used with varying success.

ONE METHOD, MANY APPROACHES

Economists were probably the first to ask "What makes a difference in schooling effectiveness?" However, they have been joined in recent years by social researchers from other disciplines, notably sociology. Economists and other social researchers have some common interests in questions about the impact of schooling, and they use essentially the same statistical model although the various disciplines tend to define their research questions differently.

Economists cast their questions in terms of the *input-output model* of production, which assumes that outputs (e.g., scores on achievement tests) are produced by combining various resources (inputs), some of which are tractable and some of which are intractable. The goal is to discover the best combination of tractable inputs for optimizing the production of schooling outputs. Mathematically, a *production function* specifies how inputs combine to produce outputs.

Other social researchers—chiefly sociologists—take a different tack. They begin implicitly or explicitly with the question—"How do people attain the social, occupational, and income positions they come to hold in adulthood?" The empirically determined answer is that educational attainment mediates social attainment. Social scientists therefore feel justified in addressing a second question—"What family background factors, characteristics of children, and school arrangements facilitate or restrain educational attainment and hence social attainment?" Unlike economists, sociologists have been less concerned (perhaps even *unconcerned*) with cost factors, and they have not limited their attention to tractable inputs to the schooling process.

Sociologists in particular have been concerned with some variables that economists view as givens and therefore of marginal importance, for example, family structure, sex, and ethnicity. Sociologists and psychologists also rarely use the vocabulary of the input-output approach. Inputs may be labeled *independent variables*, and outputs may be labeled *dependent variables* or outcomes. Some independent variables may be classified as *mediating variables* (or intervening variables) according to their temporal position in a causal chain.

Despite differences in short-term goals, theoretical emphases, vocabularies, and preferred levels of analysis, economists, sociologists, and psychologists all have a common interest in the general determinants of educational outcomes. Moreover, the various disciplines rely upon essentially the same statistical model (although they typically emphasize different aspects of the model). In this book we try to meld the different vocabularies and emphases of economics, sociology, and psychology into a single comprehensive consideration of the determinants of educational outcomes.

OBJECTIVES AND ORGANIZATION

This book has five objectives. Specifically, we hope to:

1. Describe the basic input-output approach to questions of schooling effectiveness and to identify the assumptions, strengths, and weaknesses of this approach,

2. Identify, summarize, and evaluate the major studies of schooling effectiveness that have been done to date,

3. State some propositions about what makes a difference in schooling and draw out the policy implications of these findings,

4. Specify the methodological and theoretical issues that should be considered in future research on schooling effectiveness, and

5. Provide readers with the ability to understand and criticize studies of this genre when they encounter them in the future.

The next chapter introduces the general idea of input-output studies of schooling effectiveness. The objective is to summarize in a non-statistical manner the critical assumptions underlying this research strategy. Here we consider the way that characteristics of children and combinations of school resources interact to produce schooling outcomes. The emphasis is on the input side of the input-output model.

Chapter 3 raises the debate over what constitutes a valid outcome of schooling. The outputs that are examined in detail include norm-referenced achievement tests, IQ tests, and measures of higher order cognitive skills and affective outcomes.

Chapters 4 and 5 describe the statistical techniques used in input-output studies. Readers who already have some training in statistics may skip over Chapter 4, which introduces the idea of multiple regression analysis. Chapter 5 extends the discussion of Chapter 4 to cover specific issues raised by the use of multiple regression analysis to determine the relative importance of various inputs to the schooling process.

Chapter 6 compares and contrasts two strategies of input-output research, which we have labeled the *variance partitioning* strategy and the *effects testing* strategy. The former has been used most often by sociologists and psychologists, while the latter has been used most often by economists. For technical reasons, which will be detailed in Chapter 6, the effects testing approach is rapidly becoming the standard method of input-output research.

Chapter 7 describes the methods and findings of the landmark Equality of Economic Opportunity (EEO) survey,[2] which is usually referred to as the "Coleman report" after its first author sociologist

2. The EEO survey, which was mandated by the Civil Rights Act of 1964, involved 639,650 students in grades 1, 3, 6, 9, and 12 and their teachers and administrators in over 3,000 schools. This represents an approximately 5 percent sample of all U.S. schools. The study resulted in a multi-volume report (*Equality of Educational Opportunity*. Washington, D.C.: U.S. Government Printing Office, 1966) that was coauthored by James S. Coleman, Ernest Q. Campbell, C.F. Hobson, J. McPartland, Alexander M. Mood, and others. The report has come to be known popularly as the "Coleman report," a fact James Coleman has bemoaned repeatedly. Coleman (1970) writes: "[T]he report is not a 'Coleman Report': Ernest Campbell and I were co-directors of the project that culminated in the Report, and Alexander Mood had overall supervision of the study. All three of us, together with other persons in the Office of Education (some of whom are coauthors), spent much time and effort in the analysis and preparation of the report, and the report was a joint product." In recognition that such a massive report involved the contributions of many people, as Coleman notes, we have eschewed the shorthand term "Coleman Report." Instead we refer to the study by its original title, Equality of Educational Opportunity or EEO, or by the somewhat clumsy term "Coleman et al. report."

James S. Coleman. The data generated by the EEO survey were re-analyzed by George Mayeske and his colleagues at the U.S. Office of Education. Their results, along with the original Coleman et al. findings, are discussed in detail because the EEO survey has had a wide-spread impact, and these analyses are prime examples of the variance partitioning strategy in input-output research.

Chapter 8 summarizes the findings of a decade of research and points to possible policy implications of these findings. All of the re-search reviewed in this chapter used the effects testing approach, which is most suited for identifying the impact of particular inputs. Over thirty-five different inputs are considered in this chapter, and they are grouped into five categories: individual inputs, family inputs, peer group influences, teacher inputs, and school inputs.

The summary chapter, Chapter 9, identifies methodological problems and substantive issues that future researchers will need to address. The chapter also conveys our beliefs about the potential strengths and shortcomings that this type of research holds for the formation of effective social policy and the accumulation of scholarly understanding about the impact of social institutions such as schools.

EDUCATION VS. SCHOOLING

In trying to explain so-called schooling outcomes—even traditional indicators like achievement test scores—we are forced to consider nonschool inputs, namely, individual student characteristics, family characteristics, and peer group influences, as well as school inputs like teacher characteristics and school program and plant factors. In subsequent chapters, we will review research that suggests that "school outcomes" like achievement test scores are less a product of school program and plant inputs than nonschool factors; but this is not to say that schools do not make a difference. It is simply that they make *less* of a difference than other nonschool inputs. Of the five classes of inputs we have identified, individual student characteristics seem to contribute the most to achievement, followed by family background factors, peer group influences, teacher characteristics, and school plant and program factors in that order. It makes little sense, however, to talk about the unique effects of different inputs because the real impact of particular inputs accrues from the way they combine and interact with one another to determine outcomes.

In short, so-called schooling outcomes are a product of many things besides schools, and for this reason we prefer the term *educational outcomes* to the more common term schooling outcomes. This distinction highlights the theoretical difference between schooling and education. Education, according to historian Lawrence Cremin (1977:viii), may be defined as "the deliberate, systematic, and sustained effort to transmit or evoke knowledge, attitudes, values, skills, and sensibilities." Given this definition, it is obvious that many institutions other than schools "educate." Families, religious organizations, libraries, social clubs, factories, military organizations, theaters, and the mass media, including books, television, and even advertising, may be viewed as educational institutions, and it is their combined influence that is measured in test performance and other school output measures. Because these output measures reflect the impact of all of the institutions that educate, not simply schools, we will use the term educational outcomes or educational outputs rather than schooling outcomes unless the discussion specifically concerns the effectiveness of school resources.

The next chapter introduces the basic input-output model and describes the problems of conceptually and operationally defining and interpreting inputs.

Chapter 2

The Input-Output Approach

What makes a difference in schooling outcomes? Ideally we would tackle this question through a series of true experiments. That is, we would (a) create school situations that varied systematically in terms of the factors we thought made a difference, (b) randomly assign students to these schooling "treatment" conditions, and (c) compare the performance of students in the various conditions. The hallmark of a true experiment is the random assignment of "subjects" (e.g., students) to "treatments" (e.g., instructional arrangements) or vice versa as randomization overcomes some of the major threats to the internal validity of the research results. (See Campbell and Stanley, 1966, or Cook and Campbell, 1976.)

Unfortunately, true experiments are difficult, if not impossible, to implement on a large scale for a number of reasons. For one thing, researchers do not know exactly which factors (inputs) to focus on in experiments; in fact, identifying the important variables is one of the goals of input-output studies. Moreover, it is unlikely that parents are going to permit their children to be randomly assigned to treatment groups. They believe that they "know" what makes a difference in schooling, and understandably they want it for their children. Finally, experimentation raises some ethical problems where children are exposed to potentially harmful treatments, or services are withheld for experimental reasons even when sufficient resources are available.[1]

1. In recent years, experimental and quasi-experimental research designs have been used to evaluate a number of policy interventions in schooling, housing,

Large-scale studies of schooling effectiveness are necessarily non-experimental (i.e., correlational) at this time. The idea is to measure a dependent variable—an output of schooling—and then try to find the independent variables—inputs—that "explain" the variation in the dependent variable. Some of the schooling outputs that have been investigated include standardized achievement test scores, IQ test scores, retention rates (percent completing high school), and college admission rates (percent going on to college). Measures of other school outputs are available (e.g., affective, noncognitive outcomes), but until recently they have not been used.

Many factors have been viewed as inputs in the schooling process, and in subsequent chapters we will consider the following clusters: (a) *student characteristics* (e.g., IQ, sex, age, personality, aspirations), (b) *family background characteristics* (e.g., ethnicity, socioeconomic status, wealth, family size), (c) *student body characteristics* (e.g., racial composition, study habits), (d) *teacher characteristics* (e.g., training, experience, age, sex), and (e) *school characteristics* (e.g., physical plant, per pupil expenditure, curriculum).

Once we have a school output measure (a dependent variable) and a large set of *possible* inputs (independent variables), the task is to determine how much each variable contributes to the output measure, either alone or interacting with other inputs. In principle, potential input variables will be included in our deliberations according to some theoretically derived propositions, but this is not typically the case. Anything and everything, including the proverbial kitchen sink,[2] is usually thrown into the hopper in the search for inputs that make a difference. To determine the relative importance of each input, multiple regression analysis is used. This technique will be introduced in Chapter 4. Regression methods assume that output values can be represented as a weighted combination of input values, and these weights can be interpreted to show how important a variable is, that is, how much of a contribution it makes to outcome values.

PRODUCTION FUNCTIONS ILLUSTRATED

To see how outputs can be described in terms of weighted combinations of inputs, consider this simple illustration: Every year thousands of high school students who are applying for admission to college take the Scholastic Aptitude Test (SAT), which produces two

---

social welfare, health care, and criminal justice. Reviews of these experiments may be found in Riecken and Boruch (1974), Cook (1978), and Guttentag (1976, 1977).

2. The Equality of Educational Opportunity (EEO) survey, which is often called the "Coleman Report," asked questions about the family's ownership of household appliances, encyclopedias, and other indicators of family wealth.

subscores, a verbal subscore and a quantitative subscore. Conceivably, a school might view SAT scores as major indicators of how well it is doing in preparing students for college. Many factors contribute to a student's SAT performance, including the student's initial IQ, the school's teacher-pupil ratio, the quality of the teaching staff, the "academic atmosphere" of the school, and so on. Let us look at how the first factor—IQ test performance—contributes to SAT verbal scores.

In Chapter 4, we will explain the statistical principles of linear regression analysis, but it will suffice here to say that by regressing verbal SAT scores on IQ scores, the following equation was found to be the best predictor of SAT verbal scores for students in one eastern public school district:

$$\text{Predicted SAT Verbal Score} = 6.42 \, (\text{IQ Score}) - 266 \quad (2\text{--}1)$$

Using this equation, the school district can estimate how students of different IQ levels will perform on the SAT verbal subtest, and Table 2—1 summarizes these output predictions.

The strong relationship between IQ and SAT verbal "aptitude" scores is to be expected since IQ tests are themselves a kind of general achievement test, and we would expect one measure of achievement to be highly correlated with a second measure of achievement.

Table 2—1. Output Predictions of Student Performance on SAT Verbal Subtest.

Output	Input
Predicted SAT Verbal Score	Measured IQ Test Score
376.0	100
440.2	110
504.4	120
536.5	125
568.6	130
600.7	135
632.8	140
664.9	145
697.0	150
729.1	155
761.2	160

The real issue is what determines performance on both tests? In short, IQ should probably be treated as another output measure rather than as an input (but more about this debate in Chapter 3).

This example does not capture the complexity of the production function that one would need to "explain" schooling outcomes. At least, however, it illustrates the general idea of input-output studies, that is, we are trying to find the "best" recipe for schooling by measuring the outputs that result from different combinations of inputs. A final example will illustrate an actual educational production function. This is merely an extension of the ideas that were presented in the SAT score–IQ score example above, and the chief difference is that instead of one independent variable we will have six independent variables. The dependent variable in this case is another measure of verbal achievement.

Bowles (1970) examined the data for 1,000 black twelfth graders who were surveyed in the Equality of Educational Opportunity study, and his secondary analyses involved these variables:

Y Verbal achievement test score

X_1 Reading materials in the home

X_2 Number of siblings

X_3 Parents' educational level

X_4 Family stability

X_5 Teachers' verbal ability scores

X_6 Presence of science laboratories in the school

Note that the independent variables have been identified by the letter X plus a subscript, while the dependent variable has been identified by the letter Y. This convention will be observed elsewhere in the book. Note too that conceptual variables need to be operationalized and researchers commonly distinguish between four categories of measurement: *nominal, ordinal, interval,* and *ratio scales.* (Box 2–1 describes these levels of measurement.)

Bowles found that the following equation provided the "best explanation" of verbal achievement scores,

$$Y = 1.928X_1 - 1.8512X_2 + 2.465X_3 + 0.8264X_4 + 1.255X_5 + \qquad (2-2)$$
$$0.0505X_6 + 19.456$$

Note that there are seven terms on the right side of the equation even though we have only six independent variables. The seventh term is *not* a weight that is applied to an independent variable; rather it is a

Box 2—1. Scales of Measurement.

Measurement consists of assigning symbols, usually numbers, to the elements in a set. The elements themselves are not measured; characteristics or properties of the elements are measured.

The symbols in a *nominal* scale, even when they are numbers, have no numeric meaning. They cannot be ordered, nor can any arithmetic operations be performed on them. The symbols serve simply to differentiate or classify items, to divide them among two or more mutually exclusive categories. All animals can be labeled as either "male" or "female," for example. Athletes often wear jerseys that are colored to identify which teams they play on, or numbered to identify them as individual players, but an athlete with the number "60" is not thought to be twice as big or twice as good as another with the number "30." The numbers or colors serve merely as labels.

An *ordinal* scale reveals some underlying ordering of the items in a set. For example, when we line up children according to height with the shortest at the front and tallest at the back, we have created an ordinal scale. Beginning with the first child, each succeeding child in the line is as tall as or taller than the preceding child; however, the *difference* in heights between the first and second children is not necessarily the same as that between any other two, adjacent children in the line. An ordinal scale tells us that one item is "larger than," "smaller than," or "equal to" another item, but it does not tell us "how much larger" or "how much smaller" it is.

On an *interval* scale, equal numerical distances represent equal distances in the characteristic or property being measured. For example, on the Celsius scale of temperature, the difference between 15°C and 30°C is equivalent (in terms of the expansion of mercury in a tube) to the difference between 30°C and 45°C. A reading of 0°C, however, does not represent the absence of temperature. The absence of temperature ("absolute zero") exists only in theory and cannot be observed. The zero point on the Celsius scale has been set arbitrarily to correspond to the freezing point of water. Thus, it makes no sense to say that 30°C represents "twice as much temperature" as 15°C.

A *ratio* scale possesses an absolute zero point. Unlike values on an interval scale, which can only be added and subtracted, values on a ratio scale can also be multiplied and divided. Height is an example of a ratio scale variable. It has an absolute zero point, which represents the absence of height. Thus, we can divide one height by another, and it is meaningful to state, "Richard is 10 percent taller than Howard."

The four levels of measurement—nominal, ordinal, interval, and ratio—are hierarchical in that each successive level incorporates the properties of the preceding level(s). For example, with a ratio scale (the highest level) we are able to differentiate items, to order items, to compare the intervals between items, *and* to compare quantities per se.

constant that is added to the sum of the weighted variable values. The interpretation of this kind of production function is of no concern to us now. It will be discussed in Chapters 4 and 5. All that is important to understand now is that (a) an output can be represented as the sum of a weighted set of input values, and (b) the purpose of regression studies is to find the proper weights so that the contribution of each input can be determined.

CENTRAL ISSUES

In the remainder of this chapter we will try to identify, in a nonstatistical manner, the major issues involved in studies of schooling effectiveness, and the emphasis will be on the input side of the production function. The questions that will be treated in this chapter are as follows:

1. How can we estimate the relative impact of an input or input mix that is found in all schools or in very few schools? If an input shows very *little variation across schools*, it is impossible to see how that input makes a difference in outputs.

2. How do inputs *interact?* By themselves, some inputs may be unimportant, but when combined with other inputs in the proper proportions, they may become important.

3. Must inputs be combined in a particular *sequence* in order to have an effect on outputs? Are there *critical periods* during which the presence (or absence) of key inputs affects subsequent outputs?

4. Are there minimum amounts of inputs—*thresholds*—that must be achieved before inputs can have any effects? How are we to deal with this possibility and other *nonlinear relationships* between inputs and outputs?

5. Can we *substitute* some inputs for others and still get the same output? For example, can we substitute paraprofessionals for certified teachers without adversely affecting achievement?

6. How should we interpret relationships in which a variable is clearly correlated with outputs and yet the variable is merely a *proxy*, that is, standing in for unknown underlying processes or more difficult to measure variables?

7. How are policymakers to decide, on the basis of input-output studies, *what actions* should be taken?

These are questions to which we shall return again and again, and unfortunately, they are questions that many schooling effectiveness studies answer ambiguously or only by default. One reason for this state of affairs is that these studies are often atheoretical exercises, not guided by clearly delineated assumptions. Such an approach may be appropriate—even necessary—during the early stages of development in a new research area, but eventually theory becomes a requisite for cumulative advances in the field. One objective of this chapter (and the next) is to sensitize the reader to the general theoretical considerations researchers must deal with—implicitly or explicitly—before any data are collected or analyzed.

One obvious question is missing from our list: "What is a valid outcome of education?" This is such a complex issue that we have devoted an entire chapter to it. The outcomes described in Chapter 3 include: (a) *norm-referenced (standardized) achievement tests*, which measure performance on cognitive tasks such as reading, vocabulary knowledge, arithmetic computations, spelling, and so on; (b) *intelligence* ("IQ") test scores; and (c) *noncognitive, affective outcomes* (e.g., self-esteem and locus of control expectancies).

Norm-referenced achievement tests are by far the most frequently used outcome measures in input-output research, but recently there has been increased interest in noncognitive, affective outcomes, which appear to be powerful predictors of success in other settings. Chapter 3 reviews the technical details of these outcome measures. It also explains why dynamic, bidirectional relationships and feedback loops must be hypothesized in order to account for the observed relationships between inputs, and both cognitive and affective outcomes.

But first we must examine the input side of the education production function, addressing each of the central issues raised above. We will consider the way inputs combine in certain amounts, at certain times, or in certain sequences to produce educational outcomes.

RARE INPUT MIXES AND ATTENUATED VARIANCE

The general strategy of input-output studies is to examine which mixes of inputs are associated with which levels of outputs. This approach presupposes that (a) individuals vary widely in terms of the outcomes they produce and (b) individuals differ widely in terms of the inputs they receive. The latter assumption may be invalid in many cases, especially for variations in *school* inputs.

Some inputs show very little variation. For example, most school districts in a given region make approximately equal per pupil expenditures, and thus the impact of different levels of spending cannot be detected. In statistical terms, this is described as the problem of *attenuated variance.* If there is no variation in an input, there is nothing it can explain. For one reason or another there is very little variation in some school and teacher inputs, like the qualifications of teachers (in terms of academic degrees), per capita expenditures within a region, minutes of instruction per day, and so on.

Another problem is that some mixes of inputs occur so rarely that we cannot make valid inferences about their impact. For example, it is difficult to find examples of children from highly educated families who attended financially destitute schools that are staffed by highly trained teachers. These combinations of family background characteristics (highly educated parents), school characteristics (low pupil expenditures), and teacher characteristics (highly trained) simply do not occur very frequently unless they are made to happen experimentally.

INTERACTIONS BETWEEN INPUTS

Often it is not the presence of an input by itself that is important. Rather it is the presence of two (or more) inputs that makes a difference in the production process. This is the phenomenon of *interacting inputs.* To give an example, easily verified in one's own kitchen, we note that vinegar by itself is stable and inactive and by itself baking powder is also stable; but when vinegar and baking powder are mixed together, there is a chemical reaction—an *interaction.*

Or consider an agricultural example. Fertilizer placed on a field of corn in the proper amount will have no impact unless there is water present in the proper amount as well. The water acts as a transport medium, making it possible for the fertilizer to be absorbed into the plants' root systems. If there is too little water, the fertilizer is not carried to the plants' roots; too much water, and the fertilizer is simply washed away. To be successful (i.e., to stimulate plant growth), the farmer must apply *both* fertilizer *and* water *in the proper amounts.*

Sometimes graphical representation makes interactions easier to grasp. Figures 2–1 and 2–2 are not intended to reflect known relationships; they illustrate only hypothetical interactions. In both examples, achievement in school is the dependent variable. It is measured on the vertical axis. In Figure 2–1, the interacting variables are (a) family income and (b) percent of specialized teachers in the

Figure 2—1. Hypothetical Illustration of Interaction between Student's Family Income and School's Level of Teacher Specialization.

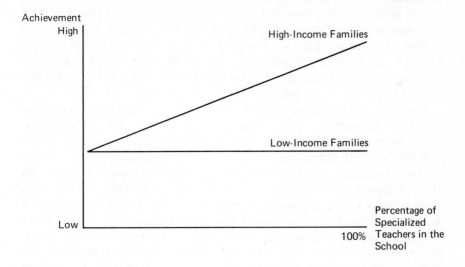

Figure 2—2. Hypothetical Illustration of Interaction between Student's Test Anxiety and Teacher's Pressure for Test Performance.

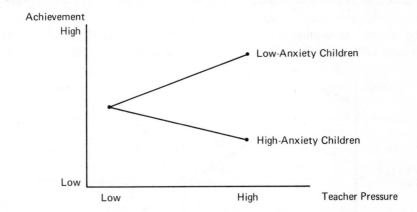

child's school. The form of the relationship is suggested by Perl's (1973, p. 176) finding that the percentage of specialized teachers in a school has no impact on low-income children but has a significant positive effect on children from high-income families.

Figure 2—2, which uses hypothetical data, shows how achievement might be affected by (a) a child's level of test anxiety and (b) the teacher's emphasis on test performance. Children who are characterized by a low level of test anxiety respond positively to the teacher's demands; but children who have a high level of test anxiety fall apart under pressure, and their achievement deteriorates as the teacher's demands increase. This example, as depicted in Figure 2−2, demonstrates an extreme kind of interaction in that the effect of teacher pressure on student performance changes in *direction* (it is positive for one group and negative for the other) and not just in *magnitude* as we look from one group of children to the other.

Figure 2−3 illustrates a different kind of interaction, a so-called *crossover interaction*. The data in this case are real, not hypothetical. They come from a teacher training experiment that compared different methods of increasing the number of analytical questions that student teachers asked (Koran, 1969). Students were assigned to three different treatment groups. Everyone taught three mini-lessons with a break between lessons. During the breaks, people in one group watched a videotape of a master teacher giving a model lesson. Subjects in a second experimental group read a transcript of the model lesson rather than seeing it on the videotape, and the remaining subjects served as a control group and received no model lessons. Before the experiment, all the subjects had taken a number of aptitude and personality tests, one of which used "hidden figures" to measure a particular perceptual style. As the data in Figure 2−3 show, people

Figure 2−3. Illustration of Interaction between Instructional Mode and Student Teacher's Perceptual Style, Suggested by Findings of Koran (1969).

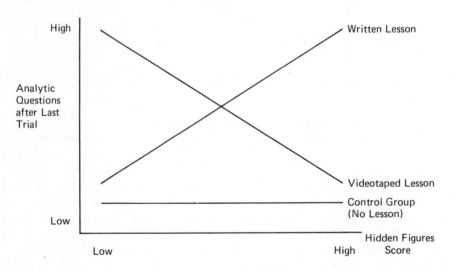

who scored high on the hidden figures test asked more analytical questions after reading the transcript than after watching the videotape. And people who scored low on the hidden figures test were more influenced by the videotaped presentation than the written transcript. The important point here is that different kinds of people—defined here by a perceptual style variable—reacted differently to different teaching methods.

The importance of interactions in the process of learning has long been suspected, but only recently have educational researchers begun to document examples of the way inputs interact. Interactions between student characteristics and instructional arrangements have been detected in a number of experiments, but the evidence is often contradictory from experiment to experiment. This is due at least in part to methodological shortcomings of the research, as Cronbach and Snow (1977) have demonstrated in their comprehensive review of the literature.

The importance of interactions is well illustrated by Bronfenbrenner's (1974) review of the empirical evidence on the effectiveness of early childhood interventions. The outcome measures in most of these studies were IQ score gains. Bronfenbrenner concluded that (a) IQ scores can be raised by a combination of "ecological interventions" (i.e., changes in the family's situation) and preschool training of cognitive skills, but (b) these training programs are effective only if parents are involved.

David Hunt (1971, 1975) has argued that student outcomes can be enhanced by matching students' "accessibility characteristics" with teaching arrangements. The chief student characteristic is what he calls *conceptual level*, an outgrowth of earlier personality research by Harvey, Hunt, and Schroder (1961). "Conceptual level is a person characteristic, indexing both cognitive complexity (differentiation, discrimination, and integration) as well as interpersonal maturity (increasing self-responsibility)" (Hunt, 1975, p. 218). The chief instructional variable is *classroom structure*, and according to Hunt's theory, low conceptual level children need high classroom structure, and high conceptual level children either benefit from low structure or are unaffected by the level of structure.

The interactions that one might be interested in examining in input-output studies include questions like these:

- Do black children achieve higher test scores when they attend desegregated schools rather than equivalent racially isolated schools? That is, does the racial composition of the school interact with the student's race to affect achievement?

- Do minority children learn more when they are taught by teachers of their own race or ethnic group? That is, is achievement affected by an interaction between child's race/ethnicity and the teacher's race/ethnicity?

- Is "open education" more effective with some kinds of children than others? That is, do certain characteristics of children interact with the instructional arrangement to determine outcomes?

- Do children from disadvantaged social backgrounds benefit more from school expenditures than advantaged children? In other words, is there an interaction between school expenditures and social background that determines achievement?

THE SEQUENCE OF INPUTS AND "CRITICAL PERIODS"

By and large, input-output studies have ignored the sequence in which inputs are applied, but some psychological theories (e.g., Piaget's theory of cognitive development or Kohlberg's theory of moral development) and a growing body of experimental evidence suggest that *when* an input is introduced may be very important. Two related but distinct ideas are involved here. One has to do with the actual *sequencing* of inputs, and the other has to do with the *timing* of inputs so that they are applied during certain "critical periods."

Sequencing. The argument that "compensatory education" funds should be concentrated in the early school years rather than in the later secondary school period is built on the supposition that "an ounce of prevention is worth a pound of cure." Proponents of this position ask what sense does it make to apply extra funds at the high school level in order to remediate problems that developed throughout the first six years or so? If we wanted to add a certain amount to a child's education, would not the money have a bigger impact if applied in the first grade instead of the senior year in high school? The state of California seems to accept this argument, for they have reallocated compensatory education funds to favor early grades. Implicit in this approach is the assumption that children learn by accumulation, a view favored by environmentally oriented learning theorists. The earlier children start accumulating the skills that contribute to school performance, the better they will do throughout the school years. But this position could also be justified by an assumption of learning sequences (stages) or critical periods.

The maturationist view is that cognitive development follows a set of invariant stages, and shifts from one state to another are contingent upon both environmental events and biological development (which is why cognitive development is so highly correlated with age according to maturationists). Piaget's stage developmental theory is probably the best known approach to cognitive development (Piaget, 1970; Piaget and Inhelder, 1969; Kamii, 1973).

According to the stage theorists such as Piaget, it makes no sense to try to teach skills that the child is not biologically ready to acquire. For this reason, many interpreters of Piaget (e.g., Furth, 1970) argue against early reading readiness programs because they believe that children will be ready to read when they are ready to read, and there is nothing gained by trying to push the biological readiness (basically neurophysiological readiness) that must precede reading.

"Critical Periods." In education there may be certain critical periods or "windows of time" during which inputs will have an impact, but at other times the same inputs will be ineffective. This hypothesis follows directly from the ethological evidence for critical periods in animal learning and imprinting (Bowlby, 1969; Hinde, 1970; Scott, 1962; Hess, 1972, 1959; Caldwell, 1962). The white-crowned sparrow, for example, must hear its species specific song before it is four months old, or it will never learn it. Schutz (1965) has shown in his work with different species of ducks that there are at least three critical periods between the time a duckling is hatched and the time it reproduces as an adult. In the first stage—which occurs between forty-eight and seventy-two hours after hatching—the duckling identifies (imprints) a "mother object," and if an animal of another species is the only one present during this time, the duckling may accept this animal as its "mother." The second stage involves social bonding to the species; the duckling learns to identify with its own species. The final stage occurs when the duckling forms a bond with a particular mate.

Some comparative psychologists (e.g., Scott, 1963; Gray, 1958) believe that a process akin to imprinting occurs in humans, but this cannot be accepted unquestioningly yet. Indeed there may be critical periods during which the child is especially sensitive to certain kinds of learning experiences, but this fact has been totally ignored in input-output studies of schooling effectiveness.

The psychoanalytic or Freudian theory of development is probably the best known critical periods theory. Briefly summarized, the major tenets of this theory are as follows: (a) development follows a set of immutable stages, (b) the stages unfold as a result of biological development (e.g., the acquisition of language, the ability to walk, refined perceptual skills) and action of the environment (e.g., the nature of the family's child-rearing practices, the family composition during different periods), (c) development can be arrested (i.e., there is nothing that guarantees that the highest level of development will be attained), and (d) the personality characteristics of adulthood, one's propensity for certain psychopathologies, and one's preferred mechanisms of ego defense (coping mechanisms) can be traced to early childhood experiences during specific periods of development. This cursory description of psychoanalytic thought cannot describe the complexities or robustness of this theory. The developmental stages posited by psychoanalytic theory are well described by Erikson (1963) and White (1960).

Psychoanalytic thought emphasizes the importance of learning experiences that occur during early childhood (particularly before about age six), but adolescence may also be a critical period during which certain key social attitudes are formed. Mannheim's theory of political socialization, for example, holds that the social attitudes of each generation are formed by the political and economic conditions prevailing during their adolescent years. Hence, people who were teenagers during the Great Depression of the 1930s are very likely to hold different political and economic philosophies from their children who reached adolescence during the late 1950s and early 1960s. Adolescence is also the period during which religious beliefs are solidified (cf. McGuire, 1969, p. 166).

It is not our purpose to review the evidence for or against the "critical periods" or "natural readiness vs. acceleration" positions; rather the point is simply to show that in assessing the impact of various schooling inputs, we must consider the sequence and timing of the inputs. Conceptually, sequence effects or critical periods may be viewed as statistical interactions between time (or age) and particular independent variables. In other words, these effects are merely a specific kind of interaction, a time-related interaction.

THRESHOLD EFFECTS AND NONLINEAR RELATIONSHIPS

Throwing a bucket of water on a raging fire will not keep a building from burning to the ground, but no one would argue on the basis of this experience that water has no value in firefighting. The value of water is apparent only when enough is applied to overcome the fire by reducing the heat below a critical point, degrading the fuel, or temporarily removing the air needed for combustion. An analogous situation often occurs in education. Frequently we judge an intervention strategy to be ineffective before we have really implemented a program that is intense enough to achieve the desired effects. "Compensatory education" is a case in point.

Critics like Arthur Jensen (1969) claim that compensatory education has not and *cannot* increase IQ test scores of minority children (because, he argues, the chief determinants of IQ test scores are genetic, not environmental). One counterargument to this position is that we have not really tried sufficiently intense school interventions to cause a change in IQ, but intensive "ecological interventions" that involve both families and schools have been successful (Bronfenbrenner, 1974).

That compensatory education has not worked dramatically does not mean that it cannot. This argument rests upon an assumed threshold effect. The idea is that children must receive a sufficiently strong dose of some input (e.g., "compensatory education") or the input will have no effect. Threshold effects are best illustrated graphically. Figure 2—4 describes the hypothetical relationship between IQ gains (the output) and hours per week spent in a preschool program (the input). Remember that these are hypothetical data. They were constructed to suggest that anything less than four hours a day in preschool has no effect on IQ, *but* after four hours a day, each additional hour of preschool is related to IQ gains.

A threshold effect is simply an example of a nonlinear relationship. For example, the hypothetical relationship between IQ gains and hours in preschool is *not* described by a straight line. Input-output studies generally assume linear relationships, and thus threshold

Figure 2—4. Hypothetical Illustration of Nonlinear Relationship between Time in Preschool and Gains in Intelligence.

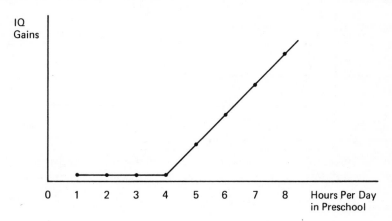

effects may be overlooked. This problem is discussed in more detail in Chapter 5.

Threshold effects are only one kind of nonlinear relationship. Figures 2–5 and 2–6 illustrate other commonly observed nonlinear relationships. Figure 2–5 illustrates a plausible but hypothetical relationship between bookkeeping performance and training in accounting. The argument might be made that people who have too little

Figure 2–5. Hypothetical Illustration of Nonlinear Relationship between Bookkeeping Performance and Training in Accounting.

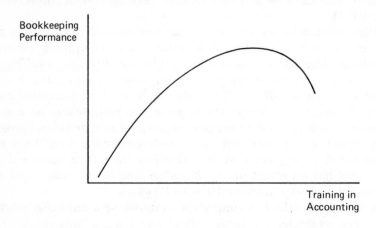

Figure 2–6. Hypothetical Illustration of Nonlinear Relationship between Attitude Intensity, Direction, and Magnitude.

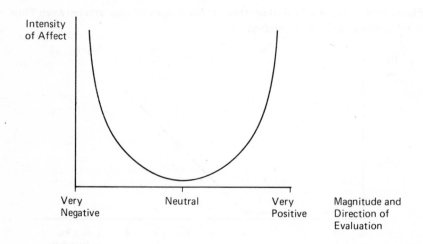

experience are ineffective bookkeepers but that people who have too much training for a particular task are also ineffective, perhaps because they become bored or because they do not take the task seriously.

Figure 2−6 shows the relationship between three dimensions of attitudes: the direction and magnitude of the evaluation component and the affective intensity with which the attitude is held (cf. Lane and Sears, 1965). The more *extreme* a person's evaluation, the more *intensely* the person holds this evaluation.

These illustrations are not of substantive importance to this discussion. They are included merely to illustrate the notion of nonlinear relationships. The important thing to remember is that most input-output studies use a statistical model that assumes linear relationships, and therefore nonlinear relationships between inputs and schooling outcomes may go undetected.

SUBSTITUTABILITY OF INPUTS

To some extent, a cook can substitute one ingredient for another (e.g., margarine for butter) and yet end up with essentially the same finished product. This is also true of the schooling process, although this point has escaped many social scientists who are concerned only with "explaining" achievement outcomes in terms of the percentage of variance accounted for by identifiable inputs of all types. Most sociologists, for example, have not paid much attention to costs although costs provide the primary impetus for substituting one resource for another. Economists have been more sensitive to the theoretical possibilities for substitution in the schooling processes, but in practice they have done little to test empirically the tradeoffs between different inputs.

Schooling is a highly labor-intensive enterprise; salaries account for about 80 percent of the average school's budget. The introduction of computer-assisted instruction (CAI), teaching machines, and other individualized instruction methods has not really altered the demand for teaching personnel. The ratio of teachers to pupils remains relatively constant regardless of which instructional arrangement is used. Substitution of capital for labor is difficult in education, but schools can substitute one kind of labor for another, and this is exactly what is happening. Perhaps the most significant current trend in school personnel practices is the substitution of relatively cheap paraprofessionals for relatively expensive certified teachers, or the replacement of relatively expensive experienced teachers with relatively inexpensive new teachers.

The scheduling of school hours may be another area in which sub-stitution is possible. If we want to have children in school a certain number of hours per year, we can choose between longer days but fewer of them, or shorter days and more of them. If there are large costs associated with the number of days schools operate (e.g., trans-portation costs, cleaning costs per day), school administrators may be under pressure to open the schools on as few days as possible with a subsequent requirement that classes be held for longer periods. On the other hand, some people argue that total costs can be reduced by the more intensive utilization of the school physical plant. The so-called "All Year School" is predicated at least in part upon this as-sumption. Assuming that children should attend school for a total of nine months a year, three school buildings can do the work of four *if* schools are used all twelve months of the year.

In principle, substituting one input for another is an effective way to reduce total school costs without reducing the quantity or quality of outcomes, and in the ideal situation this would be done by (a) identifying inputs that contributed to outcomes, (b) determining how much of a difference each input makes and at what relative cost, and (c) substituting effective resources for less effective ones. This situation assumes positive evidence that an input makes a difference, and the issue is how much of an impact it has per a given unit of cost. But input-output studies more often turn up a different set of results, null results. That is, variations in an input appear to contrib-ute little or nothing to outputs, and thus a question arises as to why we cannot simply drop this input or at least substitute the least ex-pensive equivalent. The substitution of paraprofessionals for certified teachers is a case in point.

The interpretation of null results is problematic. If we find that two variables—an input and an outcome—are unrelated statistically, it may be because (a) the data are accurate and in fact the two vari-ables are unrelated; (b) the variables are related but one (or both) of the measures is insensitive (not detecting variance that actually exists) or is producing random values; or (c) the variables are unre-lated as the data show, but we have failed to measure a relevant out-come that the input does contribute to in some significant manner.

For example, one might argue that if we cannot show that teach-ers are definitely "more effective" than paraprofessionals, there is no reason not to replace teachers with paraprofessionals; but this argu-ment is viable only if it can be demonstrated that we have accurately measured the relevant schooling outcomes. Maybe experienced or certified teachers make a very big difference, but we have not measured the particular outcomes they affect. This, of course, again raises the debate about the outcomes of schooling.

THE PROXY PROBLEM

Many of the variables we can measure and that we call inputs are actually only representatives of some underlying variables or processes. These observable, representative variables are usually called *proxy variables* or simply *proxies* because they "stand in" for more important but unmeasured variables. In the Equality of Educational Opportunity (EEO) survey, for example, Coleman (1966) and his colleagues asked questions about the presence of certain electrical appliances in students' homes; and ownership of a vacuum cleaner was significantly correlated with verbal achievement as one might expect. But this does not mean that ownership of a vacuum cleaner *caused* student achievement; rather vacuum cleaner ownership and student achievement both reflect the family's socioeconomic status. Vacuum cleaner ownership is simply a proxy for family wealth, which in turn is a proxy for home inputs of goods and time.

Strictly speaking, almost all of the variables used in input-output studies are proxies because researchers usually do not have a clear understanding of the processes underlying the relationships they uncover. Few input-output studies have been empirical tests of explicit theories; most have been scientific fishing expeditions. Hence the findings are often difficult to interpret causally, and their policy implications are often ambiguous.

For example, if we find that the quality of a teacher's graduate training instruction makes a significant contribution to student achievement, it does not tell us *why*. It may be that high quality institutions have discovered a way to teach people particularly effective teaching methods. On the other hand, it may be that graduation from a prestigious college gives one social credit, and students may pay more attention to high status teachers. Or perhaps teachers who graduated from highly selective colleges are assigned to or attract the better, more able students. Or as a fourth possibility, perhaps teachers from selective colleges are better placed in national networks that communicate the latest curriculum innovations. The possible explanations are endless, and we are not going to settle this question here. But this example does illustrate the important point that we are working with correlational relationships, and causal effects are difficult to establish. Without an explicit theory of education, we have little basis for assessing alternative explanations. Many input variables, like teacher quality, are really only labels or proxies for complex underlying processes or more central variables, and knowing that an input makes a difference does not automatically tell us *why*.

POLICY IMPLICATIONS

Earlier sections in this chapter described the problem of defining educational outcomes and identified some of the thorny theoretical and methodological considerations involved in locating inputs that make a difference. The complexity of these problems will become even more apparent when we shift our attention to how outcomes are measured (Chapter 3). But let us assume for the time being that all of these problems are behind us, and we have succeeded in locating a production function that "explains" most of the variance in some important educational outcome. What are we to do with these findings? How can they be used to improve public policy?

The remainder of this chapter discusses the considerations that must be made in translating research results into policy recommendations. These considerations can be summarized as follows:

1. Only tractable sources of variance matter when it comes to policy formation.

2. Having identified the tractable inputs, the policymaker must take into account (a) the magnitude of each input's effect on output and (b) the unit price of each input. Ideally, policy interventions are determined by combining price information with information about the magnitude of effects in order to *minimize the cost per unit of change in the output measure.*

3. Interventions have multiple consequences, some planned and some unforeseen, and one shortcoming of most contemporary production function studies of schooling is that no provision has been made for bidirectional effects or feedback processes across time.

Tractable Inputs.   At the outset, it is apparent that not all inputs are of equal interest to policymakers, and the tractability of an input is the criterion for deciding its practical importance. If a variable is intractable, that is, if the situation cannot be manipulated, there is little reason for even considering the variable in forming policy.

The first principle in translating research results into policies is to look for tractable sources of variance; inputs are considered only if they can be manipulated or if they interact with tractable inputs. But one problem with this simplistic idea is that it provides no concrete definition of what is and what is not tractable. What is potentially tractable to one person may not be tractable in another's opinion. What is intractable today may be brought under control by technological advances tomorrow. Some inputs may be tractable in a technical sense, but their manipulation is politically unfeasible. Others may be both technically tractable and politically innocuous, but these are ruled out as being "too costly." The criterion of *cost-effectiveness* is developed in the following section.

Cost-effectiveness. Having ruled out those factors that cannot be manipulated for technological or political reasons, policymakers need next to distinguish those tractable inputs that have a large relative impact on outputs from those that have a small relative impact. The question you should be asking is, "Large and small *relative to what?*" And the answer, which constitutes the fundamental decision rule of economics, is necessarily, *"Relative to the unit price of the input in question."*

The purpose of input-output studies is to determine the magnitude of each input's effect on outputs. For example, Bowles's equation (2−2 above) indicates that each unit of X_5 (teachers' verbal ability scores) contributes on the average about 1.25 points to Y (a child's verbal achievement test score), whereas each unit of X_6 (school science laboratories) contributes only about 0.05 of a point. In other words, the average effect on output of a unit change in teachers' verbal ability scores is twenty-five times greater than the average effect of a unit change in laboratory facilities. Therefore, in the absence of information on the relative costs of implementing such changes, it might seem reasonable to presume that school administrators should devote more money to hiring better educated teachers (i.e., to raise the average verbal ability score) and less on constructing, equipping, and maintaining science laboratories.

Whether to reallocate expenditures in favor of teaching personnel or science laboratories or not at all depends on the price of a one unit change in teachers' verbal ability scores as compared with the price of a one unit change in laboratory facilities. Let us suppose that these prices were estimated to be $300,000 and $10,000, respectively, for a school of average size. Then it would cost $240,000 in additional teachers' salaries to raise the output of the school by an average of one point on the verbal achievement test for students, but only $200,000 to achieve the same result via the addition of science laboratories. Clearly, our tentative conclusion as to the correct course of action, which was to increase the expenditure on teachers at the cost of reduced expenditure on science laboratories, would have been incorrect.

A shortcoming to date of most input-output studies of educational effectiveness is their omission of any discussion of input prices. Simply to compare the regression weights of inputs in the production process without explicit reference to relative input prices is to risk misinforming public policy decisions. The likelihood of public officials being misled by research in this way and making suboptimal expenditures was perhaps greater in the "fat" days of the 1960s when public funds were abundant and all social goals appeared achieveable. In the lean days of the 1970s, money is tighter, and calls for "accountability" are heard increasingly in the political arena. As the financial well dries up, researchers who look for public funding may be forced to make the cost implications of their research more explicit.

Multiple Outcomes. Policy interventions usually have more than one effect on outcomes, and it is often impossible to predict all of these consequences in advance. For example, in 1974 the federal government mandated a maximum fifty-five miles per hour speed limit on all interstate roads. The chief objective was to reduce the nation's consumption of motor fuels, but this policy had other effects. For one thing, traffic fatalities declined significantly.

One problem with most schooling effectiveness studies is that they examine only one outcome at a time. Understanding how input variations affect an outcome is important, but it is not enough. Policymakers would be ill-advised to manipulate inputs in order to increase one kind of achievement without first considering the consequences for other important outcomes. For example, increasing the proportion of time spent on math instruction may increase math achievement, but this policy would probably result in lower verbal achievement scores. Unfortunately, input-output studies do not often deal with multiple outcomes simultaneously, and therefore planners will experience some frustration when they try to translate research results into action plans.

An input may affect more than one outcome, and it is also true that inputs and outputs may have reciprocal effects. That is, the direction of effects is not necessarily one-way. In some cases, changes in an input will cause changes in an output, which in turn will set off changes in the original input variable. These reciprocal or bidirectional effects can be tested empirically with modern statistical models, but this has not been done very often in schooling effectiveness studies.

SUMMARY

After introducing the idea that educational outcomes can be represented as weighted combinations of inputs, this chapter examined the input side of the education production function, and the following points were stressed:

- Probably no single input or small set of inputs acting alone accounts for differences in children's educational outcomes; rather outcomes are the product of combinations of interacting inputs. For example, "good schools" may foster achievement, but even good schools cannot do much if the family does not lay the foundation for the schools to build upon. That is, family background characteristics and school characteristics *interact* to produce student achievement. The methodological implication is that statistical interactions should be tested in explicit models.

- Some inputs may be effective (or act as a catalyst for other inputs) only if they are applied during certain *critical periods* or in certain immutable *sequences*. Conceptually, sequence effects and critical period effects are simply statistical interactions between time or age, on the one hand, and particular inputs, on the other.

- Similarly, some inputs may be totally ineffective unless certain minimum amounts are applied; that is, some inputs display a *threshold effect.*

- In theory, *some inputs can be substituted for others* without degrading educational outcomes, and substitution is desirable if it reduces costs while maintaining the same level of outputs. Of course, policymakers should always be sensitive to this possibility, particularly when substitution promises significant savings. Unfortunately, however, the ambiguous null results that often accrue from input-output studies provide a poor basis for substituting one input for another.

- When research shows that a particular variable makes a significant difference in outcomes, our work is just beginning because many of the inputs we study are merely *proxies* for more complex underlying processes, and these processes must be understood in order to bring them under experimental control.

- Translating research results into policy recommendations involves three principles: (1) tractable sources of variance are all that matter when it comes to policy formation, (2) obviously the magnitude of an input's effect (i.e., *how much* of a difference it makes in outcomes) is important, but by itself this is an insufficient basis for choosing leverage points, because cost factors must be combined with information about magnitudes in order to minimize total cost per unit of output, and (3) interventions have multiple consequences—some planned and some unforeseen—and feedback effects must be anticipated and tested experimentally before large-scale changes are promulgated. That is, the results of input-output studies are the beginnings of more highly controlled, experimental tests of relationships.

✳ *Chapter 3*

The Outcomes of Education

What exactly are schools supposed to produce and how can we measure these outcomes? Obviously, we cannot go about specifying production functions for schools until we have first determined exactly what we are trying to produce, and this raises some thorny questions of values.

It is clear that families vary in their child-rearing values and also that these values are closely tied to background factors like parents' education, occupational status, race/ethnicity, and the "structure" of their jobs (Kohn, 1969; Bridge and Blackman, 1978; Rokeach, 1973). Box 3–1 provides an illustration of how child-rearing values vary with parents' education. Because parents vary in their child-rearing values, they also tend to vary in their expectations for the school and their beliefs about what the schools should accomplish. Occasionally, differences in parents' expectations for the schools end in violence (e.g., the Kanawha County "textbook wars"). Because of the conflicting goals that parents and other citizens hold for the schools, there is a tendency for schools to think in terms of the lowest common denominator of various groups' expectations—reading, writing, and arithmetic achievement.

The outcome measures considered in this chapter include: (a) norm-referenced, standardized achievement tests, (b) intelligence (IQ) tests, and (c) higher order cognitive and affective outcomes. Table 3–1 identifies the outcome measures used in the studies reviewed in this book. Even a cursory inspection of these data will show that in the vast majority of cases, the outcome measures have been scores on norm-referenced achievement tests and, furthermore,

33

Box 3—1.   Social Class Differences in Childrearing Values.

The values that parents hold for their children vary with family background factors such as parents' education. Sociologist Melvin Kohn (1969)
has hypothesized that parents' work experiences, especially the degree of
structure in their jobs, leads to different views of how to get ahead in the
world, and parents pass these lessons on to their children. Kohn's theory
predicts certain social class differences in how much parents emphasize
obedience and respect for authority (*politeness*) versus *independence* and
imagination. Working-class parents tend to value obedience and politeness
because these are qualities that lead to job security. In contrast, middle-
class parents tend to hold jobs that require problem solving under conditions of uncertainty, and they value imagination and independence because
they contribute to success in these occupations. These different value
emphases are inculcated in working-class and middle-class children from
birth.

Survey data collected by Bridge and Blackman (1978) (see Figure 3—1:
Box 3—1) show how parents' rankings or two values in the eighteen-item
Rokeach (1973) *Value Survey*—independence and obedience—vary with
parents' education, a proxy for social class in this case. As predicted, the
data show that the relative importance attached to children's obedience
decreased motonically with parents' education, and the relative importance of children's independence increased monotonically with parents'
education.

Median Rankings of Two Instrumental Child-rearing Values, Obedience and Independence, for 757 Mothers of K–6 Children (Bridge and Blackman, 1978).

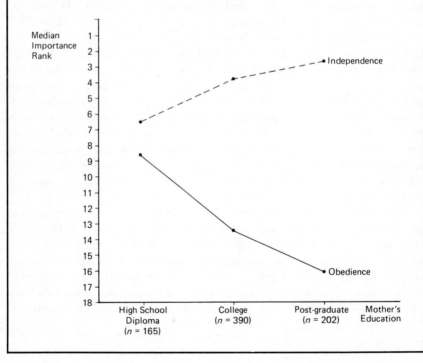

most of these tests measure "verbal achievement" including vocabulary recognition and reading ability.

Few input-output studies (Michelson, 1970; Levin, 1970; Cohn and Millman, 1975) have tried to account for more than one kind of outcome at a time although it is obvious that education produces multiple outcomes. Education affects people in many ways, and these outcomes are often reciprocally related over time. For example, children with low self-esteem may avoid achievement situations so that their test performances are poorer than they might be had they tried harder. The poor performance merely reinforces low self-esteem, and this cycle tends to become self-maintaining. Researchers have avoided dealing with more than one outcome at a time mainly for methodological reasons; the statistics required to relate *sets of inputs* to *sets of outcomes* exist in principle, but in practice they are unwieldy. In the last part of this chapter we will consider the theoretical issues involved in describing the dynamically related multiple outcomes of education, but most of our attention will be devoted to single outcome measures, beginning with norm-referenced achievement tests. First, however, we must review the desiderata of a "good" measure.

Test Reliability and Validity

Any measure or test must have two properties if it is to be useful: *reliability* and *validity*. Reliability concerns questions of consistency; does the test produce the same score for a given individual when he or she is tested on two or more occasions? Reliability can be determined in at least three ways, but obviously all involve correlations between two scores for each individual. The idea of the *test-retest method* is to administer the same test to the same individuals on two different occasions, separated by some period of time (say two weeks). Another approach, the *parallel forms method*, involves giving two different, but highly similar alternative forms of a test to the same individuals. Scores on these parallel tests can be correlated to estimate the reliability of the tests. Finally, the most commonly used method of estimating test reliability is the *split-half method*. In this case, a long version of a test is administered and the items are randomly divided into two subgroups, separate scores are computed for each subgroup of items, and then correlations are computed between these pairs of scores.

In theory, reliability increases with the length of the test. That is, the more items in a test, the higher the overall reliability of the test, but of course there is some point at which boredom or fatigue begins to interfere (see Anastasi, 1976; Thorndike and Hagen, 1977; or

Table 3–1. Summary of Outcome Measures Used in Major Input-Output Studies in Education.

OUTPUT / STUDY	Verbal Achievement, Reading, and Vocabulary	Math Achievement	Science Achievement	Academic Ability	General Information	Self-concept and Self-esteem	Locus of Control	Intelligence (IQ)	Completion/Noncompletion of High School	Educational Aspirations	Other
Bidwell and Kasarda (1975)	*	*									
Bowles (1969)	*	*		*							
Bowles (1970)	*										
Burkhead, Fox, and Holland (1967) Study 1	*							*	*	*	
Study 2	*								*		
Study 3	*								*		
Cohn (1968)											Composite Achievement
Cohn and Millman (1975)	*	*				*					
Coleman et al. (1966)	*	*			*	*	*			*	

	Latin School Exam	Composite Achievement	Composite Achievement, Language	Composite Achievement, Study-habits, Parents Attitudes	Spelling	Abstract Reasoning	Composite Achievement	French, Literature, Civics
Hanushek (1972, Chapter 4, 5)								
Hanushek (1972, Chapter 3)								
Katzman (1971)	*							
Kiesling (1969)								
Kiesling (1970)								
Levin (1970)	*							
Mayeske et al. (1972, 1973a, 1973b, 1975)	*	*						
Michelson (1975)	*							
Murnane (1975)								
New York State (1972-75)								
Perl (1973)								
Summers and Wolfe (1974)								
Winkler (1975)								
Wolf (1977)								
Wiley (1976)								

Cronbach, 1970, for an explanation of the theoretical relationship between test length and reliability).

Validity concerns the question, what does the measure really measure? There are several kinds of validity. The weakest kind is known as *face validity*, and this simply means that the content of the test "looks" like it ought to measure the concept in question. By itself, face validity is an insufficient basis for using a test.

Criterion-related validity involves correlating test scores with another known measure of the same behavior; this second measure is referred to as the *criterion measure*. *Predictive validity* is the most important kind of criterion-related validity; that is, a good test will accurately predict future behavior that it is designed in theory to measure. For example, college entrance examinations like the Scholastic Aptitude Test (SAT) are designed to predict success in college. Therefore SAT scores gathered from high school students should be highly correlated with actual college performance, including grade point averages, or the SAT would be said to lack validity, specifically predictive validity.

The *item validity* of particular questions within a single test may be estimated by another kind of criterion-related validity. In this case the criterion is the total score on the test, and the individual test items are correlated with this score, one at a time. Items that show a poor relationship to the overall test score are abandoned because it is assumed that they do not measure the concept that the test was designed to measure.

Finally, the *construct validity* of a measure is inferred from the pattern of relationships between the test and many other constructs or known facts about behavior. For example, the concept of "intelligence" has been operationally defined by a number of "IQ tests." To have construct validity, the IQ test must not only be correlated with other purported measures of intelligence, but it must also be correlated with behaviors that are supposedly related to intelligence. For instance, the higher a person's intellectual ability, the better that person should do in school, so a good IQ test should be highly correlated with school grades, teachers' ratings, and achievement test scores (assuming, of course, that these measures are themselves reliable and valid).

Convergent and *discriminant validity* refer to the pattern of interrelationships that should be found among different tests if they have construct validity (Campbell and Fiske, 1959). To find these relationships, one must have at least two different *methods* of measuring at least two different *traits*. Convergent validity occurs if two measures of the same trait are highly intercorrelated; they must be measuring the same thing, the same trait. On the other hand, tests that are intended to measure different traits should *not* be correlated; if they have discriminant validity, measures of different traits will be uncorrelated or very weakly correlated.

These comments about test reliability and validity apply to all kinds of measures, not just achievement tests or other output measures. Inputs must also be measured reliably and validly if input-output studies are to produce meaningful results. On the whole, the reliability and validity of output measures are probably better known quantities than the reliability and validity, particularly the validity of input measures. Norm-referenced achievement tests are by far the most frequently used output measures in I−O studies, and we will examine these measures next.

NORM-REFERENCED ACHIEVEMENT TESTS

Standardized achievement tests (more properly called norm-referenced tests) are typically administered in group sessions and usually contain several short subtests that measure cognitive skills such as mathematical concepts, computational skills, reading comprehension, vocabulary, and so on. Box 3−2 describes the subtests that comprise one of the more popular norm-referenced tests, the *Metropolitan Achievement Test* (MAT−70). Each year this test is administered to over one million students in grades K through 9, and another test from the same publisher, the *Stanford Achievement Test* (SAT−73), is administered annually to an even larger number of students. Other popular norm-referenced tests include the *California Achievement Test* (CAT) and the *Iowa Test of Basic Skills*.

The idea of *norm-referenced* tests is to place each person's performance in relation to others. Relative standing, not some absolute accomplishment, is the important thing in norm-referenced tests. In

Box 3−2. The Metropolitan Achievement Test.

The *Metropolitan Achievement Test* (MAT−70) covers grades K−9 with six tests, each of which contains between three and nine different subtests. The *Elementary Level* battery, for instance, contains tests of (a) word knowledge (vocabulary), (b) reading, (c) language, (d) spelling, (e) math computations, (f) math concepts, and (g) math problem solving. The sample items shown below illustrate each of these subtests.

(Reproduced with permission of Harcourt, Brace, Jovanovich, publisher of the *MAT-70.*)

WORDS

☞ WHAT TO DO: *Read* the beginning part of each sentence, paying particular attention to the *underlined* word(s). *Pick* the word which best completes the sentence. *Mark* the space for that word.

1. To **trot** is to . . . . ○ run   ○ sew   ○ prize   ○ cook

2. A **painting** is a . . . . ○ picture   ○ brush   ○ person   ○ work

READING

☞ WHAT TO DO: *Read* each story. Then read each question about the story. *Pick* the best answer to the question. *Mark* the space for that answer.

Joe and Tom are in the house. They are playing with Tom's trains. They build bridges and hills with the track. Joe likes to watch the engine pull the trains across the bridges.

4. Joe and Tom are playing in the—
   ○ yard   ○ house   ○ car

5. They are playing with—
   ○ trains   ○ toy autos   ○ blocks

6. Joe likes to see the engine go—
   ○ over the hills
   ○ through the town
   ○ over the bridges

MATHEMATICS: PART A

☞ WHAT TO DO: *Work* each example. *Pick* the right answer. *Mark* the space for your answer. Mark NG if a right answer is NOT GIVEN. Mark DK if you DON'T KNOW the right answer.

1

$$\begin{array}{r} 2 \\ 2 \\ +4 \\ \hline \end{array}$$

○ 5
○ 7
○ 9
○ NG
○ DK

2

$$\begin{array}{r} 5 \\ -0 \\ \hline \end{array}$$

○ 0
○ 5
○ 15
○ NG
○ DK

MATHEMATICS: PART B

2. If you buy the baloon and the lollipop below, how much would you spend?

5¢	10¢	25¢	NG	DK
O	O	O	O	O

3. Fill in the space under the date of the third Sunday in this month.

Sun	Mon	Tue	Wed	Thur	Fri	Sat
						1
2	3	4	5	6	7	8
9	10	11	12	13	14	15
16	17	18	19	20	21	22
23	24	25	26	27	28	29
30	31					

9	15	16	NG	DK
O	O	O	O	O

MATHEMATICS: PART C

3. My brother has 10 marbles. He is going to give me half of them. How many marbles will he give me?

8	12	20	NG	DK
O	O	O	O	O

4. Five children are playing in the pool. Two more children come to play. How many children are there now?

3	7	10	NG	DK
O	O	O	O	O

5. A boat went 15 miles the first hour and 6 miles the second hour. How many miles did it go in 2 hours?

9	17	21	NG	DK
O	O	O	O	O

contrast, *criterion-referenced* tests are designed simply to describe the individual's skill level or behavior. For example, a teacher might make the statement that Sue is able to add any two positive whole numbers that sum to 10; this is the kind of statement that might accrue from a criterion-referenced test. In contrast, when Sue's performance is compared to others, it may be described as being as good as or better than that scored by 90 percent of the people who have taken the test (i.e., in the 90th percentile), but this is only one way of describing the results of norm-referenced tests.

Expressing Norm-Referenced Test Scores

A *raw test score* (i.e., the number of correct answers) is usually transformed into a *standard score* or a *scaled score* or expressed as a *percentile* or *grade equivalent* (GE) or a *stanine score*. To transform a raw score, the researcher refers to a set of published *norms* that shows how samples of children of different ages performed on the same test during its development. Table 3−2 presents the norms for the *Elementary Level* of the *Metropolitan Achievement Test*. These vocabulary subtest norms will be used in the illustrations that follow.

A *percentile* score shows the individual's relative position in a set of 100 ranked scores; the percentile tells how many people received the same or a lower score than the individual in question. For example, a third grader who correctly answers 18 of the 50 items on the Word Knowledge (vocabulary) subtest of the MAT−70 will have a percentile score of 54, meaning that 54 out of every 100 third graders who took the test scored the same as or lower than this individual.

A *grade equivalent* (GE) score shows the grade (school year and month) at which 50 percent of the children achieve or exceed a given score. For example, on the vocabulary subtest, the raw score of 18, which corresponds to a percentile score of 54, has a grade equivalent of 2.7, meaning that by the seventh month of the second grade, 50 percent of the students achieve a score of 18 or higher on the vocabulary subtest.

The term *stanine* stands for "standard nine," and it refers to a system by which individuals, rank ordered by their raw scores, are grouped into nine categories. This simple grouping makes it possible to describe raw scores with a single digit, and this presents some advantages over percentiles in many cases. Figure 3−1 shows the percentage of scores that fall into each stanine. Note that the fifth category contains the average score; a low stanine indicates a relatively poor performance, and a high stanine indicates a relatively good performance.

Figure 3–1. Distribution of Scores Expressed in Terms of Stanine Scores.

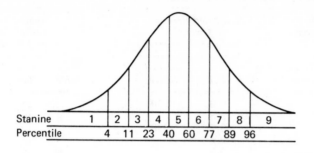

Stanine	1	2	3	4	5	6	7	8	9
Percentile		4	11	23	40	60	77	89	96

Standard scores are difficult to explain without referring to basic statistical principles. Since we do not introduce these statistics until Chapter 4, the present description of standard scores will be quite superficial. Simply stated, the idea is to show how far a raw score is above or below the average. The average in this case is called the arithmetic *mean*, and it is simply the sum of all of the scores divided by the number of scores involved. The mean of the scores 13, 14, 15, 16, and 17 is 15 (i.e., 13 + 14 + 15 + 16 + 17 = 75, and 75 ÷ 5 = 15). The *standard deviation* is a statistic that measures how tightly the scores cluster around the average. The greater the dispersion of the scores, the larger the standard deviation will be. A raw score is converted to a standard score (*z*-score) by subtracting the mean from the raw score and then dividing this dividend by the standard deviation. That is,

$$\text{Standard Score} = \frac{\text{Raw Score} - \text{Mean}}{\text{Standard Deviation}} \qquad (3-1)$$

The advantage of standard scores is that they permit us to compare raw scores on tests that are very different. The tests may vary in length, content, or format; but we can compare scores on these tests by converting the raw scores to standard scores. The standard score tells us how many standard deviations above or below the average (mean) each score is.

Scaled scores, which are often mistakenly called standard scores, are becoming increasingly popular with test manufacturers. The reason is that scaled scores permit direct comparisons between any two scores on a single subtest, including comparisons across different grade levels or alternative test forms. Scaled scores, which originated with Thurstone (Edwards and Thurstone, 1952), are difficult to

Table 3-2. Sample Norms for the MAT-70 Word Knowledge Subtest, Elementary Level Forms F, G, and H.

Raw Scores to Scaled Scores

Raw Score	Scaled Score
60	
59	
58	
57	
56	
55	
54	
53	
52	
51	
50	116
49	99
48	92
47	87
46	83
45	80
44	78
43	76
42	74
41	73
40	72
39	70
38	69
37	68
36	67
35	67
34	66
33	65
32	64
31	64
30	63
29	62
28	61
27	60
26	60
25	59
24	59
23	58
22	57
21	57
20	56
19	55

Scaled Scores to Grade Equivalents (GE)

G.E.	Scaled Score
9.9	130
9.8	
9.7	98
9.6	
9.5	
9.4	97
9.3	96
9.2	
9.1	95
9.0	
8.9	
8.8	94
8.7	
8.6	93
8.5	
8.4	92
8.3	
8.2	
8.1	91
8.0	
7.9	90
7.8	
7.7	89
7.6	
7.5	88
7.4	
7.3	87
7.2	86
7.1	85
7.0	
6.9	84
6.8	
6.7	83
6.6	
6.5	82
6.4	
6.3	81
6.2	
6.1	80
6.0	79
5.9	
5.8	78
5.7	
5.6	77
5.5	

Scaled Scores to Percentiles and Stanines

Stanine	%ile Rank	Scaled Score
	99	87
9	98	83
	96	80
8	94	77
	92	75
	90	73
	89	72
	88	71
	86	70
7	84	69
	82	68
	80	67
	78	
	77	
	76	66
	74	
	72	65
	70	
6	68	
	66	64
	64	63
	62	62
	60	
	58	61
	56	
	54	60
	52	59
	50	58
5	48	
	46	57
	44	
	42	56
	40	
	38	55
	36	54
	34	
	32	53
	30	
4	30	
	28	52
	26	
	24	51

Table 3-2. continued

Raw Scores to Scaled Scores		Scaled Scores to Grade Equivalents (GE)		Scaled Scores to Percentiles and Stanines		
Raw Score	Scaled Score	G.E.	Scaled Score	Sta-nine	%ile Rank	Scaled Score
18	54	5.4	76		23	
17	53	5.3	75		22	
16	52	5.2	74		20	50
15	51	5.1			18	
14	49	5.0	73	3	16	49
13	48	4.9			14	48
12	47	4.8	72		12	47
11	45	4.7	71		11	
10	43	4.6			10	46
9	42	4.5	70		8	44
8	40	4.4	69	2	6	42
7	38	4.3			4	41
6	35	4.2	68	1	2	39
5	33	4.1	67		1	33
4	30	4.0				
3	27	3.9	66			
2	23	3.8	65			
1	17	3.7	64			
		3.6	63			
		3.5	62			
		3.4	61			
		3.3	60			
		3.2	59			
		3.1	58			
		3.0	57			
		2.9	56			
		2.8	55			
		2.7	54			
		2.6	53			
		2.5	52			
		2.4	50			
		2.3	49			
		2.2	47			
		2.1	46			
		2.0	45			
		1.9	42			
		1.8	40			
		1.7	38			
		1.6	36			
		1.5	34			
		1.4	31			
		1.3	27			
		1.2	24			
		1.1	21			
		1.0	18			

explain without referring to the statistical principles that will be described in Chapter 4. But the idea in essence is this: groups of children matched for basic ability according to their IQ scores are given different grade level tests. One group of first graders takes the Grade 1 level test while another group of first graders takes the Grade 2 level test. Say that the average score on the Grade 1 level test was 20 correct out of 30 possible answers, and for the Grade 2 level test the average correct was 10 out of 30 possible answers. It is safe to conclude, given that the two groups are similar, that a score of 10 on a Grade 2 level test is "the same as" a score of 20 on a Grade 1 level form.

To create a continuum of scaled scores, the test developers must use the overlapping testing pattern for all grades to be covered by the test. That is, some first graders will take a Grade 1 test, others will take a Grade 2 test, and still others will take a Grade 3 test, and so on. With these data in hand, the test maker can compute a single continuum of scaled scores that runs from the lowest score on the lowest grade level test through the highest score on the highest grade level test. This is valuable because it permits comparisons of scores across test forms and grade levels, and this is important when it comes to measuring change over time. Note, however, that *scaled scores do not permit comparisons between different subject areas*, say vocabulary and mathematics subtests.

The way a researcher chooses to express test scores can make a difference in the conclusions he or she reaches, and in the next section we will examine this and other potential problems of using norm-referenced tests as outcome measures.

Potential Problems

Achievement test scores are relatively easy to collect, and they seem to have "face validity," that is, they appear to measure skills that most people feel are basic to the school's task. But using norm-referenced achievement test scores as output measures raises some potential problems.

1. *The Wrong Curriculum.* Good standardized tests are expensive to develop, and therefore they are designed to serve a broad market; test makers of necessity must assume that all children have been exposed to essentially the same curriculum. This is a tenuous assumption, especially in the case of secondary school students. If the school's curriculum and the test's assumed curriculum are markedly incongruent, the achievement measures for that school will be dis-

torted even though the students may be achieving at a very high level in some skills that the test does not measure adequately. To obviate this possibility, test developers can follow one of two strategies; they can (a) limit their tests to very basic curriculum objectives ("the common denominator approach") or (b) assume a broad spectrum curriculum ("the something for everyone approach"). Test reliability increases with test length. However, longer tests raise test construction costs, and thus there is a tendency to prefer the common denominator approach to test construction.

2. *Inadequate or Obsolete Norms.* Standardized achievement tests do not measure absolute knowledge, but rather they are intended to determine the relative standing of test takers. An individual's raw score is interpreted by referring to a set of published test norms that show the scores that children in different grade levels obtained during the norming of the tests. The accuracy of these norms determines at least in part how well a person's relative standing is measured, and the accuracy of the norms depends in large part upon the kinds of pupils who were tested during the development of the test norms. Ideally, the test manufacturers should administer the new tests to large samples of randomly selected students so that the norming samples are highly representative of all 49 million American elementary and secondary school students. Large samples are easy to obtain, but the samples sometimes fail to represent the whole population of American students. Some evidence suggests that, especially in the past, norming samples systematically underrepresented certain difficult to test groups, particularly inner-city and minority populations. As a result, the published norms for some tests overestimate the national distribution of scores since inner-city and minority status are negatively correlated with test performance at this point in our social history. One consequence is that the scores of lower ability, inner-city, minority populations who take the tests will be relatively worse than they would have been if the norming samples had been more representative of all students. This is serious, given that much of the educational research that uses the I—O approach is aimed at improving the schooling of low-income, low-ability, minority students in inner-city schools. The use of inadequate norms is only one of the problems that has an impact on the measurement of these students' achievement. The net result of these problems is that achievement is measured less accurately for low-ability students than others, and hence the ability of input-output studies to determine what works with these populations is reduced.

3. *Grade Equivalent Scores.* The grade equivalent scores (GE), which are often used in input-output studies (e.g., Summers and Wolfe, 1975; Churchman, et al., 1975), may be inappropriate, especially if the sample includes junior high or senior high school students. Even the authors of many achievement tests argue against the use of GE scores (but they publish them anyway because teachers seem to want them). The authors of the MAT—70, for example, provided this succinct summary of the dangers inherent in grade equivalent scores (Durost, et al., 1971, p. 5):

> Grade equivalents are losing the popularity they once had as a means for interpreting pupils' performances. This is due to several special difficulties which grade equivalents create for the teacher. First, grade equivalents are not directly comparable from one test to another for pupils who are above or below average in performance. For example, if a pupil in grade 4 obtains a GE of 6.8 in Reading and 7.2 in Mathematics Concepts, the pupil may actually be doing better in Reading than in Concepts in relation to other grade 4 pupils. Such odd phenomena can be noted in the norm tables for Metropolitan or for any other test which gives both grade equivalents and percentile ranks. Second, grade equivalent units are not equal throughout the scale. An increase in raw score of 10 points may amount to only three months growth in one part of the scale and to three years in another part of the scale. Third, laymen frequently think that a pupil ought to be in the grade corresponding to the grade equivalent obtained by a pupil. For example, if a pupil in grade 3 gets a grade equivalent of 5.2, some people cannot understand why the pupil is not placed in grade 5 in the school. There are, of course, many things to be considered in double-promoting a pupil. Most importantly the pupil's emotional and physical maturity and his mastery of specific skills and knowledge in each grade must be considered. A pupil in the beginning of grade 4 could obtain a grade equivalent of 6.7 in mathematics and have almost no ability to work with fractions. To place such a pupil in the second half of grade 6 for mathematics instruction would probably be a disaster.

4. *Bottoming-and-Topping Out.* If children are behind in school, they may "bottom out" on tests that are assigned to them on the basis of their grade or age. In effect, they produce "chance" scores since the tests are too hard for them. On the other hand, children who are far ahead in school will obtain maximum scores ("top out") on the tests that are intended for their age or grade level. The tests are simply too easy for them even though they are appropriate for the majority of children their age. "Bottoming out" is a more common phenomenon than "topping out," but both situations result in reduced variance in the output measures, and as a result, the true impact of some inputs will be underestimated.

5. *Group vs. Individual Testing Situations.* Group administrations of achievement tests probably produce lower scores than individual administrations of the same test because more distractions occur in the group situation. This would pose no problem if everyone suffered equally—it would be like reducing all scores by a constant—but it appears that educationally disadvantaged children show a larger decline in scores than advantaged children do when tests are administered in large groups. This proposition has not been tested empirically, but it is certainly plausible. If it occurs, the differential impact of the test situation causes lower ability children to look relatively worse than they really are, and statistically this means that the variance of the test scores is inflated artificially. As a consequence, the apparent impact of variables correlated with the differential impact of the situation (e.g., initial ability) will be overestimated.

6. *Scoring Media.* Group-administered achievement tests are usually presented to children in the form of test booklets. Sometimes the children are asked to write their answers in the booklets, and other times they are told to record their answers on separate answer sheets. These answer sheets, which can be scored by computerized optical scanners, reduce testing costs by leaving intact the most expensive materials, the booklets. But research shows that children often make clerical errors in using separate answer sheets, and the errors appear to be most likely to occur: (a) on items in the mathematics area, (b) among children in kindergarten through third grade, and (c) among below average fourth graders.

This is suggested by one experiment with the MAT−70 battery (Harcourt, Brace, Jovanovich, 1973). Third and fourth graders were randomly assigned to groups that used either separate answer sheets or test booklet scoring media. The median *reading* score for third graders who used booklets was 25 (GE = 3.2) while those who used separate answer sheets had a median score of 23 (GE = 3.1). Similarly, on the *mathematics concepts* subtest, fourth graders who used the test booklets had a median score of 25 (GE = 4.2) while those who used the separate answer sheets had a median of 23 (GE = 3.9). In grade equivalent terms, the answer sheets shaved about three months off the average math test score. Since a school year is only nine months long, three months is quite an impressive apparent loss.

The message should be clear to school districts that wish to maximize test scores; saving money on test materials means lowering the average performance for children in grades K through 4. But what is the implication for input-output research? If everyone uses the same scoring media, does it really matter which one is used? The answer would be no *if* everyone were equally susceptible to clerical errors, but we suspect that errors are correlated with ability; lower ability children probably commit more clerical errors than average and above average ability children. As in the case of group vs. individual test administrations, these differential effects of the test situation probably inflate the apparent contributions of inputs that are associated with ability (e.g., social class, IQ, and other student characteristics).

7. *Testing Times.*   Norm-referenced test scores may be distorted if the tests are administered during a time in the school year that is different from the time the test manufacturers developed the norms. Distortions, if they occur, are due to the way midyear norms are produced through linear interpolations between the fall norms and the spring norms. If children learn at a nonconstant rate across the school year, the linear interpolation of midyear norms may over- or underestimate actual achievement although this is only a hypothesis.

Figure 3-2 illustrates the problem of interpolated/extrapolated norms. The broken line is merely a linear interpolation between the fall and spring standardization periods and a linear extrapolation thereafter. The solid curve indicates a plausible record of how children may accumulate skills. According to this model, the first few months of school are a warm-up and review period, and the last few months are a period of consolidation (and getting ready for vacation). The diagram shows how much the interpolated/extrapolated norms might under- and overestimate actual achievement.

The easiest solution, of course, is simply to give the tests at the prescribed times, but this is not always possible (e.g., when testing hundreds of thousands of children as the EEO survey did). The impact of off-time testing is probably small when it comes to input-output studies *unless the test times are somehow related to characteristics of the schools or the students.* For example, if different grades are tested in different months, a spurious age effect (or age interaction) may be introduced. That is, inputs may falsely appear to work better with some age groups than others when in fact the real source of the differences may simply be errors in outcome measures that accrued from off-time testing.

8. *Tester-Student Interactions.*   Ideally, we would like a test to measure an individual's knowledge or skill and nothing more. We are forced to assume that everyone is equally motivated to perform well on the test, and therefore test performance reflects capacity and only capacity. Unfortunately other, extraneous factors may reduce per-

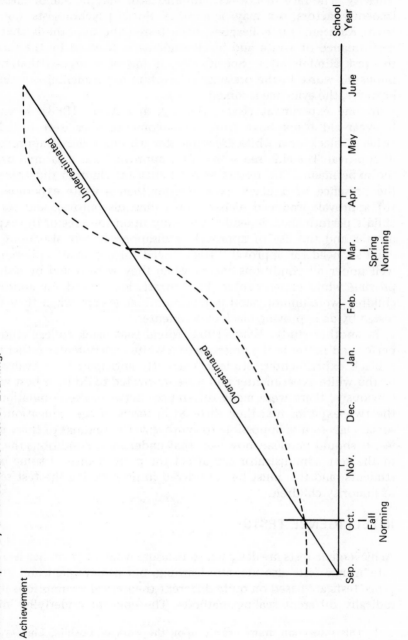

Figure 3–2. Hypothetical Curves Comparing Achievement Implied by Linear Interpolation of Midyear Norms and Possible Achievement Implied by a Nonconstant Rate of Learning.

formance so that we are likely to underestimate the individual's capacity. The race of the test administrator may be one of these extraneous factors; sex may be another. Social psychologists, notably Irwin Katz and his colleagues, have tested the hypothesis that the performance of white and black students is affected by the race of the test administrator. Specifically, it has been argued that black pupils do worse in the presence of a white experimenter or teacher; however, the evidence is mixed.

In one experiment (Katz, Henchy, and Allen, 1968), seven- to ten-year-old black boys from low-income families were tested by either a black or a white experimenter who gave either approval or disapproval. The children's "need for approval" was measured before the experiment. The results showed that (a) children did better in the presence of a black experimenter than a white experimenter, (b) approval produced higher scores than disapproval, and (c) the child's performance depended not only upon the race of the experimenter and the use of approval or disapproval, but also upon the child's "need for approval." High "need for approval" children did well under all conditions except when they were tested by a disapproving white experimenter. In contrast, low "need for approval" children were unmotivated in all conditions except when they were tested by an approving black experimenter.

In another study, Katz (1964) found that black college students performed better in the presence of a white experimenter rather than a black experimenter. Students evidently anticipated the evaluation of the white experimenter and were motivated to do their best work. Obviously, there were many differences between the populations in the two experiments; they differed in terms of age, education, and social class so it is impossible to synthesize the findings of these studies. It should be clear, however, that under some conditions the race of the test administrator can affect the performance of some black students, and this must be considered in interpreting the test scores of minority children.

INTELLIGENCE TESTS[1]

Achievement tests are designed to measure what a person has learned. Intelligence tests also measure learning, but achievement and intelligence tests are based on quite different theoretical assumptions if not radically different scaling methods. The concept underlying intelli-

1. This subsection draws heavily upon the work of Loehlin, Lindzey, and Spuhler (1975); Kamin (1974); Lewis (1976); Anastasi (1976); Thorndike and Hagen (1977); and Cronbach (1970).

gence tests is that people who do well on one kind of task will do well on all (or many) other tasks because there is a general ability or aptitude (or a small set of basic abilities) that can be called "intelligence."

Intelligence tests have not been used as output measures in many input-output analyses, but they have been the chief dependent variable in some studies of early childhood education and the effects of desegregation. Intelligence test scores have been at the center of the long running debate over the contributions of "nature" (genetic givens) and "nurture" (environmental experiences) to human behavior. Estimates of the genetic contribution to intelligence test scores run from a low of 50 percent to a high of approximately 80 percent (e.g., Jensen, 1969; Herrnstein, 1971; Pearson, 1904), but methodological problems make it difficult to produce precise estimates of the relative contributions of nature and nurture.[2] To understand the current nature-nurture debate, one must understand the nature of the intelligence construct and the historical context in which intelligence tests were developed.

The Historical Context

The idea that people are either "bright" or "dull" and that these characteristics run in families has been around for a long time (e.g., Galton, 1869), but it was a French psychologist, Alfred Binet, who produced the first workable operational definition of "intelligence." In 1905 in response to a request of the French Minister of Public Instruction, Binet produced a thirty-item test that was supposed to identify children of "low aptitude" who could benefit from instruction in special schools. The original Binet test was revised in 1908, and by 1911 tests were available for ages three through adult. It is important to note that Binet did *not* assume that "intelligence" was a fixed factor that was insensitive to training or schooling.

Several translations of the Binet test were made in the United States, but the version developed by Lewis M. Terman (1916) and his colleagues at Stanford University proved to be the most viable. Terman expanded the item pool by 30 percent, rewrote many of the original Binet items, and discarded others. Moreover, in 1937 Terman introduced the idea of an IQ quotient. Intelligence quotients, or IQ scores, express intelligence in terms of a ratio of "mental age" to "chronological age." For convenience, the quotients are multiplied by 100, and a score of 100 is average. A person who performs like the average member of his or her age group is said to have an IQ

2. For an overview of three methods of determining genetic contributions to human behavior, see Jinks and Fulker (1970).

score of 100. For example, a six-year-old that performs like the average eight-year-old child will have an IQ score of 133 (i.e., 8/6 × 100 = 133). It is important to note that these IQ scores cannot be compared directly across age groups since the computation of IQ scores depends upon the variation (the standard deviation) of scores within a given age group.[3]

The Stanford-Binet Intelligence Test was standardized in 1937 with a population of 3,184 people between the ages of 1½ and 18 living in seventeen cities selected from eleven states. The norming sample was diverse, but it was not a probability sample; hence we cannot assume that it was representative of the entire U.S. population in 1937. In fact, the sample seems to have seriously overrepresented higher socioeconomic status groups. The scale was renormed in 1960 using 4,498 people between the ages of 2½ and 18 living in six states, but again these people did not represent a scientific sample of all Americans.

At the same time Terman was developing the individually administered Stanford-Binet IQ Test, World War I provided the impetus for the development of group-administered tests, and the Army Alpha Test, designed in large part by Arthur Otis, was used to screen and classify over 1,500,000 army recruits. The apparent success of this diagnostic instrument provided the foundation for the mental test movement that evolved into the psychometric technology of today.

What Is "Intelligence"?

For various reasons the theoretical distinctions between achievement tests and intelligence tests have been exacerbated as IQ testing has matured. Many people now assume that it has been demonstrated that (a) individuals possess a general intellectual ability that causes them to perform about the same way on a wide range of intellectual tasks, (b) this general intellectual ability—which Cattell labeled g—is "intelligence," and (c) it is stable and largely insensitive to environmental interventions. How reasonable are these assumptions?

The fact that the various IQ subtest scores are highly intercorrelated has been mentioned as evidence that IQ tests measure a unitary, general intellectual ability. However, this overlooks an important fact—the items were selected on the basis of their demonstrated high correlations, and thus it is tautological to offer this as evidence of a general intellectual ability. Considerable empirical evidence (e.g., McCall et al., 1972; Lewis, 1976) raises serious questions about the

---

3. Stanford-Binet IQ scores have been computed in a new way since 1960, and these so-called deviation IQ scores do permit direct comparisons between the IQs of children of different ages (see Edwards, 1972; Anastasi, 1976).

concept of a single unitary intellectual ability factor that remains constant across age groups.

We are forced to assume a position of extreme operationalism. That is, intelligence is defined as whatever it is that IQ tests seem to measure. To be sure, IQ tests predict school performance; that is, of course, what they were designed to do. But this merely illustrates the ability of test makers to estimate performance (e.g., school achievement) on the basis of samples of behavior (i.e., IQ test performance). This leads to a concept of intelligence tests that is not burdened with the unproven theoretical stance assumed by some IQ test builders. That is, we view IQ tests as merely samples of achievement, and we do not have to argue that they measure a unitary, general "intellectual ability" per se. This is not to say that individuals do not differ in their learning abilities. IQ scores reflect both innate ability and learning experiences, and the effects of these two factors cannot be separated empirically.

Parenthetically, we must note that IQ tests may lead to spurious conclusions if they are misapplied to groups that differ from the norming population in terms of language or culture. One of the strongest characteristics of most of these tests is that they measure *verbal skills*. What defines tasks as "intellectual activities" is that they require verbal skills, and this is especially true of the tests for older children and adults. The Stanford-Binet, for instance, contains subscales that involve vocabulary items, analogies, scrambled sentences, and the interpretation of proverbs.

This heavy emphasis on verbal achievement poses a problem if the subjects have not grown up with the language of the test. If researchers realized that they were dealing with verbal achievement measures rather than unitary measures of problem-solving ability, there would be no problem. But in America, IQ tests have sometimes been misapplied to groups that did not grow up speaking English, and it is unreasonable to label this lack of exposure to the language as a sign of dullness. Difficulty with English is one thing; "low aptitude" or dullness is an entirely different matter.

The problem is not simply one of language, but also of cultural symbols. Inner-city, black children grow up with English, the standard English spoken by TV performers and the nonstandard English they speak with friends, but they do not share the same set of cultural symbols and experiences that white, suburban children have. It is this body of information that the test constructors—highly educated, white, males by and large—consider when they choose items for IQ tests. Some test makers have tried to create nonverbal IQ tests in order to avoid the problems described above. The Porteus mazes, the Bender-Gestalt, and the Draw-a-Man Test are examples of largely nonverbal IQ measures.

The point is quite simple. Most IQ tests involve verbal skills, and to some extent they measure (a) children's exposure to the vocabulary and language of the test makers as well as (b) children's ability to learn from their experiences. These two factors are confounded, and in some cases it is difficult to determine whether a low score is due to a lack of exposure or inability to learn. This suggests that we must be very careful in comparing the achievement or intelligence scores of various racial, ethnic, and cultural groups.

The Uses of IQ Scores in Input-Output Research

IQ scores, being highly correlated with achievement test scores by design, should not be used as input measures when achievement tests are used as output measures. In this case, IQ will appear to account for all or most of the explained variance in the achievement outputs, and the impact of other inputs, notably teachers and schools, will pale in relation to individual inputs. This would foster an unwarranted feeling of futility among school policymakers. In short, IQ tests are simply general achievement tests. They do "explain" much of the variance in achievement scores, but these explanations are tautological and add little to our understanding of the causes of achievement outcomes.

Intelligence tests may be useful in certain input-output analyses. Specifically, when researchers wish to see the effects of current inputs, they may use initial IQ scores as a proxy for previous achievement. By partialing out "initial achievement" (e.g., earlier achievement scores or IQ scores), it may be possible to get better estimates of the effects of variations in current inputs. For example, if one is interested in the effects on verbal achievement of tracking vs. not tracking at the junior high school level, it may be useful to control statistically for differences in what pupils learned before they went to junior high. IQ scores (or other achievement test scores) from Grade 6 can be used to represent initial achievement levels before the pupils entered the tracked or untracked junior high schools that are the prime subject of interest.

A tremendous amount has been written in recent years about possible abuses of standardized testing, both IQ tests and achievement tests. Some of these criticisms are merely authors' unsubstantiated opinions, but others are the result of thoughtful critiques by professional educators, especially those identified with the so-called "humanistic education" movement (e.g., McKeena, 1977; Davies, 1976;

Perrone, 1977). The debate over the pros and cons of standardized tests is complicated, not so much by the technical complexity of the issues, but rather by the lack of hard data to address these issues. Box 3-3 summarizes some of the most often voiced criticisms of standardized tests. One thing is sure, however; standardized tests will continue to play some major role in educational research because they seem to tap the lowest common denominator of various groups' expectations for the schools. With this in mind, we conclude our consideration of standardized IQ and achievement tests and we turn now to the affective outcomes of education.

Box 3-3. The Pros and Cons of Standardized Tests.

The heated debate over the pros and cons of standardized tests seems to involve six issues:

1. *Some classroom teachers may misuse test results in making instructional decisions.* For instance, they may assign children to reading groups or classroom groups on the basis of small and uninterpretable differences in test scores.

2. *The scores on achievement subtests do not give teachers the information they need in order to make instructional decisions.* For instance, if a child cannot add 5 and 16, the teacher does not know if it is because the child (a) does not know that $5 + 6 = 11$, or (b) that the child knows that $5 + 6 = 11$, but does not know how to carry to the tens place. In this regard, criterion-referenced tests, not norm-referenced tests, would provide more information for classroom teachers. What a child actually knows, not the relative differences between children, is all that the classroom teacher needs to know according to some critics of standardized tests.

3. *If standardized tests are used to evaluate teachers, formally or informally, there will be a tendency for teachers to "teach to the test."* That is, they will spend all of their time on the fairly narrow range of skills that will be measured in the tests. This distorts the curriculum of the school to fit the form of the tests.

4. *Tests do not measure some of the most important outcomes of schooling,* and they tend to concentrate on simple recall items at the expense of more important conceptualization skills.

5. *Some of the tests, especially the early IQ tests, may have been normed with inadequate, unrepresentative samples of children.* When biases occurred, it was usually in the direction of underrepresenting minority students and urban populations. As a result, the norms were skewed toward the higher achievement students, and hence minority and urban populations looked relatively worse than they were when compared with these inadequate national norms.

6. *Many of the items in intelligence tests and achievement tests make assumptions about the child's cultural experience, and some items may be biased against minority children.* For instance, an item was excluded from a vocabulary subtest when the test manufacturers' team of black psychologists decided that the item was culturally biased against black children because it assumed that a family consists of a father and mother, whereas a larger proportion of black children than white children live in families headed by a mother only.

The important question is how the shortcomings of standardized tests, if they are indeed true, affect the conclusions of input-output studies of schooling? Given this restricted perspective, criticisms 1 and 2 are irrelevant. They have to do with the way instructional decisions are made on the basis of test results, and they do not bear directly upon the conclusions of I—O studies.

Criticisms 3 and 4 concern the fit between what tests measure and what schools intend to teach. "Teaching to the tests" would not be a problem if the tests truly represented all of the schools' instructional objectives. Test makers and their defenders claim that the tests do cover the content of most nationally published textbooks and curriculum materials, but there is little empirical evidence to prove or disprove this. However, there is some evidence (Rudman, 1977, p. 182), albeit limited evidence, that speaks to criticism 4, the argument that standardized tests concentrate on simple recall at the expense of process and concept items. At least one major tests, *the Stanford Achievement Test* (SAT—73), has been analyzed with these results: (a) the percentage of items in social science and science subtests that tap processes and concepts declines monotonically across K—9, but (b) in every form at least 44 percent (to a high of 76 percent) of the items tap concepts and processes. Is this adequate or inadequate? There is no simple way to decide, but some researchers would argue that it is unreasonable to criticize the comprehensiveness of the outcome measures used in I—O research because even explaining only one or two measures, even rudimentary things like vocabulary, is a major advance in our knowledge. This argument might be plausible if the results of I—O studies were merely academic exercises. But they are not; they have had a measurable impact on school policies, and hence we must be concerned about the coverage of the outcome measures used in input-output studies. From the scientists' standpoint, getting a statistical model to "explain" anything adequately is a major technical advance; but this is not enough from the policymaker's standpoint.

Criticisms 5 and 6 are especially important to those who use the I—O model. If the test norms underrepresent urban and minority children, a given minority or urban school child's test performance will appear to be lower than it should be. This problem, which was discussed earlier, appears to occur less frequently today than in the past, and it appears to be less of a threat to modern achievement tests than intelligence tests, especially those that have not been renormed recently. The EEO data set, which has been used more than any other data set in I–O research, certainly suffers from this problem because many urban school districts failed to participate in the study.

Cultural bias, the subject of criticism 6, is also a possible shortcoming of the standardized tests used in I–O research, although this problem is fading as test manufacturers become more sensitive to the issue. It is entirely defendable to argue that standardized tests have not measured the actual knowledge of minority students as well as the achievement of majority students, but this does not mean that cultural bias accounts for all or even most of the observed differences in achievement of these two groups.

AFFECTIVE OUTCOMES

The idea is essentially commonsensical. We all "know" that people differ in terms of motivation, attitudes, self-esteem, and personality, and it seems logical to argue that (a) these characteristics are at least partly learned through experience, (b) schools must have some impact on these characteristics since much of a person's experience is in the context of schooling, and (c) these characteristics of individuals are related to other outcome measures, including those in the cognitive domain. These noncognitive properties of the individual are often labeled the *affective domain*, a term coined by University of Chicago psychologist Benjamin Bloom (1974).

It is unclear exactly what should be classified as belonging to the affective domain, but Bloom, Hastings, and Madaus (1971, pp. 273–277) have provided some general guidelines. They argue that the affective domain involves (a) receiving (attending), (b) responding, (c) valuing, (d) organization, and (e) "characterization by a value or value complex." For example, conceivably one could observe and score students' "attentiveness" to a science demonstration and then infer their interest in the subject matter. The more interested the pupils are in the demonstration (an affective variable), the more they should learn about the scientific principles that are the subject of the demonstration (a cognitive outcome). The truth of the matter is that the affective domain is usually defined in terms of "everything that is not clearly a cognitive variable."

The conceptual definition of the affective domain may be fuzzy, but there is no shortage of measures that are supposed to represent this domain. The U.C.L.A. Center for the Study of Evaluation (1972) has collected and rated over 1,000 different measures of higher order cognitive and affective variables. Unfortunately, this is not much of a step forward for we still do not understand (a) how these variables are related to each other, how they are integrated in the individual; or (b) how they impact on the other, cognitive outcomes of schooling as measured by standardized achievement tests.

The so-called internal-external control variable, which was briefly introduced in Chapter 2, is one of the most important affective variables, and it is discussed in some detail in the following subsection.

Internal-External Control Expectancies
Extensive research has demonstrated that people vary in the extent to which they believe that their outcomes are under their control. Some people tend to believe that their successes and failures are contingent upon their own actions. In contrast, others believe that their outcomes are determined by and large by fate, luck, chance, or "powerful other people." For convenience, we can categorize people according to their relative tendencies to attribute their outcomes to internal or external causes. *Internals* tend to attribute most of their outcomes to their own actions; *externals* tend to attribute most of their outcomes to fate, luck, chance, or powerful other people. Note that no one is entirely internal or entirely external; we are talking about relative positions.

Correlates of I—E Expectancies. Twenty years of research has shown that internals and externals differ in predictable ways, and this lends some validity to the internal-external control (I—E) construct. For example, internals are more likely than externals to:

(a) Delay gratification in order to gain long-term benefits (Mischel et al., 1974).
(b) Learn task relevant information (Seeman, 1972).
(c) Take longer on skill tasks and shorter on chance tasks (Rotter and Mulray, 1965).
(d) Join civil rights demonstrations during the 1960s (Gore and Rotter, 1963).
(e) Wear seat belts when they drive (Bridge, 1971; Russell et al., 1977).
(f) Use contraceptives to prevent unwanted pregnancies (MacDonald, 1970; Lundy, 1972).
(g) Perform better on standardized achievement tests (EEO, 1966).

The last finding is dramatically illustrated by data from the EEO report. Table 3—3 shows that in every ethnic/racial group and in every region of the country, relatively internal ninth graders had higher average verbal achievement scores than relatively external pupils had.

The Distribution of I—E Beliefs. Locus of control orientations are not randomly distributed across the adult population of the United States. I—E control expectancies vary systematically with race/ethnicity, social class, and sex. In general, whites tend to be more internal than blacks (Battle and Rotter, 1963; Lefcourt and Ladwig, 1965a and 1966; Lessing, 1969; Shaw and Uhl, 1969; Strickland, 1972; Zytkoskee et al., 1971), middle-class people tend to be more internal than working-class and lower class individuals (Strodtbeck, 1958), and in most cases, males tend to be more internal than females (Rotter, 1966).[4] Obviously these patterns correspond to the distribution of privilege and power in contemporary America, and therefore peoples' locus of control expectancies reflect at least in part the actual possibilities for control over the environment. In discussing the relatively external orientation of black children, Mayeske et al. (1973b) summed it up this way:

> We concluded that the minority group students' less optimistic outlook on life was an accurate reflection of social reality, and would not be

Table 3—3. Mean Verbal Achievement Scores for Relatively Internal and Relatively External Grade 9 Pupils in EEO Survey (Coleman et al., 1966). Questionnaire Item Asked—"Agree or Disagree: Good Luck Is More Important Than Hard Work for Success."

Ethnic Group	Externals (good luck)	Internals (hard work)
Mexican-Americans	38.6	46.8
Puerto Ricans	38.5	45.5
Native Americans	39.9	47.3
Orientals	44.0	52.5
Blacks, South	36.6	43.3
Blacks, North	40.0	47.1
Whites, South	42.9	52.5
Whites, North	45.4	54.8

4. The OEO data, as analyzed by Mayeske et al. (1973b), Levin (1970), and Michelson (1970), show females to be slightly more internal than males in grades 6, 9, and 12.

changed until discrimination in employment, housing, and schooling was eliminated. We also concluded that much could be done to eliminate the random element in child rearing, since most parents have little awareness of how they are affecting their childrens' intellectual and emotional well-being, and that the dependence of a student's performance upon his fellow students' level of achievement could be lessened by changing the schools' reward and performance criteria (p. xi).

The Mayeske et al. analysis takes on added poignancy when one considers the laboratory evidence that shows that locus of control expectancies are formed early in life, and by the age of three they tend to be statistically stable in test-retest studies (e.g., Mischel, Zeiss, and Zeiss, 1974). Once these beliefs are formed, they tend to be self-perpetuating.

The Dimensions of I—E Beliefs. Up to this point we have described locus of control beliefs in terms of a single I—E continuum, but this ignores three important theoretical distinctions. First, we must distinguish between *personal control beliefs* (PC) and *control ideology* (CI). The former term refers to individuals' beliefs about their control over their own personal lives. In contrast, control ideology refers to beliefs about what determines most peoples' outcomes. This distinction, which was first reported by Gurin, Gurin, Lao, and Beattie (1969), is especially important when one considers certain subpopulations, particularly inner-city black children. Most college students, the kind of people who participated in the development of the initial I—E scales (James, 1957; Phares, 1957; Rotter, 1966), have highly correlated PC and CI scores, but Gurin et al. discovered a significant difference between the PC and CI scores of inner-city, black high school students. Among this population, it was common to find highly internal control ideology beliefs mixed with highly external personal control orientations. In effect, these individuals were saying, "To get ahead, one must work hard and exert effort, but it won't work for me because something will go awry when I try."

Second, one must distinguish between control over *positive outcomes* and *negative outcomes*. Some people take responsibility for their successes but not their failures while a few people do just the opposite (e.g., Crandall, Katkovsky, and Crandall, 1965). One might speculate that this split orientation is probably most characteristic of children under the age of twelve, but as children mature their cognitive consistency needs tend to push them toward a single, congruent set of control beliefs. Modern I–E scales for children have been designed to include separate items for control over positive and negative outcomes (e.g., Crandall et al., 1965; Mischel et al., 1974).

Third, it is important to distinguish between different *kinds of external control.* By definition, fate, luck, and chance are intractable, but the control that emanates from "powerful other people" may be offset through ingratiation (Jones, 1977) or other interpersonal strategies. This distinction, first made by Collins (1974), suggests that every I–E scale item should allow respondents to attribute causation to themselves, to powerful others, or to fate (see also Reid and Ware, 1974).

None of these distinctions has been considered in the rather crude locus of control items that have been used in input-output studies to date. Only a handful of forced choice I–E items were included in the EEO survey, but the fact that they accounted for so much of the variance in verbal achievement scores, despite their psychometric crudeness, attests to the explanatory power of the internal-external control concept.

Self-Concept and Self-Esteem

Self-esteem is not the same thing as self-concept. The latter term refers to one's *perceptions* of one's abilities and personal attributes. Self-esteem refers to one's *evaluations* of one's abilities and personal characteristics. This distinction has often been lost in the schooling effectiveness literature.

Shavelson, Hubner, and Stanton (1976, pp. 411–415) have developed a model that holds that self-concept is:

(a) *Organized.* Self-concept reflects the person's cumulative, patterned experience with significant others.

(b) *Multifaceted.* There are several groups or subareas of self-beliefs (e.g., beliefs about one's physical skills, academic abilities, attractiveness to peers).

(c) *Hierarchical.* Global self-concept, at the top of the hierarchy, is based upon the synthesis of beliefs that fall into several subareas or categories, and these beliefs are in turn based upon particular experiences in which the individual has formed personal evaluations.

(d) *Stable.* While specific experiences may shift self-perceptions in limited subareas, global self-concept is relatively stable over time.

(e) *Developmental.* Self-concept becomes increasingly differentiated as the person accrues experience, and hence there is a strong, positive correlation between differentiation of self and age.

(f) *Evaluative.* We do not just passively perceive our behaviors and physical characteristics; we evaluate them according to our expectations and the expectations of significant other people and reference groups. This evaluative dimension of self-concept is reflected in self-esteem.

One study in particular illustrates the importance of self-esteem although this is a true experiment rather than a correlational I−O study. Maracek and Mettee (1972) used two primary self-esteem scales from the *California Psychological Inventory* to determine college women's (a) self-esteem and (b) the certainty with which they held these self views. All subjects performed two blocks of ten trials on a geometric matching task, but then the subjects were randomly assigned to two conditions. In one condition, people were led to believe that their performance was determined by chance and beyond their control while the other group was led to believe that they were working on a skill task. After the initial block of ten trials, all of the subjects were told that they were doing very well, that their performance was very successful. The dependent variable of interest was how well the subjects did on the second block of trials. The experimental manipulations had little effect on the second block performance of all of the subjects except those in one group—women who were certain about their low self-esteem and who thought that the task was skill-determined did very poorly. In short, they sabotaged their performance so that they could avoid success and maintain their very low self-esteem. Why would they do this? There are several possible explanations, but the most plausible argument is that they did not want to raise their standards or expectations for their performance only to have them dashed in some other setting. It is easier simply to avoid short-term information that upsets one's self-concept and self-esteem.

Note that the skill vs. chance nature of the task was a key factor. Success was avoided only in skill-determined tasks; "success" on chance-determined tasks has no implications for one's self-esteem since it does not reflect one's behavior but rather the operation of chance. The implications for education are obvious; many children who have initially poor experiences in school and who develop highly negative self-esteem may avoid skill-determined tasks, even tasks on which they can do well, simply because they do not want to raise their self-esteem only to have it shattered later by failure.

The State-Trait Problem

Affective measures have not been used in I–O studies as often as one might expect given their demonstrated importance in the few studies in which they have been used. One thing that may account for this is that affective variables tend to be less stable, at least in theory, than the cognitive outcomes of schooling. That is, unlike cognitive skills such as reading and vocabulary recognition, affective characteristics can vary across time depending upon the person's emotional "state." Once learned, cognitive skills tend to be permanent, and they tend to accumulate over time. Once children learn how to add two integers, they do not lose this ability but go on to do increasingly more complex operations. On the other hand, we all vary somewhat in our moods—our emotional states—and we may feel we are in control of our outcomes on one occasion and less in control on another occasion. This points to a question about affective measures. Are they measuring temporal *states* or consistent, transituational *traits?* Input-output studies assume that affective variables measure stable traits.

SUMMARY

The vast majority of input-output studies in education use *norm-referenced (standardized) achievement tests* to measure schooling outputs. Raw scores on these tests (i.e., the number of correct answers) may be expressed as *percentiles, stanines, grade equivalents, standard scores (z-scores)*, or *scaled scores*. Standardized tests are easy to administer and interpret, but their use as a measure of outcomes is fraught with potential pitfalls. These include:

(a) Test makers assume that everyone has been exposed to essentially the same curriculum, but this is frequently not the case. If the school's curriculum and the test makers' assumed curriculum are markedly different, the achievement measures for that school will be distorted. Students may be achieving very well in some areas that the test does not measure.

(b) Inadequate or obsolete norms, norms that are based on unrepresentative samples of American students, may make some groups' scores look relatively worse than they really should be. Inner-city children and racial minorities are most likely to be hurt by this defect in test norms, and as a result the impact of race and correlated social factors will be overestimated.

(c) Certain distortions occur when test scores are expressed as grade equivalents because GE scores are not constant throughout a scale.

(d) A test that is too hard for a student will result in a chance score ("bottoming out") while a test that is too easy will produce an inadequate measure of what the student really knows. Both kinds of test insensitivity result in attenuated variance in the distribution of scores, and this means that the impact of various inputs will be underestimated.

(e) Group testing generally depresses scores relative to individual testing. This would be inconsequential if everyone suffered equally in group testing situations, but it is very likely, although unproven at this time, that low-ability children are more negatively effected by group testing situations than are high-ability children. The result is that the impact of everything that is associated with initial ability (especially family background factors) will be overestimated relative to other inputs.

(f) A similar problem occurs when *separate scoring media* (i.e., separate computer-read answer sheets) are used instead of test booklets. Transferring answers to a separate scoring sheet presents more problems for low-ability children (or children in early grades) than others, and hence the distribution of scores will not accurately reflect the relative achievement of all students in the population. The result is that the correlates of low ability (or young age) will appear to be more important inputs than they really are.

(g) Test scores may overestimate or underestimate achievement, depending on the time of year, if the tests are administered at points in the school year that are different from those that the test manufacturer used in norming the items. This is because linear interpolations are used to create midyear norms, but children probably do not learn at a constant rate across the school year.

(h) Tester-student interactions may affect some children's test scores. Some experimental evidence suggests that white testers may negatively affect the performance of black, inner-city children.

Intelligence (IQ) tests differ from achievement tests in important theoretical ways. The former assume that (a) there is a general, unitary "intellectual ability," (b) this general intellectual ability is largely genetically determined, and (c) intellectual ability is relatively constant across the age span. The evidence for all three assumptions is tenuous. IQ tests may simply be very general achievement tests that measure verbal skills, especially in the forms for older children. Because they are achievement tests, intelligence tests are powerful predictors of other achievement test scores and school performance.

IQ scores have rarely been used in input-output studies of schooling although they have been the chief dependent variable in some studies of compensatory early childhood education. If IQ scores are viewed as achievement test scores, it makes little sense to use IQ as an input variable in trying to explain achievement test outputs. Obviously one achievement test will predict another. However, IQ scores may be used as inputs if they were collected before an intervention and are used as measures of initial achievement.

Affective outcomes—the noncognitive results of experience—include personality variables, attitudes and values, and self-perceptions. Three affective variables in particular have been used in input-output studies. *Internal-external locus of control expectancies* involve the person's beliefs about what causes his or her successes and failures. Relatively "internal" people, those who assume responsibility for their outcomes, tend to score significantly higher on school achievement tests. *Self-concept* reflects the individual's beliefs about his or her characteristics, and these hierarchically organized perceptions are derived from day to day experiences in a number of settings (e.g., academic work, sports, and interpersonal relationships. *Self-esteem*, which is different from self-concept, refers to the individual's evaluations of his or her characteristics. In most cases, affective variables have been viewed as inputs rather than outputs of schooling, but a more refined view assumes that affective and cognitive variables are bidirectionally related.

Chapter 4

Introduction to Linear Regression Analysis

The goal of this chapter is to equip the reader with an understanding of linear regression analysis, the basic statistical tool used in input-output studies. Introduced first is simple (i.e., two-variable) regression analysis. The method used in the analysis of bivariate relationships is easily extended to take account of multivariate relationships. The generalized technique, also discussed in this chapter, is known as multiple regression analysis.

Chapter 5 demonstrates the use of *linear* regression analysis in exploring *nonlinear* relationships, and it introduces some additional statistical issues of importance to the reader who wishes to become a critical consumer of educational research of the kind reviewed in this volume. Chapters 4 and 5 cannot substitute for formal course work in statistics, but a careful perusal of these pages should help the reader to understand studies that use linear regression analysis and to appreciate many of their strengths and weaknesses. We shall assume no special mathematical skills on the part of the reader other than simple algebra (although one or two footnotes will make reference to concepts from differential calculus).

THE REPRESENTATION OF FUNCTIONS

A *function* expresses a relationship between two or more variable numbers. It is simply a rule, formula, or recipe for associating numbers. Some everyday functions are closely akin to definitions. For example, by watching the hands on a clock, children soon learn that an hour consists of 60 minutes, no more, no less. They also learn that

30 minutes equal one half-hour, and 120 minutes, two hours. The significant achievement comes when they learn to generalize this information. In algebraic terms, they learn that

$$\text{Hours} = \frac{\text{Minutes}}{60} \qquad (4\text{--}1)$$

This rule, or function, is satisfied by the three pairs of values (60 minutes, 1 hour; 30 minutes, 1/2 hour; 120 minutes, 2 hours) and by all other pairs, observed (or unobserved) on any clock in good repair.

A graph may be used as easily as an equation in displaying many functional relationships. The graph that relates hours and minutes is given in Figure 4–1. To illustrate how points are plotted in two-dimensional space, three arbitrary points have been labeled along this particular line: $A(-60$ minutes, -1 hour), $B(0, 0)$, and $C(120, 2)$.[1]

The graph relating hours and minutes is positively sloped, that is, it rises from left to right, indicating what we know to be true, that hours and minutes increase together. Such pairs are said to be "directly related." Other variable pairs, like gravitational force and dis-

Figure 4–1.   Graph Relating Hours and Minutes.

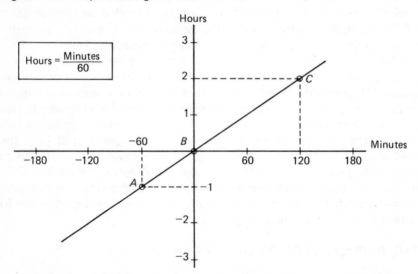

1. You may notice that Figure 4–1 introduces a concept of negative time, that is, time less than zero hours (or zero minutes). An everyday application of the concept of positive and negative time is time with reference to an appointment. A negative one hour (or 60 minutes) might indicate the earliness of someone's arrival with respect to the appointed time, in which case a positive value would indicate the lateness of arrival.

tance, are "inversely (i.e., negatively) related" to one another—the greater the distance between two objects, the smaller the force of attraction between them.

Not only is the graph of hours and minutes positively sloped, but the rate at which the graph rises from left to right is always the same —one unit of "rise" (vertical change) per 60 units of "run" (horizontal change). The ratio of rise to run is known as the *slope* of the equation. The slope of this particular equation, therefore, is 1/60. The definition of a straight-line or linear equation, such as this one, is an equation of constant slope. The ratio of rise to run in the time equation is the same between A and B (1/60) as it is between B and C (2/120 = 1/60) or between A and C (3/180 = 1/60).

Let us look at another linear relationship. Suppose that your recipe for steeped tea calls for two measures of tea leaves for every cup of the beverage desired, plus one measure "for the pot." Put differently, the function that relates measures (M) to cups (C) is

$$M = 1 + 2C \qquad (4-2)$$

The graph of the equation (Figure 4–2) has a positive slope of 2 but, unlike the graph relating hours and minutes, it does not pass through

Figure 4–2. Graph of Tea Recipe.

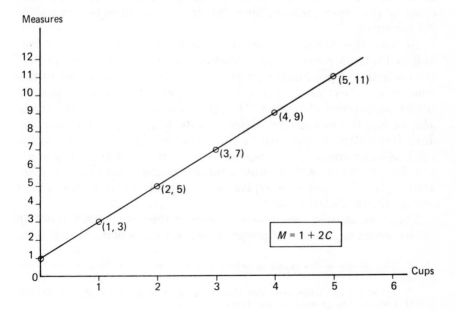

the origin.[2] Instead, it crosses the M axis one unit above the origin. The distance from the origin to the point of intersection of the graph and the vertical axis is referred to as the *intercept*.[3]

In general, a linear function of two variables, X and Y, can be expressed by the equation

$$Y = a + bX \tag{4-3}$$

where

a = the Y-intercept and

b = the slope

In (4–1), the formula relating hours and minutes, a is 0 and b is 1/60. In (4–2), the recipe for tea, a is 1 and b is 2. You should have little difficulty in understanding the implications of negative values for the letters a and b.

DETERMINISTIC FUNCTIONS VS. SCIENTIFIC MODELS

The equations given in (4–1) and (4–2) are not the kinds of functions that are subject to scientific investigation. The first is a definitional relationship and as such is indisputable. The second is one person's recipe for brewing tea. It might be called a normative relationship in that it is a prescription for action. In each of the functions, for every value of one variable there is only one corresponding value of the other variable. Such functions are said to be "exact" or "deterministic."

By way of contrast, in scientific research the outcomes of all natural and human processes are unpredictable at least to some degree. No educational production study, such as the ones reviewed in this volume, can "explain" more than a fraction of the variation that exists in educational outcomes. The job of the scientist is to demarcate and extend the boundaries between *systematic* (explained) and *random* (unexplained) variance in the world in which we live. As the random component of any phenomenon is whittled away, outcomes can be predicted with greater confidence than before, but there always remains some unexplained dispersion of outcome values around the predicted value.

There are at least two interpretations of the unexplained variation in the world around us, although whether a particular scientist leans

2. The *origin* is the point at which the axes intersect, that is, the point (0, 0).

3. Since the intercept does not change in value as X gets larger or smaller, it is also referred to as the *constant term*.

toward one interpretation or the other or favors a combination of the two is not at all critical as the particular interpretation chosen has no bearing on the appropriate mode of investigating problems. Variation unaccounted for can be interpreted as genuine haphazardness in natural phenomena and human behavior. Alternatively, it can be said to reflect the limited perception at any time of scientific investigators. For example, in studies of educational outcomes it may be unrealistic to suppose that researchers could ever identify *all* of the factors that contribute to differences in learning. Even if they could (implying that the number is finite), the manner in which these factors combine to produce outcomes—that is, the algebraic form of the relationship between inputs and outputs—is likely to be so complex as to overwhelm the algebraic skills of even the best mathematicians. The point is that for mortal beings the outcomes of all processes must remain random even if one chooses to believe that these outcomes are systematically determined from the point of view of some omniscient superhuman.

The method of science consists of specifying and testing hypothetical relationships, known also as models. A *model* is an imitation of reality, an abstract picture of the way in which variables interrelate. A model can be very simple mathematically or very complex, but in relation to the real-world phenomenon that it depicts, it is bound to be something of a caricature.

Let us illustrate the approach with a simple example. Suppose that we are researchers investigating differences in scores on a standardized achievement test within a population of pupils, and theory and experience suggest to us that differences in per pupil expenditure can account for most of the variance in the achievement variable. Although other scientists stress the importance of genetic characteristics, on the one hand, and home environment, on the other, we have failed to consider these factors or else decided a priori that they are unrelated to achievement.[4] Or we may suspect that ability and background differences are important, but we attempt to "control" for them by sampling separately from subpopulations that are homogeneous with regard to these factors (i.e., by studying groups of students who have similar backgrounds and who have shown similar abilities).

At this point, we have assumed a relationship exists between achievement and school expenditure, but the model is not testable until the particular type of relationship we suspect is made clear (i.e.,

---

4. The distorting effect of an omitted relevant variable will be discussed in the next chapter.

until the algebraic form of the function is specified). The assumed interdependence of A and E is denoted by the symbolic statement

$$A = f(E) \qquad (4-4)$$

which reads, "A is some function of E." By convention, the variable on the left-hand side of a functional expression is termed the "dependent" variable and the variable to the right the "independent" or "explanatory" variable. Although these terms are not intended to imply a causal relationship,[5] it is intuitively appealing in this case to cast school expenditure in the "explanatory" role since it is the antecedent of pupil achievement.[6] Moreover, while prudence is called for in interpreting the nature and (when causation *is* inferred) direction of any relationship, if researchers in the area of school effectiveness were not *thinking* "cause" and "effect," they would want to avoid the labels "input" and "output" and substitute some neutral term for talking about the two sides of the equation, a term such as "correlates" or "associated variables."

The correct algebraic form of the relationship between A and E is problematic. There is little theory, based either on deductive reasoning or previous research, to guide us. Often in such cases, the researcher assumes that the variables in the model are related linearly, the simplest assumption. The linear specification of $(4-4)$ is the equation

$$A = a + bE \qquad (4-5)$$

The intercept, a, and the slope, b, are referred to as *parameters of the model.*

Having specified the model, the researcher seeks to find estimates of the parameters. The estimates of a and b may be denoted by the symbols $\hat{a}$ and $\hat{b}$ (a-hat and b-hat) to distinguish them from the population parameters. Needed "to estimate the equation" specified in

---

5. Mathematically, an inverse formulation is always possible. The inverse of $(4-4)$ is $E = g(A)$, in which g and f are related functions. If $A = a + bE$, then $E = -\dfrac{a}{b} + \dfrac{1}{b}A$. In g, expenditure is the "dependent" variable, and achievement is the "independent" variable.

6. For one event to cause another, antecedence is a necessary condition but not a sufficient condition. Achievement in time t cannot be a cause of expenditure in time $t-1$. However, a relationship between the two variables does not imply necessarily the reverse causation either. Some prior variable, for example, parental wealth, may account causatively for both school expenditure and pupil achievement.

(4–5) are observations of values of A and E for some random selection of pupils in the population under investigation.[7] Whereas the parameters are fixed in the population, the estimates will vary depending not only on the particular selection of pupils, but also on the method used to summarize the observed values of A and E.

SIMPLE REGRESSION ANALYSIS

To demonstrate a powerful and deservedly popular method of estimating linear relationships, we may begin with an illustrative set of paired numbers. The numbers are concocted as the sample size (five cases) is too small to be used in testing most relationships based on actual data. The paired values of X and Y are given in Table 4–1. The subscript j refers to the case number. Depending on the study, *the case* could be an individual (e.g., a pupil) or a group of individuals (e.g., all of the pupils in a school or district), or the number could refer to a month or year in a study that analyzed variables over time. In experimental research, the case is often a particular trial. No matter what the study, Table 4–1 tells us that 1 and 12 are the observed values of Y and X for the first case, 3 and 9 for the second case, and so on.

The values of X and Y are plotted in Figure 4–3. The data points lie more or less in a straight line. Thus, the assumption of linearity appears not unreasonable. The slope of the line is clearly negative ($b < 0$). However, which of the very many negatively sloped graphs that lie in the vicinity of these five points summarizes the information contained in these points better than any other?

Table 4–1. Illustrative Data Set.

j	Y_j	X_j
1	1	12
2	3	9
3	4	7
4	8	3
5	9	4

7. A *random sample* of items is a group whose composition has been determined by chance. When this principle is followed, we can expect the presence of any characteristic or subgroup to be large or small in the sample according to whether it is large or small in the population. This expectation is the basis of any inferences we make about population parameters.

One method of fitting the equation in X and Y is to connect two extreme points, those representing the minimum and maximum values of X or the minimum and maximum values of Y. The line that defines the range of X is AB in Figure 4–4. The line that does the same for Y is BC. However, because this method ignores the information contained in all intermediate points, we should hope that there is a better method of fitting the equation to a sample of observations.

Figure 4–3. Plotted Data Points from Table 4–1.

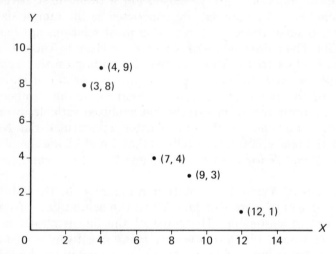

Figure 4–4. Linear Equations Defined by Minimum and Maximum Values of X and Y.

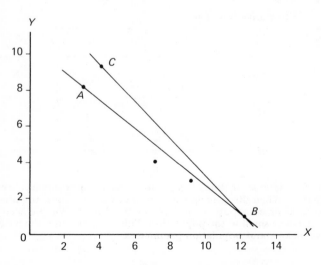

Given that Y is not a perfect linear combination of X, there is no straight-line equation satisfied by all five data points. In other words, some (if not all) of the observations must lie off the line, even in the case of the "best" estimating equation. Given any equation, therefore, associated with each X_j are two values of Y; (1) the observed Y-value, Y_j, and (2) the Y-value of the point that lies on the equation, call it $\widetilde{Y}_j$ (Y-tilde, sub-j). The vertical distance between the two is known as the *residual*, and it is represented by the symbol u_j. Another name for the residual is the *random error* since it represents the component of Y_j that cannot be explained by the specified model and the observed data set. The definitions of $\widetilde{Y}_j$ and u_j in terms of any observed point (X_j, Y_j) can be expressed graphically as in Figure 4–5, or algebraically as follows (where $\hat{a}$ and $\hat{b}$ define the particular estimating equation):

$$Y_j = \hat{a} + \hat{b}X_j + u_j \tag{4-6}$$

$$\widetilde{Y}_j = \hat{a} + \hat{b}X_j \tag{4-7}$$

$$u_j = Y_j - \widetilde{Y}_j \tag{4-8}$$

An estimating equation, since it must summarize a set of observations, will have data points that fall both above it and below it.

Figure 4–5. The Residual or Random Error Term (u_j).

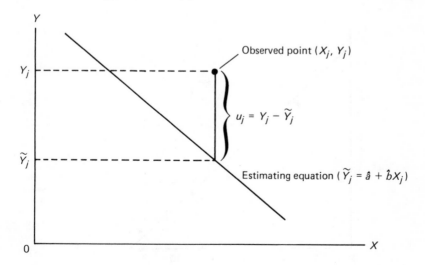

Stated differently, the error term will assume both positive values (for points that fall above the line, as does the example in Figure 4–5) and negative values (for points that fall below the line). Since we are looking for the line that summarizes the information in these points most accurately, we might wish to find the line that minimizes the total of these residual error terms. Any line for which the residuals sum to zero might seem to be a good candidate for our selection of the "best" estimating equation.

Unfortunately, there are many lines for which the positive and negative error terms just cancel one another, resulting in a net sum of zero. Which of these many equations do we take to be the "best" estimating equation? For the solution to this problem, we look beyond the sum of the residuals themselves to a related sum, the sum of the *squared* residuals. Since the square of any number (positive or negative) is a positive number, the sum of the squared residuals in the case of any equation must be greater than zero (unless all of the data points fall exactly on the line, in which case the equation summarizes the data set perfectly and the sum of the squared residuals is equal to zero). When an equation fits the data well (i.e., when the distances between the points and the line are small), the sum of the squared distances is small. The smaller this sum, the better is the fit.

Therefore, when looking for the line that best summarizes a set of data points, we choose the one that *minimizes the sum of the squared error terms*. The equation that meets this criterion in the case of the five data points taken from Table 4–1 is graphed in Figure 4–6. The equation that minimizes the sum of the squared resid-

Figure 4–6.   Linear Equation that Minimizes the Sum of Squared Residuals.

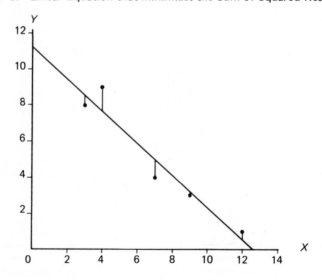

uals is uniquely related to the underlying data set and is generally accepted by statisticians as the "best" summary of the data set.

The criterion just described for fitting a bivariate (two-variable) relationship is referred to somewhat cryptically as *least-squares*. This label, like many others in statistics, makes sense once the principle behind it is understood. The estimating procedure based on the least-squares criterion is known as *linear regression analysis*. In our example, we are "regressing Y on X." Before proceeding to a full description of least-squares regression analysis, it is necessary in order that we be able to understand the formulas involved to introduce three fundamental statistical constructs: the mean and variance of a single variable and the covariance between two variables.

MEAN, VARIANCE, AND COVARIANCE

The *arithmetic mean* of a set of numbers is what is known in everyday usage as "the average." It is the most widely employed measure of central tendency.[8] The mean is computed as the sum of the values in a set of numbers $(X_1, X_2, \ldots, X_N)$ divided by the number of cases in the set (N). If we use $\overline{X}$ (X-bar) to denote the mean,

$$\overline{X} = \frac{X_1 + X_2 + \ldots + X_N}{N} = \sum_{j=1}^{N} X_j/N = \frac{\Sigma X_j}{N} \qquad (4-9)$$

The Greek letter Σ (capital sigma) is the standard symbol in mathematics for the summation operation. The ornate symbol $\displaystyle\sum_{j=1}^{N}$ tells us to take the sum (of whatever expression follows) for all cases from the first to the last (N-th). Unless à different summation is indicated explicitly, in the pages that follow Σ will be used in abbreviated fashion to represent $\displaystyle\sum_{j=1}^{N}$, the summation of case values from 1 to N.

The *variance* is a measure of the dispersion (scatteredness) of a set of numbers about the mean. The sets $(5, 5, 5, 5, 5)$ and $(3, 4, 5, 6, 7)$

---

8. Other widely used "averages" (i.e., measures of central tendency) include the mode and the median. The *mode* is simply the most frequently observed value in a set of observations. For example, in the set of observations $(3, 3, 5, 5, 5, 7)$ the mode is 5 because a score of 5 was observed three times and no other score was observed more than twice. The *median* is the point that divides an ordered set of values into two equal sized groups. Like the median strip on a highway, the median in descriptive statistics divides a distribution in half. For example, in the set of values $(3, 4, 5, 6, 8)$ the median is 5.

have the same mean, 5, but the latter set is clearly more scattered. A third set (1, 2, 8, 9), also with a mean of 5, is still more scattered. The formula for the variance is closely related to the formula for the mean since as already stated the variance measures how closely the different numbers in the set are clustered around the mean. Moreover, the variance is itself a kind of mean. It is "the mean of the squared deviations from the mean":

$$\text{Var}_x \ = \ \frac{\Sigma\,(X_j - \overline{X})^2}{N - 1} \tag{4-10}$$

where Var_x stands for the variance of the set $(X_1, X_2, \ldots, X_N)$, and $(X_j - \overline{X})^2$ is the squared deviation of the j-th score from the mean, $\overline{X}$.[9] The reason for dividing the sum of the squared deviations by $(N - 1)$ rather than by N is to make Var_x an "unbiased estimator" of the variance in the population from which the set $(X_1, X_2, \ldots, X_N)$ is drawn. Technical explanations of this fact together with definitions of the term "unbiased" in the context of statistics can be found in many textbooks[10] and will not be reproduced here.

An illustration may help to clarify the statistics presented in (4-9) and (4-10). The values of X from Table 4-1 are reproduced in column 2 of Table 4-2. To find the mean score, we sum the observed values and divide by N; these two steps yield the value 7. This value, the mean of (12, 9, 7, 3, 4), is used in column 3 to compute the deviation of each of the five scores from the mean. Note that the sum of the deviations of any set of numbers from their mean is zero. In column 4, the deviations are squared to get rid of negative signs since we are only interested in the absolute distance of each score from the mean, not in the direction of this distance. The squared deviations are then summed and divided by $N - 1$ to give us the variance, in this case 13.5.

Also given in the list of summary measures in Table 4-2 is the standard deviation of X. The standard deviation (SD_x) is simply the square root of the variance. That is,

$$SD_x \ = \ \sqrt{\frac{\Sigma\,(X_j - \overline{X})^2}{N - 1}} \tag{4-11}$$

9. Once again squares are used because if the positive and negative deviations are unsquared, they just cancel one another, that is, sum to zero, even when the absolute deviations are very large.

10. See, for example, Kmenta (1971, pp. 137–139).

Table 4-2. The Mean, Variance, and Standard Deviation of X.

(1)	(2)	(3)	(4)
j	X_j	$(X_j - \overline{X})$	$(X_j - \overline{X})^2$
1	12	5	25
2	9	2	4
3	7	0	0
4	3	-4	16
5	4	-3	9
Σ	35	0	54

$$\overline{X} = \frac{\Sigma X_j}{N} = \frac{35}{5} = 7$$

$$\mathrm{Var}_x = \frac{\Sigma (X_j - \overline{X})^2}{N-1} = \frac{54}{4} = 13.5$$

$$SD_x = \sqrt{\mathrm{Var}_x} = \sqrt{13.5} = 3.6742$$

The standard deviation is used as an alternative measure of the dispersion of a set of scores. It is somewhat easier to interpret than the variance since it is measured in the same units as the scores themselves and as the mean of the scores (e.g., in test points rather than squared test points, dollars rather than dollars squared).

In conclusion, whereas the mean refers to a single point on a scale, the variance measures dispersion along the scale. The smaller the variance (and the standard deviation), the more closely bunched are the values of the variable on either side of the mean. To test your understanding of these statistics, Table 4-3 reproduces in column 2 the values of the Y-variable in our hypothetical data set. Using Table 4-2 as the model, you should be able to fill in the missing information in Table 4-3.

The final construct to be defined in this section is the *covariance*. The statistics $\overline{X}$ and Var_x relate to the variable X alone; similarly, $\overline{Y}$ and Var_y relate to Y alone. The mean and variance (and standard deviation) are single-variable measures. In contrast, the covariance is a measure of the simultaneous changes in two variables, that is, a measure of their relationship.

In its computation, the covariance, Cov_{xy} (or Cov_{yx}), is fully analogous to the single variable measure of dispersion defined in (4-10).

Table 4-3.   The Mean, Variance, and Standard Deviation of Y.

(1)	(2)	(3)	(4)
j	Y_j	$(Y_j - \overline{Y})$	$(Y_j - \overline{Y})^2$
1	1	⬭	⬭
2	3	⬭	⬭
3	4	⬭	⬭
4	8	⬭	⬭
5	9	⬭	⬭
Σ	⬭	⬭	⬭

$$\overline{Y} = \frac{\Sigma\,Y_j}{N} = \frac{\boxed{}}{\boxed{}} = 5$$

$$Var_y = \frac{\Sigma\,(Y_j - \overline{Y})^2}{N - 1} = \frac{\boxed{}}{\boxed{}} = 11.5$$

$$SD_y = \sqrt{Var_y} = \sqrt{\boxed{}} = 3.3912$$

The formula for the covariance tells us to divide the sum of the cross-products of the X and Y deviations by the number of cases less one:

$$Cov_{xy} = Cov_{yx} = \frac{\Sigma\,(X_j - \overline{X})\,(Y_j - \overline{Y})}{N - 1} \qquad (4\text{-}12)$$

Computation of the covariance is illustrated in Table 4-4 using X and Y values from our hypothetical data set.

In columns 4 and 5, we begin by subtracting the mean of X from the first X-value and the mean of Y from the first Y-value, and then in column 6 we multiply the differences one by the other. The result for the first pair of values is -20. We proceed in the same manner with all subsequent cases, sum the column of cross-products, and divide the sum by $(N-1)$ just as we did in calculating the variance of X or the variance of Y.

How is the covariance statistic to be interpreted? When in a set of paired numbers, lower than average values of X are associated in most cases with lower than average values of Y and, as must follow, higher than average values of X with higher than average values of Y, the cross-products will usually be positive and the covariance will be

Table 4-4. The Covariance Between *X* and *Y*.

(1)	(2)	(3)	(4)	(5)	(6)
j	X_j	Y_j	$(X_j - \overline{X})$	$(Y_j - \overline{Y})$	$(X_j - \overline{X})(Y_j - \overline{Y})$
1	12	1	5	−4	−20
2	9	3	2	−2	−4
3	7	4	0	−1	0
4	3	8	−4	3	−12
5	4	9	−3	4	−12
Σ	35	25	0	0	−48

$$\text{Cov}_{xy} = \frac{\Sigma(X_j - \overline{X})(Y_j - \overline{Y})}{N-1} = \frac{-48}{4} = -12$$

positive. When, on the other hand, lower than average values of *X* tend to be paired with higher than average values of *Y* and vice versa, the cross-products will tend to be negative and the covariance will be negative.

In other words, a positive covariance indicates a direct relationship between *X* and *Y*. As one goes up, the other usually goes up as well. A negative covariance, as in Table 4-4, indicates an inverse relationship. As *X* goes up, *Y* usually goes down and vice versa. A covariance of zero indicates that there is no systematic relationship between *X* and *Y*. As one goes up, the other may go up, but it is equally likely to go down. The larger the absolute value of the covariance statistic, the stronger is the relationship between the two variables (i.e., the closer it is to being perfectly linear).

However, comparing the magnitudes of covariances based on different sets of paired numbers is not meaningful because the covariance statistic reflects the units in which the two variables are measured. In other words, the sum of cross-products will change if the units of either *X* or *Y*, or both, are changed (e.g., from dollars to francs, or feet to inches). Thus, in general, it is not possible to tell whether a covariance of a given magnitude indicates a strong relationship between *X* and *Y*, or whether it arises from the units used to measure *X* and *Y*.

The influence of units is eliminated if we replace the covariance with a closely related statistical construct known as the *correlation coefficient*. The correlation coefficient expresses the strength of linear association in "standard" terms (i.e., free of units), and it is this ingenious measure, to be discussed in some detail below, that is used most often to compare relationships.

ESTIMATORS OF a AND b IN
SIMPLE REGRESSION

You will recall that the equation graphed in Figure 4−6 is the equation that minimizes the sum of the squared residuals. This line is said to summarize the scatter of the five observations better than any other straight-line equation. In order to identify a particular estimating equation, we need to know its slope, $\hat{b}$, and its intercept, $\hat{a}$. What are the $\hat{a}$ and $\hat{b}$ values of the equation in Figure 4−6? In general, what are the formulas (or *estimators*) for $\hat{a}$ and $\hat{b}$ that satisfy the least-squares criterion?

The solution to the general problem is found in the methods of differential calculus.[11] Although the algebra will not be reproduced here, it can be shown[12] that

$$\hat{b} = \frac{\Sigma(X_j - \overline{X})(Y_j - \overline{Y})}{\Sigma(X_j - \overline{X})^2} = \frac{\text{Cov}_{xy}}{\text{Var}_x} \tag{4−13}$$

and

$$\hat{a} = \frac{\Sigma Y_j}{N} - \frac{\hat{b}\Sigma X_j}{N} = \overline{Y} - \hat{b}\overline{X} \tag{4−14}$$

In words, the slope estimator is the ratio of the X-Y covariance to the variance in X. In terms of our example,

$$\hat{b} = \frac{\text{Cov}_{xy}}{\text{Var}_x} = \frac{-12}{13.5} = -0.8889 \tag{4−13'}$$

This value is the slope of the graph in Figure 4−6. As X increases by one unit, Y decreases by nearly nine-tenths of a unit. The slope estimator, known also as the regression coefficient (of Y) on X, indicates the change to be expected in Y as X increases by one unit.[13] For the sample of observations, it measures the average effect on Y of a one-unit change in X.

11. The procedure is to take the first partial derivatives of $SSR = \Sigma(Y_j - \hat{a} - \hat{b}X_j)^2$ with respect to $\hat{a}$ and $\hat{b}$, set the derivatives equal to zero (implying that SSR is at a minimum), and solve the two equations for $\hat{a}$ and $\hat{b}$.

12. See Kmenta (1971, pp. 206−209).

13. Symbolically, $\hat{b} = d\widetilde{Y}/dX = dE(Y \mid X)/dX$.

Equation (4−14) highlights an interesting fact about the linear regression model. It informs us that the least-squares equation is "constrained" to pass through the sample means. In other words, one point on any regression line is the point $(\overline{X}, \overline{Y})$. To substantiate this fact, you might check the graph in Figure 4−6 to see if it contains the point (7, 5).

The formula for the estimator of the intercept enables us to complete the regression equation in our numerical example. Plugging in our estimates for the mean of Y, mean of X, and slope of Y on X, we get an estimate of the intercept,

$$\hat{a} = \overline{Y} - \hat{b}\overline{X} = 5 - (-0.8889)7 = 11.2223 \qquad (4-14')$$

and the regression equation, in the form of (4−7), becomes

$$\widetilde{Y}_j = 11.2223 - 0.8889X_j \qquad (4-15)$$

The regression equation indicates the value of Y, $\widetilde{Y}_j$, to be expected given a particular X-value, X_j.[14] It "predicts" or "estimates" Y from X.

For example, when X is 4 the equation estimates Y to be 7.6667:

$$\widetilde{Y}_j = 11.2223 - 0.8889(4) = 7.6667 \qquad (4-15')$$

However, from Table 4−1 you will recall that there is an observation ($j = 5$) for which X is 4, and the observed Y-value for this observation is not 7.6667; rather, Y_5 is 9. In other words, whereas the X-value of the fifth case would lead to a *predicted* Y-value of 7.6667,

$$\widetilde{Y}_5 = 11.2223 - 0.8889(4) = 7.6667 \qquad (4-15'')$$

the *actual* Y-value is known to be 9. The difference between the two has been defined in (4−8) as the random error or the residual. In this case, the residual is 1.3333:

$$u_5 = Y_5 - \widetilde{Y}_5 = 9 - 7.6667 = 1.3333 \qquad (4-16)$$

There are no other cases in our small data set where X assumes the value 4. However, were we to continue to sample indefinitely from the population, we would select eventually a number of observations at every value of X, including 4. The cases where X equaled 4 would

14. In symbols, $\widetilde{Y}_j = \hat{a} + \hat{b}X_j = E(Y \mid X_j)$.

Figure 4−7. Assumed Distribution of Actual Y Values around Predicted Y Value.

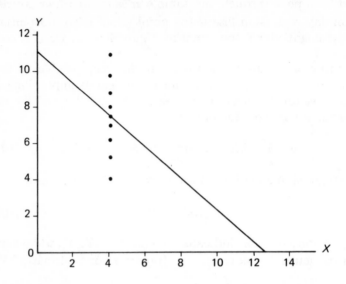

display different values of Y. The points could be plotted as in Figure 4−7. An assumption of regression analysis is that the mean of the residuals at each value of X is zero. In other words, the mean value of Y at any value of X is the value predicted by the regression equation, in this case 7.6667. It is in this sense that $\widetilde{Y}_j$ is the "expected value" of Y when X takes the value X_j.

EXPLAINED AND UNEXPLAINED VARIATION IN Y

You will recall the formula for the variance of Y, $\Sigma (Y_j - \overline{Y})^2/N - 1$. The expression in parentheses is the deviation of the j-th case from the mean value of Y. The deviation is shown in Figure 4−8 to be made up of two components:

$$(Y_j - \overline{Y}) = (Y_j - \widetilde{Y}_j) + (\widetilde{Y}_j - \overline{Y}) \qquad (4-17)$$

The equality in (4−17) is maintained if we square both sides of the equation and then sum over all js:

$$(Y_j - \overline{Y})^2 = (Y_j - \widetilde{Y}_j)^2 + 2(Y_j - \widetilde{Y}_j)(\widetilde{Y}_j - \overline{Y}) + (\widetilde{Y}_j - \overline{Y})^2$$

$$(4-18)$$

Figure 4–8. Partitioning the Deviation of Y_j from the Mean of Y.

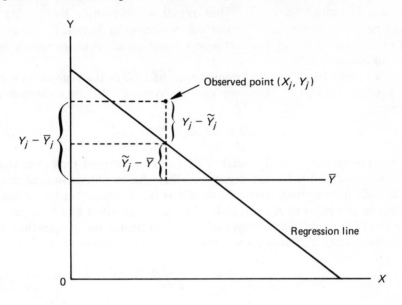

$$\Sigma(Y_j - \overline{Y})^2 = \Sigma[(Y_j - \widetilde{Y}_j)^2 + 2(Y_j - \widetilde{Y}_j)(\widetilde{Y}_j - \overline{Y}) +$$
$$(\widetilde{Y}_j - \overline{Y})^2] \qquad (4\text{–}19)$$

$$\Sigma(Y_j - \overline{Y})^2 = \Sigma(Y_j - \widetilde{Y}_j)^2 + 2\Sigma(Y_j - \widetilde{Y}_j)(\widetilde{Y}_j - \overline{Y}) +$$
$$\Sigma(\widetilde{Y}_j - \overline{Y})^2 \qquad (4\text{–}19')$$

It can be proved[15] that the cross-product terms sum to zero so that (4–19') can be rewritten:

$$\Sigma(Y_j - \overline{Y})^2 = \Sigma(Y_j - \widetilde{Y}_j)^2 + \Sigma(\widetilde{Y}_j - \overline{Y})^2 \qquad (4\text{–}20)$$

The left side of (4–20), the sum of the squared deviations from the mean (*SSD*), is a measure of the variation or dispersion in Y.[16] It is this variation in the dependent variable that we attempt to explain by regression analysis. The first term on the right side of (4–20) is by now an old friend, the sum of the squared residuals (*SSR*). The *SSR*, minimized by the least-squares regression line, is a

15. For the proof see, for example, Kane (1968, p. 234).
16. Compare the formula for the variance of Y,
$$\mathrm{Var}_y = \Sigma(Y_j - \overline{Y})^2/N - 1$$

measure of the variation in u. It is, in short, a measure of the "un-explained" variation in Y. What remains, therefore, $\Sigma(\widetilde{Y}_j - \overline{Y})^2$, must be a measure of the "explained" variation in Y, that is, the variation accounted for by the regression equation or, in other words, by the variation in X.[17]

If we refer to the second component of SSD as the regression sum of squares (RRS),[18] then we can rewrite (4−20) in abbreviated form:

$$SSD = SSR + RSS \qquad (4-20')$$

The total variation in Y consists of the unexplained part plus that part accounted for by the regression line. An excellent indicator of how well a particular scientific model is borne out by a set of data points is the ratio of RSS to SSD. This ratio, denoted by r^2, is called the *coefficient of determination*, and it indicates *the proportion of the variation in Y that is accounted for by the variation in X*:[19]

$$r^2 = \frac{RSS}{SSD} = 1 - \frac{SSR}{SSD} \qquad (4-21)$$

Since the whole (SSD) must equal the sum of its parts (RSS and SSR) and since each part is greater than or equal to zero (as each is formed by summing squares), we know that r^2 ranges from zero (no explained variation) to one (fully explained variation). Figure 4−9 illustrates the two extremes (rarely encountered in empirical research) and an intermediate value of r^2. Notice in (c), the case of no relationship between Y and X, that the regression line is horizontal at the value, $Y = \overline{Y}$. In other words, when Y and X are unrelated, the best prediction of Y at any value of X is the mean of Y.

---

17. The relation between $\Sigma(\widetilde{Y}_j - \overline{Y})^2$ and the variation in X may be clarified by the following:

$$
\begin{aligned}
\Sigma(\widetilde{Y}_j - \overline{Y})^2 &= \Sigma(\hat{a} + \hat{b}X_j - \overline{Y})^2 \\
&= \Sigma(\overline{Y} - \hat{b}\overline{X} + \hat{b}X_j - \overline{Y})^2 \\
&= \Sigma(\hat{b}[X_j - \overline{X}])^2 \\
&= \hat{b}^2 \Sigma(X_j - \overline{X})^2
\end{aligned}
$$

18. In experimental research, this component is sometimes called the "between group" sum of squares, while the SSR is called the "within group" sum of squares.

19. An alternative definition of r^2, reflected in (4−21), is 1 minus the proportion of the variation in Y that is *not* accounted for by the variation in X.

Perhaps more familiar to many readers than r^2 is the square root of r^2, known as the (zero-order product-moment) *coefficient of correlation*. Whereas r^2 ranges from 0 to 1, r ranges from -1 to 1, a negative value signifying an inverse relationship (correlation) between X and Y. In other words, r has the same sign as $\hat{b}$. There are many formulas for the linear correlation coefficient, but one that appeals intuitively is

$$r = \frac{\text{Cov}_{xy}}{\sqrt{\text{Var}_x\ \text{Var}_y}} = \frac{\text{Cov}_{xy}}{SD_x\ SD_y} \tag{4-22}$$

Equation (4-22) demonstrates the close kinship between the covariance (Cov_{xy}) and the correlation coefficient. The latter, unlike the former, is expressed in standard units and thus may be used to compare relationships among different variables or among the same variables measured on different scales.

The coefficients of determination and correlation between X and Y for the data in Table 4-1 are computed in Table 4-5.

Figure 4-9. The Coefficient of Determination (r^2).

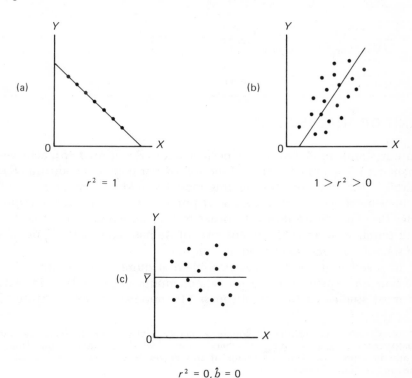

(a)

$r^2 = 1$

(b)

$1 > r^2 > 0$

(c)

$r^2 = 0, \hat{b} = 0$

Table 4-5. Computing r^2 and r.

j	Y_j	X_j	$\widetilde{Y}_j$	$(Y_j - \widetilde{Y}_j)$	$(Y_j - \widetilde{Y}_j)^2$	$(\widetilde{Y}_j - \overline{Y})$	$(\widetilde{Y}_j - \overline{Y})^2$
1	1	12	0.5555	0.4445	0.1975	-4.4445	19.7535
2	3	9	3.2222	-0.2222	0.0494	-1.7778	3.1606
3	4	7	5.0000	-1.0000	1.0000	0.0000	0.0000
4	8	3	8.5556	-0.5556	0.3087	3.5556	12.6423
5	9	4	7.6667	1.3333	1.7777	2.6667	7.1113

$$SSR = 3.3333 \qquad\qquad RSS = 42.6677$$

$\widetilde{Y}_j = 11.2223 - 0.8889 X_j$ (Equation 4-15)

$SSD = SSR + RSS = \Sigma(Y_j - \overline{Y})^2 = 46$ (Table 4-3)

$Cov_{xy} = -12$ (Table 4-4)

$Var_x = 13.5$ (Table 4-2)

$Var_y = 11.5$ (Table 4-3)

$$r^2 = \frac{RSS}{SSD} = \frac{42.6677}{46} = 0.9275$$

$$r = \frac{Cov_{xy}}{\sqrt{Var_x \, Var_y}} = \frac{-12}{\sqrt{(13.5)(11.5)}} = -0.9631$$

$$r = \sqrt{r^2} = \sqrt{0.9275} = -0.9631$$

UNIT OF ANALYSIS AND r^2

In our simple model of school performance (Equation 4-5), achievement (A) is assumed to be a function of per pupil expenditure (E). Ideally, the data for testing this model would consist of a set of achievement scores for a sample of pupils paired with a set of *pupil-specific* expenditure levels. In other words, we would know that the j-th pupil, with an achievement level of A_j, has had exactly E_j dollars of school resources expended on him/her.

In practice, it has not been possible to acquire pupil-specific information on expenditure (or on school inputs in general).[20] In fact, in most studies on the effectiveness of schooling, the expenditure of

20. Clearly, expenditure in dollars is merely a proxy for the quantity and quality of the various inputs—teachers, books, and so on—in the educational production process. Some criticisms of this aggregate variable are discussed in the next section of this chapter.

educational resources is measured not even at the classroom level, but rather at the level of the school or the district or (imagine it!) the state. In other words, the achievement of a particular pupil is paired with the *average* level of expenditure in his (or her) school, district, or state. To use a group measure of this kind is to ignore all of the variation that exists within the administrative or geographic unit. The particular pupil may have had more or fewer resources expended on him (or her) than has the average pupil because, as we know, per pupil expenditure is not constant within a state across districts, or within a district across schools, or within a school across classrooms. (It is not even constant within a classroom across pupils, as it will vary according to the assertiveness of the pupils and the preferences of the teacher.)

Thus, it is useful to distinguish between the validity of a model and the validity of the measures of the variables in the model. It could be that (4–5) is a close approximation of the real-world determination of differences in pupil achievement. However, average expenditure is a proxy for the independent variable in the model, and presumably not a very good one. The greater the variation in expenditure around the average, the poorer is the group measure as an indicator of the pupil-specific variable, and as a consequence, the smaller will be the r^2 of the regression equation. In summary, the use of proxy variables tends to reduce the proportion of total observed variation in output explained in the analysis.

In some studies, both the dependent and the independent variables are measured as averages. For example, the researcher may choose to regress mean district achievement on mean per pupil expenditure. This procedure is quite different from the one described above. There the unit of analysis was the individual pupil, and a group measure of expenditure was used as a proxy for the amount expended on the individual. Here the group becomes the unit of analysis.

The effect of using group data instead of individual data in estimating a relationship is usually to increase the r^2 of the regression equation. The reason for this is best understood by examining the regression equations based on both kinds of data. Let

$$A_j = \hat{a} + \hat{b}E_j + u_j \qquad (4\text{–}23)$$

be the equation for N individual pupils, and

$$\overline{A}_g = \hat{a} + \hat{b}\overline{E}_g + u_g \qquad (4\text{–}23')$$

the equation for some smaller sample of pupil groups, made up of the individual pupils. You will recall that u_j in (4–23) is the "random error" in achievement of the j-th individual about the regression line. It can be said to measure the net effect on the achievement of this individual of all of the explanatory variables omitted from the model. As the N individuals are grouped in (4–23') by school district or by any other criterion assumed to be unrelated to achievement, the random errors within groups tend to cancel one another out. As a result, the group means tend to be less dispersed about the regression line than are the individual observations, and the r^2 based on group data is larger as a consequence.

EXPENDITURE A PROXY FOR THE QUANTITY AND QUALITY OF INPUTS

Implicit in our model of school performance, $A = f(E)$, is an intermediate step in the educational production process—the conversion of E, a dollar figure, into teachers' services, classroom supplies, library facilities, and other factors that touch pupils more or less directly. Each of these factors is available at different prices in the marketplace, and price differentials are assumed to reflect differences in the productiveness of inputs or, loosely speaking, differences in input "quality." If, for example, teachers with master's degrees are 10 percent more effective at augmenting achievement test scores than teachers with only baccalaureate degrees, efficiency-minded school boards should be willing to pay them at a 10 percent higher rate of salary.

There is nothing new in using factor prices as weights in aggregating, for purposes of analysis, the inputs in a production process. "Capital" and "labor" are constructs based on this principle. Economists rely on "dollars of capital" to avoid having to distinguish in manufacturing among lathes, presses, wedges, and winches, or in agriculture, among barns, silos, harnesses, and hoes. Similarly, instead of counting separately the hours worked by individuals (40 hours of Harriet's time, 38 hours of George's time, . . .) or by categories of individuals (5,000 hours of machinists' time, 2,000 hours of file clerks' time, . . .), economists argue that "the labor bill," a single measure, serves just as well for many purposes.

The validity of this procedure for adding together dissimilar factor inputs rests on a belief that those who purchase inputs are engaged in a competitive struggle and are impelled to maximize the output produced from a given dollar expenditure lest they be undercut in their sales and driven out of business. Whereas this behavioral model may apply in a rough fashion to manufacturers and farmers, the men and women who manage systems of education would seem to be much less accountable to market forces.

"Economic efficiency" has meaning only with reference to a clearly defined and measurable goal (such as the augmentation of pupil scores on a standardized achievement test).[21] There is, however, among the consuming public (or their legislative representatives) no single educational goal or set of goals universally subscribed to. A school administrator judged efficient with respect to one criterion may rate as grossly inefficient in relation to another.

It might make sense to use E as a proxy for all of the inputs in our model of school performance if we were certain that the single goal of every school administrator was the development of cognitive skills, as measured by the particular test scores (A), and if we could assume that all administrators were efficient in pursuing this goal. However, if it were true that schools everywhere were efficiently run, then there would be no reason to conduct this kind of study. The ultimate purpose of input-output studies of school effectiveness should be to identify *inefficiency* in the present system of education.[22] Wherever there is inefficiency, it is possible to increase the output of the system at no increase in cost simply by reallocating resources, that is, by using more of some inputs and less of other inputs.

Thus, for our model of school effectiveness to have implications for the improvement of resource allocation, it is necessary that the measure of inputs (E) be disaggregated. Since teachers' salaries make

---

21. The "efficient" producer is one who maximizes the goal (output) produced from a given dollar expenditure or, conversely, one who minimizes the cost of producing a given level of output. It follows from this definition that

$$\frac{MP_1}{P_1} = \frac{MP_2}{P_2} = \ldots = \frac{MP_k}{P_k}$$

where

MP_i = the marginal product of input i (the additional output produced by the addition of the last unit of this input to the production process)

P_i = the market price of input i

k = the number of inputs in the production process

In other words, the efficient producer equates the ratio of marginal product to factor price across all inputs in the production process.

22. To repeat, efficiency (and inefficiency) cannot be measured without reference to a specific goal or set of goals. Perhaps the most valuable contribution of input-output studies is that it forces policymakers to *make explicit* the goals of the educational system.

up the lion's share of most educational budgets, let us direct our attention to the input of teachers' services. What are some direct measures of this input into the production process? Two that come quickly to mind are class size (S), a measure of the *quantity* of pupil-teacher interaction, and teacher's verbal ability (V),[23] a measure of the *quality* of the interaction.

We now have a model in three variables—A, S, and V. Treating A as the dependent variable, we can write

$$A = f(S, V) \qquad (4-24)$$

Specifying further that the relationship between the dependent variable and the two independent variables is "linear," we have

$$A = a + b_1 S + b_2 V \qquad (4-25)$$

The meaning of "linearity" was readily understood when we were dealing with a two-variable model because the relationship could be represented by a two-dimensional graph. With three variables, three dimensions are needed to represent the full relationship, and the solutions to the equation lie not in a line but rather in a plane.[24]

The model in $(4-25)$ can be reduced to a two-dimensional relationship if either S or V is held constant at some particular value; that is, for every value of S, there is a line in A and V that satisfies the equation, and similarly, for every value of V, a line in A and S. For example, if S is held constant at its mean, $\overline{S}$, then $(4-25)$ becomes

$$A = (a + b_1 \overline{S}) + b_2 V \qquad (4-25')$$

The expression in parentheses is the intercept term of the equation in A and V (see Figure 4-10).

The method for estimating the values of a, b_1, and b_2 is a straightforward extension of the least-squares method already described for just two variables. Although the formulas become more complicated, the principles remain the same. In the following section, we will look at the general case of least-squares regression analysis,[25] paying

23. A test of verbal ability would need to be given to the teachers of the pupils in the same sample.

24. When more than three variables are involved, there is no meaningful geometric representation. The solutions to an equation of four or more variables are said to lie in a "hyperplane," the multivariate analogue of the bivariate straight-line graph.

25. The general case may be said to involve k independent variables. Equations $(4-5)$ and $(4-25)$ then become special cases in which $k = 1$ and $k = 2$, respectively.

Figure 4–10. The Intercept when Class Size Held Constant at Its Mean Value.

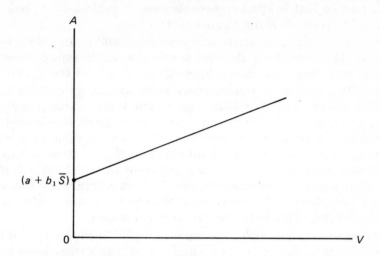

particular attention to the interpretation of the regression coefficients.

MULTIPLE REGRESSION

The *general* regression equation, consisting of a dependent variable (Y) and k independent variables ($X_1, \ldots, X_k$), may be written as follows:

$$Y_j = \hat{a} + \hat{b}_1 X_{1j} + \ldots + \hat{b}_k X_{kj} + u_j$$
$$= \hat{a} + \sum_{i=1}^{k} \hat{b}_i X_{ij} + u_j \qquad (4-26)$$

As before, the subscript j indicates the case number ($1, \ldots, N$), and the new subscript, i, refers to the input number ($1, \ldots, k$). The value of Y predicted by the regression equation ($\widetilde{Y}_j$) differs from the observed value (Y_j) by u_j (the residual, or random error):

$$\widetilde{Y}_j = \hat{a} + \sum_{i=1}^{k} \hat{b}_i X_{ij} \qquad (4-27)$$

$$u_j = Y_j - \widetilde{Y}_j \qquad (4-28)$$

The least-squares regression equation minimizes the sum of the squared residuals (Σu_j^2).

The estimator of the Y-intercept, $\hat{a}$, has an interpretation fully analogous to that in the two-variable case. It indicates the predicted value of Y when *all* of the X_i are equal to zero.

It may be in a given study that points containing zero input levels are outside the range of observed points, that is, the sample does not include any cases with nonpositive values for any of the X_i. For example, in a sample of pupils, every individual is, by definition, attending school, and zero values for S and V (the explanatory variables in Equation 4–25) are not possible. Because this is true, we should have very little confidence in the predicted value of A when we plug zero values of S and V into the equation.[26] If the researcher were interested in predicting the achievement of children *not* in school, it would be necessary to sample from a population that contained such children (virtually impossible in the United States if we are considering children in the 5 to 16 age bracket).

The interpretation of $\hat{b}_i$, the regression coefficient on X_i,[27] is very important to understand. This estimator indicates the change to be expected in Y as X_i increases by one unit—*ceteris paribus, other things remaining the same.* An illustration using the model of pupil achievement may help to make the point.

The regression equation implied by the model is of the form,

$$\widetilde{A}_j = \hat{a} + \hat{b}_1 S_j + \hat{b}_2 V_j \qquad (4\text{--}29)$$

Let us say that we have estimated the parameters a, b_1, and b_2 from a sample of pupils by the method of least-squares, giving us the specific equation,[28]

$$\widetilde{A}_j = 50 - 0.5 S_j + 0.8 V_j \qquad (4\text{--}30)$$

This equation tells us that the expected difference between the achievement score of one pupil in a class of, say, thirty-four pupils and another in a class of thirty-five pupils, the teachers of both classes demonstrating *the same level of verbal ability*, is half a point

26. The best prediction of the dependent variable in any regression equation is at the sample means of the independent variables. For a demonstration of this, see Kane (1968, pp. 240–241).

27. To be precise, $\hat{b}_i$ is the *partial* regression coefficient (of Y) on X_i but, except where there is the likelihood of confusion with the *simple* regression coefficient, this label is normally abbreviated.

28. The *computation* of multivariate estimates involves matrix algebra, which the reader need not understand in order to be able to *interpret* such estimates.

(the pupil in the larger class having the lower score). Similarly, *holding class size constant*, the average effect (in a statistical sense, if not causatively) of a one-unit increase in teacher's verbal ability is to increase pupil achievement by eight-tenths of a test point.

Of course, an alternative to the use of multiple regression analysis might be to control *physically* for S or V and then to measure the relationship between A and the remaining explanatory variable. In other words, it would be possible (though probably more costly and less revealing of the pupil population) to include in our sample only pupils who are in a given sized class or pupils whose teachers are of a given level of ability. Moreover, if S and V were unrelated to each other and the researcher were interested only in the effect of the one on A, it would not be necessary to control for the other since its omission would not bias the estimator of the desired parameter.[29]

In our example, however, the effects of both S and V on A are of interest, and what is more, it is likely that S and V are related (wealthier districts can afford smaller classes *and* better teachers) so that to ignore either would be to risk biasing the estimator of the other's effect on A. The principal merit of multiple regression analysis is that it enables the researcher to sort out the complicated tangle of relationships typically encountered in nonexperimental research situations. Multiple regression allows us to control *statistically* for other variables when physically explicit control is either impossible or undesirable and when the lack of a control threatens to bias an estimate of what we really want to know—the independent (partial, or *ceteris paribus*) effect of one variable on another.

The proportion of the variation in the dependent variable accounted for by the several independent variables in a multiple regression problem is referred to as the *coefficient of multiple determination*, and its denotation is R^2. This measure is an exact analogue of r^2 in bivariate regression. Its square root is known as the *coefficient of multiple correlation*, and R is sometimes reported together with or in lieu of R^2. Unlike simple r, multiple R is always nonnegative by convention. Both R and R^2 range from 0 to 1.

BETA COEFFICIENTS

A question that may have arisen as you scrutinized the discussion of regression coefficients is, "What constitutes a *large* or an *important* $\hat{b}_i$?" Unfortunately, the answer to this perfectly reasonable question

---

29. This point will be returned to in the next chapter.

is relative to the given situation since the size of any regression coefficient depends very much on the units in which the dependent variable and particular independent variable are measured.

For example, the hypothetical coefficients on S and V in (4-30)
were -0.5 and 0.8, respectively. Neither of these may seem very
"large," that is, different from zero (in either a positive or negative
direction). However, since a regression coefficient measures the ratio
of change in the dependent variable to change in the independent
variable, the importance of a *given sized coefficient* is greater the
larger are the measurement units of the dependent variable and the
smaller the units of the independent variable.

To illustrate, let us say that the variable S, class size, was measured
as the number of pupils. Instead, if it had been measured as the number of *tens* of pupils,[30] the regression coefficient on S, $\hat{b}_1$, would
have been ten times larger than it was (-5 instead of -0.5). Whereas
before the coefficient on S was smaller than the coefficient on V, the
measurement of S in larger units has reversed (in absolute terms) this
ranking of coefficients.

If we wish to compare directly the coefficients in a multiple regression equation, it is necessary to use equivalent units in measuring
all of the variables in the model.[31] What standard unit might we use
to make equivalent the measurement of pupil achievement, class size,
and teacher's verbal ability, variables so diverse physically? One answer is to use the *standard deviation* of its distribution for each variable in turn.[32]

To be more precise, the values observed on all variables are converted into *standard scores*. A standard score is the deviation of the
original (or "raw") score from the sample mean divided by the standard deviation of the sample values. In symbols, the formula that
transforms a raw score, X_j, into a standard score, X'_j (X-prime,
sub-j), is written as

$$X'_j = \frac{X_j - \overline{X}}{SD_x} \qquad (4-31)$$

30. That is, a pupil in a class of thirty-five pupils would have scored 3.5 on
this variable.

31. Strictly speaking, it is necessary to standardize only the explanatory variables since the dependent variable is the same for each $\hat{b}_i$ in the equation. However, by convention the dependent variable is standardized as well. This makes it
possible to compare coefficients, not only within equations, but also across
equations where the dependent variables are different.

32. Remember, the standard deviation of X is the square root of the variance
of X:

$$SD_x = \sqrt{\text{Var}_x}$$

Table 4-6 demonstrates the computation of standard scores, using the illustrative data already encountered in earlier tables. Because the sum of the deviations of any set of numbers from their mean is zero (columns 4 and 5), the sum of the standard scores must be zero (columns 6 and 7), and therefore the mean of any set of standard scores is zero. You will note that the squared deviations of standard scores from their mean add up to $N - 1$ (columns 8 and 9), and thus the variance and standard deviation of any set of standard scores equal unity.

When standard scores replace raw values in a regression equation, the intercept term disappears,[33] and the resultant regression coefficients, known as *standardized regression coefficients* or *beta coefficients* (β_i), may be compared across variables (and even across different regression equations):

$$Y'_j = \sum_{i=1}^{k} \beta_i X'_{ij} + u'_j \qquad (4-32)$$

The relationship between the standardized and nonstandardized regression coefficients is shown in the following equation:

$$\beta_i = \hat{b}_i \frac{SD_i}{SD_y} \qquad (4-33)$$

We can illustrate this relationship with our bivariate example:[34]

$$\beta_x = (-0.8889) \frac{3.6742}{3.3912} \qquad (4-33')$$

$$= -0.9631$$

---

33. Since $\hat{a} = \overline{Y} - \hat{b}\overline{X}$ (Equation 4-14) and, by extension, $\hat{a} = \overline{Y} - \sum_{i=1}^{k} \hat{b}_i \overline{X}_i$, and since the mean of each set of standard scores is zero, the intercept equals zero in the standardized regression equation.

34. You may notice that in the case of a bivariate relationship, β_x is equal to the zero-order correlation coefficient (r) between X and Y. This is not generally true in the multivariate case.

Table 4–6.   Standard Scores Computed from Data in Table 4–1.

(1) j	(2) Y_j	(3) X_j	(4) $(Y_j - \bar{Y})$	(5) $(X_j - \bar{X})$	(6) Y_j'	(7) X_j'	(8) $(Y_j' - \bar{Y})^2$	(9) $(X_j' - \bar{X})^2$
1	1	12	-4	5	-1.1795	1.3609	1.3913	1.8519
2	3	9	-2	2	-0.5897	0.5443	0.3478	0.2963
3	4	7	-1	0	-0.2949	0.0000	0.0870	0.0000
4	8	3	3	-4	0.8846	-1.0887	0.7826	1.1852
5	9	4	4	-3	1.1795	-0.8165	1.3913	0.6666
Σ	25	35	0	0	0.0000	0.0000	4.0000	4.0000

$$\bar{Y} = 5 \quad \text{(Table 4-3)}$$

$$\bar{X} = 7 \quad \text{(Table 4-2)}$$

$$SD_y = 3.3912 \quad \text{(Table 4-3)}$$

$$SD_x = 3.6742 \quad \text{(Table 4-2)}$$

$$\bar{Y}' = \frac{\sum Y'_j}{N} = \frac{0}{5} = 0$$

$$\bar{X}' = \frac{\sum X'_j}{N} = \frac{0}{5} = 0$$

$$Var_{y'} = \frac{\sum(Y'_j - \bar{Y}')^2}{N-1} = \frac{4}{4} = 1 \qquad SD_{y'} = \sqrt{Var_{y'}} = 1$$

$$Var_{x'} = \frac{\sum(X'_j - \bar{X}')^2}{N-1} = \frac{4}{4} = 1 \qquad SD_{x'} = \sqrt{Var_{x'}} = 1$$

TESTS OF HYPOTHESES CONCERNING
POPULATION PARAMETERS

We have concentrated on three least-squares measures of linearity—
$\hat{a}$, $\hat{b}_i$ (or β_i), and R^2. These are the essential elements of linear regression analysis. With these three measures alone, the researcher has
a good "picture" of any "scatter" of observation points.

Regression analysis is similar to the work of a navigator on a ship
or in an aircraft. The constant term, $\hat{a}$, locates a set of data points
(fixes its *position*) by measuring its vertical distance from the origin.
The regression coefficient, $\hat{b}_i$, identifies the *direction* of the scatter's
"motion." A northeasterly (southwesterly) direction is indicated by
a positive $\hat{b}_i$, a southeasterly (northwesterly) direction by a negative
$\hat{b}_i$. The greater is $\hat{b}_i$ in absolute value, the more pronounced is the
north-south motion in relation to the east-west motion. Finally, the
coefficient of determination, R^2, tells us the *directness* of the scatter's motion. An R^2 close to one indicates a beeline progression in
the direction indicated by the regression coefficient(s). A smaller
R^2 signals a more circuitous route. An R^2 of zero indicates so much
rambling motion (so much random variation in the dependent variable)[35] that all direction is lost ($\hat{b}_i = 0$).

The ultimate purpose of regression analysis, however, is seldom
the description of a scatter of data points. Instead, the researcher is
interested ultimately in making *inferences about the population* from
which the observations are taken. In the scenario developed in this
chapter, we are interested in arriving at some conclusions about the
relationship between pupil achievement and specific measures of
school inputs. In particular, we wish to know (1) the average effects
in the population of given changes in class size and teacher's verbal
ability on a pupil's achievement test score and (2) the proportion of
variation in test scores of pupils *in the population* accounted for by
differences in class size and teacher's ability.

If we had observations of A, S, and V for every pupil in the population, then the values of $\hat{b}_i$ and R^2 would constitute precise measures of (1) and (2), respectively. However, to have observations for
every pupil in the population is unfeasible if the population is very
large and impossible if the population is taken to consist of all pupils
past, present, and future. Assuming that we have data for only a *sam-*

---

35. ... so much "noise," borrowing a favorite noun from the vocabulary of
systems technicians, in fields that range from stereophonic equipment to com-
puter programs to social scientific models.

ple of the population, the values of $\hat{b}_i$ and R^2 are simply *estimates* of the desired population parameters, b_i and ρ^2.[36]

The evaluation of such estimates is the essence of *inferential statistics*, and researchers are obliged to engage in this kind of statistical analysis to safeguard the consumers of research against "chance results," that is, results based on the vagaries of sample selection and not reflecting actual patterns in the population. The principles of inferential statistics can be summarized in a few sentences. Although the researcher relies on a single sample to make a particular estimate, that sample is just one of very many samples of N cases that could have been drawn from the population, all of them equally likely.[37] Each of these samples would yield an estimate (of the parameter under consideration), and the many estimates of the parameter constitute a random variable, called the *estimator* of the parameter.

Some of the estimates would be at or very close to the true value of the parameter; others would be farther away. The way in which the estimates are distributed around the actual value of the parameter is referred to as the *sampling distribution* of the estimator. Statisticians have developed a body of knowledge about different sampling distributions based on some plausible assumptions about sample randomness and relevant population characteristics. The sampling distribution enables the researcher to specify the probability that a particular estimate falls within a given acceptable range of values on either side of the true (but unknown) value of the population parameter.

---

36. The Greek letter ρ (rho) is used here to distinguish this population parameter (the coefficient of determination) from its sample estimate, R, just as b_i and a have been used throughout to distinguish these parameters from their respective estimates, $\hat{b}_i$ and $\hat{a}$.

37. The number of possible samples (NPS) depends on the population size (P) and the sample size (N). NPS is the number of combinations of P items taken N at a time:

$$NPS = \frac{P!}{N!(P-N)!}$$

To illustrate, let us take a sample of five cases from a population of fifteen items. There are more than 3,000 such samples that could be selected:

$$NPS = \frac{15!}{5!(15-5)!} = \frac{15 \cdot 14 \cdot 13 \cdot 12 \cdot 11}{5 \cdot 4 \cdot 3 \cdot 2 \cdot 1} = 3{,}003$$

Clearly, for a given N, NPS increases with P. Thus, for example, there are more than two and a half million five-card poker hands in a fifty-two card deck. For a given P, NPS increases as N increases to $P/2$ (and then NPS decreases as N increases further). There are more than six hundred billion thirteen-card bridge hands!

A common variant of the general procedure, which was just out-lined, for evaluating a statistical estimate is the so-called *test of the null hypothesis*. Recall Equation (4–25), our model of pupil achieve-ment:

$$A = a + b_1 S + b_2 V \qquad (4-25)$$

In specifying a model, the researcher usually has certain expectations for the slope parameters, b_i (and less often for the constant term, a). On the basis of casual observation and previous research, let us say that we have hypothesized the following about the slopes on S and V:

$$b_1 < 0 \qquad (4-34)$$

$$b_2 > 0 \qquad (4-35)$$

These are the specific *research hypotheses* that we choose to test. We next turn to our data set to see if the hypotheses are confirmed or not.[38]

In trying to confirm a particular research hypothesis, the research-er assumes the role of "devil's advocate" and sets up an opposing hypothesis, called the *null hypothesis*, that must be rejected if the research hypothesis is to be accepted. The null hypotheses corre-sponding to (4–34) and (4–35) are

$$b_1 = 0 \qquad (4-34')$$

$$b_2 = 0 \qquad (4-35')$$

These hypotheses state that there is no relationship between achieve-ment and class size (b_1, the partial effect of S on A, is zero) and none between achievement and teacher's verbal ability (b_2 is zero).[39]

Set down above (4–30) are illustrative values of the estimates $\hat{b}_1$ and $\hat{b}_2$, −0.5 and 0.8, respectively. In a simple, *numeric* sense, obviously both of these estimates are consistent with the research hypotheses (4–34 and 4–35). However, from a *statistical* point of view for an estimate to be "significantly different from zero"

---

38. To be discreet, researchers should avoid all claims of "proof" and be con-tent with having "confirmed" or "supported" hypotheses since, by the very nature of probabilistic tests, the possibility, however remote, of opposite conclu-sions can never be ruled out.

39. We need not necessarily set the parameter equal to zero in a null hypoth-esis. Although zero is assumed in (4–34') and (4–35'), we can hypothesize any value as the true value of the parameter in a null hypothesis. Letting μ (mu) rep-

(greater than or less than, depending on the research hypothesis), more is required than just numeric inequality.

Take the first estimate, $\hat{b}_1 = -0.5$. Remember that this is just one of many estimates in a sampling distribution of the estimator of the parameter b_1. The null hypothesis asserts that the actual value of b_1 is equal to zero. Accepting for the moment the null hypothesis as correct, we ask the question: "What is the probability of selecting a sample that yields an estimate negative by as much as 0.5 unit when b_1 is actually equal to zero?" If this probability is sufficiently small —less than or equal to some predetermined level, often 0.05 or 0.01 —then the null hypothesis ($b_1 = 0$) can be rejected and the estimate ($\hat{b}_1 = -0.5$) labeled *statistically significant* at the 0.05 or 0.01 level. In other words if the probability is small, then the research hypothesis, that is, that b_1 is negative, is said to be supported by the data.

In a closer look at the test of the null hypothesis, we find that it involves a comparison of the estimate with its *standard error*, which is an estimate of the standard deviation of the sampling distribution. A small standard error implies that the many estimates of the parameter are bunched closely together around the actual value of the parameter. Thus, a *given sized estimate* is more significant the smaller is its standard error. The ratio of an estimator to its standard error forms a *test statistic*, and the significance level of an estimate is determined by locating the computed value of the test statistic in a table of values that describes the assumed distribution of this statistic.

The ratio of the regression coefficient, $\hat{b}_i$, to its standard error, SE_i, has (given the plausible assumptions referred to above) the distribution known as the t-distribution with $(N - k - 1)$ degrees of

---

resent the parameter to be estimated, we can state the null hypothesis in general terms as follows:

$$\mu = \mu_{NH}$$

where

μ = the true (but unknown) value of the parameter

and

μ_{NH} = the hypothesized value

The null hypothesis can be rewritten,

$$\mu - \mu_{NH} = 0$$

It is this "zero difference" that the "null" in null hypothesis refers to.

freedom.[40] In other words, the t-value of the i-th coefficient in a regression equation is computed as follows:[41]

$$t = \frac{\hat{b}_i}{SE_i} \quad \text{d.f.} = N - k - 1 \quad\quad (4-36)$$

The standard error of the bivariate regression coefficient in $(4-15)$ is 0.1435,[42] so that

$$t = \frac{-0.8889}{0.1435} = -6.1967 \quad \text{d.f.} = 3 \quad\quad (4-36')$$

Consulting a table of values for the t-distribution indicates that this coefficient is significant (the null hypothesis can be rejected at the 0.005 probability level).[43]

(A crude but useful rule of thumb to carry with us in our review of regression studies says that a t-value of two—that is, a coefficient twice the size of its standard error—assures the significance of a regression coefficient at about the 0.05 level, even with very small samples. For the exact probability level, of course, a table of t-values must be consulted.)

---

40. There are actually many t-distributions, distinguished from one another by the number of *degrees of freedom*. (The reader may wish to consult a table of t-values.) The t-distribution, also referred to as the Student's t, approaches the well-known normal distribution as the number of degrees of freedom becomes very large. The t-distribution has many uses in inferential statistics in addition to testing hypotheses about slopes in linear regression analysis.

41. Strictly speaking, the test statistic is the ratio of the *difference* between the estimator and the hypothesized value of the parameter (cf. note 39 above) to the standard error of the estimator. In the case of the regression coefficient,

$$t = \frac{\hat{b}_i - b_{iNH}}{SE_i}$$

However, in $(4-34')$ and $(4-35')$, b_{iNH} is zero, and thus this formula reduces to $(4-36)$.

42. In the bivariate case, the standard error is computed by the formula

$$SE_{\hat{b}} = \sqrt{\frac{\Sigma(Y_j - \widetilde{Y}_j)^2 / N - 2}{\Sigma(X_j - \overline{X})^2}}$$

In the multivariate case, the formula for the standard error, SE_i, involves notation from matrix algebra and will not be given here.

43. From a table of values, $|t_{3;0.005}| = 5.841$ and $|t_{3;0.001}| = 10.22$. Our statistic, -6.1967, falls between the two. Hence the null hypothesis, that $b = 0$, can be rejected at the 0.005 level, but not at the 0.001 level.

Another null hypothesis often tested in multiple regression relates to the significance of the entire equation. This hypothesis asserts that *all* of the slopes are zero:

$$b_1 = \ldots = b_k = 0 \qquad (4-37)$$

The hypothesis in $(4-37)$ is equivalent to another hypothesis, that is, that the coefficient of multiple determination equals zero,

$$\rho^2 = 0 \qquad (4-37')$$

to wit, that the model accounts for none of the population variation in the dependent variable.

The test statistic for $(4-37)$ is distributed according to the *F-distribution* with k and $(N-k-1)$ degrees of freedom, and the value of F for a particular equation is defined by the formula

$$F = \frac{(\widetilde{Y}_j - \overline{Y})^2/k}{(Y_j - \widetilde{Y}_j)^2/N-k-1} = \frac{RSS/k}{SSR/N-k-1} \qquad (4-38)$$

$$\text{d.f.} = k, \ N-k-1$$

Using the values of *RSS* (the regression sum of squares) and *SSR* (the sum of the squared residuals) calculated in Table 4-5, we can compute the F-ratio for our bivariate example:

$$F = \frac{42.6677/1}{3.3333/3} = 38.40 \qquad \text{d.f.} = 1, 3 \qquad (4-38')$$

As before, the null hypothesis can be rejected at the 0.005 probability level,[44] enabling us to conclude that ρ^2 is greater than zero.

SUMMARY

In this chapter we have discussed the use of linear models in the social sciences. By now the reader should be quite familiar with three

---

44. From a table of values for the F-distribution, $F_{1,3;0.005} = 34.1$ and $F_{1,3;0.001} = 104.4$. Note that, in the bivariate case, the test of the equation's significance $(4-38)$ reduces to the test of the single coefficient's significance $(4-36)$, and in this case the two tests are fully equivalent (the F-distribution with 1 and v degrees of freedom corresponds to the *square* of the t-distribution with v degrees of freedom).

parameters of the linear model: (1) the intercept, which is the value of the dependent variable (output) when all of the explanatory variables (inputs) are zero; (2) the slope, which can be interpreted as the "effect" of a particular input on output, other inputs held constant; and (3) the coefficient of multiple determination, which is the proportion of the variance in the output related systematically to the inputs of the model. The reader has learned about one technique for estimating linear models, the method of least-squares regression analysis, which yields estimates ($\hat{a}$, $\hat{b}_i$, and R^2) of the above three parameters.

In addition, this chapter has included an introduction to inferential statistics, the procedures that are used for evaluating sample estimates. In particular, we have examined the test of the null hypothesis, which establishes the statistical significance of an estimate. The statistic by which the significance of a slope estimate is determined is the t-statistic; the statistic for testing the significance of an entire regression equation is the F-ratio.

For readers with no previous acquaintance with scientific models or statistical techniques, this chapter has covered a lot of ground. For others with some prior exposure to these areas, the coverage has been of necessity superficial. No one could be expected, based on a reading of this chapter alone, to *conduct* statistical research on the educational production process. But a careful reading of this chapter and the two following chapters should enable the reader to understand studies like those reviewed in Chapters 7 and 8, and to appraise them critically.

Chapter 5

Extensions of the Linear Model

In this chapter, we shall look at the linear model in greater detail and underscore some of its weaknesses. Next we shall see how researchers are able to investigate many non-linear relationships by first changing them into linear forms and then applying, as above, the technique of least-squares regression analysis. Finally, we shall examine some of the more persistent and serious problems faced by nonexperimental researchers who rely on the regression approach.

THE LINEAR MODEL RECONSIDERED

In the preceding chapter, we considered two models of school effectiveness.[1] In the first, achievement (A) is specified as a linear function of per pupil expenditure (E):

$$A = a + bE \qquad (5-1)$$

In the second, class size (S) and teacher's verbal ability (V) replace E, the highly aggregate indicator of school inputs, but the assumed relationship in three variables remains linear in form:

$$A = a + b_1 S + b_2 V \qquad (5-2)$$

---

1. These were given in Equations $(4-5)$ and $(4-25)$. They are reproduced here as $(5-1)$ and $(5-2)$.

The general linear model, in which output (Y) is a function of k inputs ($X_1, \ldots, X_k$), is given by

$$Y = a + \sum_{i=1}^{k} b_i X_i \qquad (5\text{-}3)$$

There are several startling implications of the linear model as a description of any production process. Two of these relate to the constant slope coefficient (b_i) of Y on X_i. The constant coefficient indicates that each unit of X_i contributes a constant amount to output. Stated differently, the model implies that the change in Y associated with a one-unit change in X_i depends neither on (a) the level of this particular input (X_i)[2] nor on (b) the level of any other input (X_h, $h \neq i$).[3] Economists refer to these implicit and related assumptions of the linear model as (a) the assumption of *constant marginal products* and (b) the assumption of *perfect substitutability among inputs.*

There are grounds for doubting these assumptions of the linear model. From the economic perspective, if the slope coefficients of the inputs in a production process truly were fixed regardless of input proportions, the optimal response to this kind of production function would be to expand the use of one input indefinitely and to abandon the use of all other inputs, which is clearly ludicrous.[4]

This criticism of the linear model is somewhat unfair in that it is a case of reductio ad absurdum. The results of input-output analysis may justify and are intended to prompt small or *marginal changes* in resource allocation but should never suggest dramatic changes to points outside the existing (often quite narrow) range of observed data. Researchers who estimate linear coefficients do not intend that their policy recommendations be taken to these extremes.

2. In the language of differential calculus, the second partial derivative of Y with respect to X_i is assumed to be zero ($\partial^2 Y / \partial X_i^2 = 0$).

3. In other words, the effect of any input is simply added to the output resulting from all other inputs. Hence, the linear model is sometimes called the *additive model.* In terms of calculus, the cross derivative of Y with respect to X_i and X_h is assumed to be zero ($\partial^2 Y / \partial X_i \partial X_h = 0$).

4. The input given exclusive use would be that for which the ratio of marginal product (represented by the slope coefficient) to market price of the input was the largest. For example, if the educational output per dollar spent on classroom supplies exceeded the output per dollar spent on any other input, including teachers, and if marginal products (and prices) could be assumed to be unaffected by the expenditure patterns of school administrators, then these administrators should devote their entire budgets to paper, pencils, and chalk, and they should fire all teachers!

Nevertheless, the criticism remains that both theory and past empirical investigations of many kinds of production processes tend to belie the assumptions of constant marginal products and perfect substitutability. There are other algebraic forms that modify these assumptions, and the reader interested in better understanding input-output studies of school effectiveness should become familiar with some of these alternatives.

QUADRATIC TERMS IN CURVILINEAR MODELS

When a researcher suspects that the effect of X_i on Y is different at different levels of X_i, a quadratic or second-degree term may be added to the model. In our example of pupil achievement, it would be reasonable to suppose that the relationship between class size and achievement is *curvilinear*, which is to say that it can be graphed as a smooth (neither kinked nor broken) curve.

In particular, we might imagine that the effect of class size (S) on achievement (A) is positive when S is small but gradually declines and eventually becomes negative as S increases. As grounds for this theory, we would argue that a pupil benefits directly from the presence of additional pupils in the classroom but that the *net* effect is positive only up to a point. Beyond that point, the positive effect of more pupil-pupil interaction is outweighed by the negative effect of less pupil-teacher interaction.

The algebraic form of the revised model is a *quadratic equation in S*:

$$A = a + b_1 S + b_2 V + b_3 S^2 \qquad (5-4)$$

The quadratic term, $b_3 S^2$, is simply added to the earlier model $(5-2)$. The assumed relationship between A and S is sketched in Figure 5-1 (in which V, teacher's verbal ability, is held constant at some particular level). For the graph of $(5-4)$ to look like the graph in Figure 5-1, it is necessary that the coefficient on $S(b_1)$ be positive and the coefficient on S^2 (b_3) be negative:[5]

$$b_1 > 0 \qquad (5-5)$$

$$b_3 < 0 \qquad (5-6)$$

The estimation of the parameters in a nonlinear equation such as $(5-4)$ can be accomplished by least-squares regression analysis, the

---

5. These parameters define a *parabola* that opens downward.

Figure 5-1. Quadratic Model Relating Achievement and Class Size.

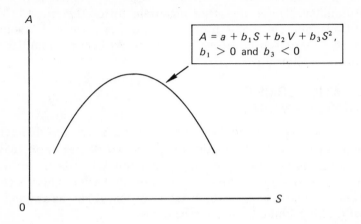

$$A = a + b_1 S + b_2 V + b_3 S^2,$$
$$b_1 > 0 \text{ and } b_3 < 0$$

method described in Chapter 5, so long as the model is *intrinsically linear*. An intrinsically linear equation is one that can be converted into an ordinary linear equation by some suitable algebraic transformation.[6] Equation (5-4) consists of a dependent variable (A) and two independent variables (S and V), but in terms of the slope parameters to be estimated, it can be treated like an equation in *four* variables (A, S, V, *and* S^2).

To make this point very clear, let us rewrite (5-4) as follows:

$$Y = a + b_1 X_1 + b_2 X_2 + b_3 X_3 \qquad (5\text{-}4')$$

where

$$Y = A$$
$$X_1 = S$$
$$X_2 = V$$
$$X_3 = S^2$$

6. The phrase, "intrinsically linear," is Kmenta's (1971). Kmenta (p. 451) distinguishes between models that are "linear with respect to the variables" and those that are "linear with respect to the parameters to be estimated." Models that are nonlinear with respect to the variables but linear with respect to the parameters to be estimated are "intrinsically linear" and can be estimated by the least-squares method, whereas models that are nonlinear with respect to both the variables and the parameters are "intrinsically nonlinear," and in such cases, there are no least-squares estimators.

Assuming that the random error term, u, enters the model additively, we can estimate $(5-4')$ in a straightforward fashion by the regression equation

$$Y_j = \hat{a} + \hat{b}_1 X_{1j} + \hat{b}_2 X_{2j} + \hat{b}_3 X_{3j} + u_j \qquad (5-7)$$

MULTIPLICATIVE TERMS
IN INTERACTION MODELS

When a researcher suspects that the effect of X_i on Y depends on the level of some other input, X_h ($h \neq i$), we say that there is an assumed *interaction* in the model between the variables X_h and X_i. For example, we might believe that the (positive) effect of teacher's verbal ability on pupil achievement is more pronounced in a small class than it is in a large class of pupils. The specification of this interaction consists of the addition to the linear model of a term that is the product of S and V:

$$A = a + b_1 S + b_2 V + b_3 SV \qquad (5-8)$$

Our hypothesis relating to the direction of this interaction is given by

$$b_3 < 0 \qquad (5-9)$$

To illustrate the interaction between S and V, let us say that the exact form of $(5-8)$ is given by

$$A = 50 - 0.5S + 0.8V - 0.02SV \qquad (5-8')$$

and we want to know the difference in the achievement levels of two pupils, one whose teacher scores 80 in verbal ability and the other whose teacher scores 90. Because of the interaction term $(-0.02SV)$, this difference will be smaller, the larger is S. To show this, we shall calculate the difference in $A - \Delta A$ (delta-A)—first with class size held constant at twenty pupils and then with class size held constant at thirty pupils.

The calculations are presented in Table 5–1. When S equals 20, the difference in output associated with a 10-point difference in teacher's verbal ability amounts to 4 points on the standardized achievement test. However, when S equals 30, the difference amounts to only 2 points.

The interaction between S and V, demonstrated in Table 5–1, can be visualized by a comparison of the two graphs in Figure 5–2. The

Table 5-1. Computing Achievement as a Function of Class Size (S) and Teacher's Verbal Ability (V) When S and V Interact.

	$V = 90$	$V = 80$	ΔA
$S = 20$	$S = 20,\ V = 90,\ SV = 1800$ $A = 50 - 0.5(20) + 0.8(90) - 0.02(1800)$ $= 50 - 10 + 72 - 36$ $= 76$	$S = 20,\ V = 80,\ SV = 1600$ $A = 50 - 0.5(20) + 0.8(80) - 0.02(1600)$ $= 50 - 10 + 64 - 32$ $= 72$	$\Delta A = 76 - 72$ $= 4$
$S = 30$	$S = 30,\ V = 90,\ SV = 2700$ $A = 50 - 0.5(30) + 0.8(90) - 0.02(2700)$ $= 50 - 15 + 72 - 54$ $= 53$	$S = 30,\ V = 80,\ SV = 2400$ $A = 50 - 0.5(30) + 0.8(80) - 0.02(2400)$ $= 50 - 15 + 64 - 48$ $= 51$	$\Delta A = 53 - 51$ $= 2$

Figure 5—2. Negative Interaction between Class Size and Teacher's Verbal Ability.

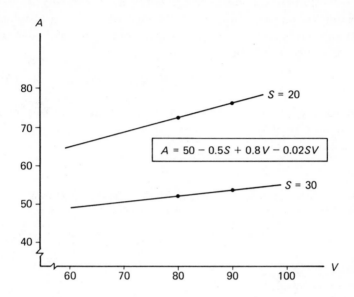

graph in which S is held constant at 20 is steeper (i.e., its slope is greater) than the graph in which S is held constant at 30. The vertical distance between them, ΔA, increases as V increases.

THE MULTIPLICATIVE MODEL

There are other nonlinear models that may be useful under certain conditions. A model especially dear to economists and thus likely to appear in an input-output study conducted by an economist is the model in which all of the independent variables enter multiplicatively:

$$Y = cX_1^{b_1} X_2^{b_2} \ldots X_k^{b_k} \qquad (5-10)$$

where c is a constant and b_i is the exponent of the i-th input (X_i). The *multiplicative model*, also called the *Cobb-Douglas model* in honor of two economists who promoted this function in production analysis, is useful in that it exhibits both (a) curvilinearity between

Y and any input, X_i[7] and (b) interaction between any one input, X_i, and any other input, X_h ($h \neq i$).[8]

The direction of the relationship between Y and any X_i is indicated, as in the additive model, by the sign of b_i. The multiplicative form of the model relating pupil achievement, class size, and teacher's verbal ability would be

$$A = cS^{b_1} V^{b_2} \qquad (5-11)$$

and, as before, let us hypothesize that the relationship between A and S is inverse (negative),

$$b_1 < 0 \qquad (5-12)$$

7. Stated differently, the partial derivative of Y with respect to X_i is a function of X_i. Demonstrating this with just two independent variables,

$$Y = cX_i^{b_i} X_h^{b_h} \, ,$$

$$\frac{\partial Y}{\partial X_i} = b_i cX_i^{b_i-1} X_h^{b_h}$$

$$= b_i(cX_i^{b_i} X_h^{b_h})X_i^{-1}$$

$$= b_i \left(\frac{Y}{X_i}\right)$$

8. In other words, the cross derivative of Y with respect to X_i and X_h varies with X_i and X_h. In terms of (5-11),

$$\frac{\partial^2 Y}{\partial X_i \partial X_h} = \frac{\partial}{\partial X_i}\left(\frac{\partial Y}{\partial X_h}\right)$$

$$\left[= \frac{\partial}{\partial X_h}\left(\frac{\partial Y}{\partial X_i}\right)\right]$$

$$= \frac{\partial}{\partial X_i}\left(b_h cX_i^{b_i} X_h^{b_h-1}\right)$$

$$= b_i b_h cX_i^{b_i-1} X_h^{b_h-1}$$

$$= b_i b_h (cX_i^{b_i} X_h^{b_h})X_i^{-1} X_h^{-1}$$

$$= b_i b_h \left(\frac{Y}{X_i X_h}\right)$$

and that the relationship between A and V is direct (positive),

$$b_2 > 0 \qquad\qquad (5-13)$$

The assumed relationship between A and S is sketched in Figure 5−3. At the two extremes (neither of which is observable), achievement tends to infinity as class size approaches zero and achievement tends to zero as class size approaches infinity.[9] In between (in the range of observable values), the negative slope of A on S flattens continually as S increases. In other words, additions to class size continue to subtract from individual achievement, but each successive subtraction is smaller than the one before it.

The graph of the positive relationship between A and V can take two forms, depending on whether b_2 is greater than or less than one, as shown in (a) and (b) of Figure 5−4. In both, achievement tends to infinity as verbal ability tends to infinity. However, in (a) the slope continually increases, whereas in (b) the slope continually decreases. Because of the well-known economic "law" that marginal returns must (eventually) diminish, we would expect the empirical relationship between A and V to look like the graph in (b) and not

Figure 5−3. Inverse Multiplicative Relationship between Achievement and Class Size.

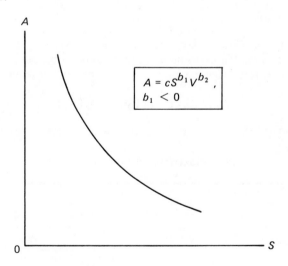

9. In geometric terms, the graph in Figure 5−3 is one branch of a *hyperbola* that is *asymptotic to the two axes.*

Box 5-1:   Logarithms.

A *logarithm* is an exponent of a constant number called the *base*. The *logarithm to the base p* of any number, X, is the exponent to which p must be raised to obtain that number. For example, since it is true that 10-squared is 100,

$$10^2 = 100 \qquad\qquad (5\text{--}14)$$

it is also true that the logarithm to the base 10 ($\log_{10}$) of 100 is 2,[10]

$$\log_{10} 100 = 2 \qquad\qquad (5\text{--}14')$$

In general, if

$$p^x = X \qquad\qquad (5\text{--}15)$$

then we may write

$$\log_p X = x \qquad\qquad (5\text{--}15')$$

We need to recall two rules concerning the properties of logarithms in order to complete the logarithmic transformation of the model in (5-11). The first is the rule giving the logarithm of the product of two numbers:

$$\log(X_1 X_2) = \log(X_1) + \log(X_2) \qquad\qquad (5\text{--}16)$$

The second is the rule giving the logarithm of an exponential expression:

$$\log(X^b) = b \cdot \log(X) \qquad\qquad (5\text{--}17)$$

---

10. Logarithms to the base 10 are called *common logarithms*, and where no base is indicated—$\log(X)$—the common logarithm is usually implied.

Figure 5—4. Direct Multiplicative Relationship between Achievement and Teacher's Verbal Ability.

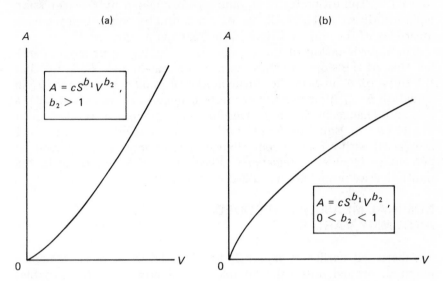

like the graph in (a). In (b), additional units of teacher's verbal ability continue to contribute to a pupil's achievement, but each successive contribution is smaller than the one before it.

Like the quadratic model in (5—4) and the interaction model in (5—8), the multiplicative model in (5—11) is intrinsically linear, although the appropriate algebraic transformation of (5—11) is by no means obvious. The trick is to express both sides of (5—11) in logarithmic form. Logarithms are described briefly in Box 5—1.

Taking the logarithm of each side of (5—11)[11] and applying the rules in Box 5—1 (Equations 5—16 and 5—17), we get

$$\log(A) = \log(cS^{b_1} V^{b_2}) \qquad (5-18)$$

$$\log(A) = \log(c) + b_1 \log(S) + b_2 \log(V) \qquad (5-18')$$

Equation (5—18') is linear in three variables—$\log(A)$, $\log(S)$, and $\log(V)$. For this reason, the multiplicative or Cobb-Douglas model is referred to also as the *log-linear model.* To estimate the model given in (5—11), we would need first to convert the observations on A, S, and V for each pupil in the sample into logarithmic values (using a

11. We can do this without upsetting the equality, since if $Y = X$, then $\log(Y) = \log(X)$.

table of logarithmic values or a computer/calculator programmed to compute logarithms). Then, we would regress $\log(A)$ on $\log(S)$ and $\log(V)$.[12] The estimates of b_1 and b_2 are yielded by the regression equation directly. The estimate of c is found by computing the *antilogarithm* of the constant term in the regression equation.[13]

The interpretation of the exponents in the log-linear model parallels that of the slope coefficients in the linear model. We know that the slope of A on S in the linear model of pupil achievement (b_1 in Equation 5–2) indicates the *absolute change* in A associated with a one-unit change in S. The corresponding exponent in the log-linear model (b_1 in Equation 5–11) indicates the *percentage change* in A associated with a one-percent change in S. Economists call a ratio of percentage changes an *elasticity*. Elasticities and their place in the multiplicative model are discussed in Box 5–2.

NOMINAL MEASURES RECODED
AS DUMMY VARIABLES

We discussed earlier (Chapter 2) the four levels of measurement—nominal, ordinal, interval, and ratio. Until now all of the variables considered for inclusion in our illustrative model of school effectiveness have been, by assumption at least, measured on interval or ratio scales.

Some critics would argue that most measures in the social sciences are ordinal at best. You will recall that an interval scale is one on which equal numerical distances represent equal distances in the property being measured. This is almost certainly *not* an accurate description of either A or V (both are test scores). Nevertheless, social scientists routinely use measures such as these in correlation/regression analysis, even though this analysis involves the summing of scores and therefore implies interval scales. The rationale is pragmatic, that is, these variables are "close enough" to being interval in scale that the assumption of equal intervals leads to useful research results.

12. To do this, we must be able to assume that the error term enters the model multiplicatively and not additively—that is,

$$A_j = \hat{c} S_j^{\hat{b}_1} V_j^{\hat{b}_2} 10^{u_j}$$

so that

$$\log(A_j) = \log(\hat{c}) + \hat{b}_1 \log(S_j) + \hat{b}_2 \log(V_j) + u_j$$

13. The constant term is $\log(\hat{c})$, and by definition, the antilogarithm of the logarithm of a number is the number itself.

Box 5−2: Elasticity.

Economists label a ratio of percentage changes — that is, the rate of change in one variable as a proportion of the rate of change in another variable — "the elasticity of the first variable with respect to the second." Thus b_1 in (5−11) is "the elasticity of pupil achievement with respect to class size." Similarly, b_2 is "the elasticity of achievement with respect to teacher's verbal ability."

That b_1 and b_2 are elasticities can be demonstrated algebraically. In general, the elasticity of Y with respect to X_i (call it $e_{y \cdot i}$) is defined as follows:

$$e_{y \cdot i} = \frac{\text{Percentage change in } Y}{\text{Percentage change in } X_i}$$

$$= \left(\frac{\partial Y}{Y} \right) \div \left(\frac{\partial X_i}{X_i} \right)$$

$$= \left(\frac{\partial Y}{Y} \right) \cdot \left(\frac{X_i}{\partial X_i} \right)$$

$$= \left(\frac{\partial Y}{\partial X_i} \right) \cdot \left(\frac{X_i}{Y} \right)$$

From footnote 7, we know for the multiplicative model that

$$\frac{\partial Y}{\partial X_i} = b_i \left(\frac{Y}{X_i} \right)$$

Therefore, for the multiplicative model we conclude that

$$e_{y \cdot i} = b_i \left(\frac{Y}{X_i} \right) \left(\frac{X_i}{Y} \right)$$

$$= b_i$$

Like the slope of a function, the elasticity is a measure of the responsiveness of the dependent variable to a small change in the level of a particular independent variable *ceteris paribus*. Unlike the slope, however, since it is defined as the ratio of two percentage changes the elasticity measure is not influenced by the units used to measure variables. Elasticity is a "pure" measure, devoid of units, which makes it a useful tool and very popular among economists.

It can be argued that the multiplicative production model is no less restrictive than the linear model in which *constant slope coefficients* are assumed. The multiplicative, or Cobb-Douglas, model assumes *constant elasticities*. The elasticity of Y with respect to X_i depends neither on the level of X_i nor on the level of any other input $(X_h, h \neq i)$.

This cavalier disregard for strict measurement assumptions cannot be extended to nominal variables. For a nominal variable, numbers, letters, or labels have been assigned arbitrarily to indicate membership in different categories or possession of different attributes. Occupation is a good example of a nominal scale variable. In a given study, the sample might be divided into four groups—"doctors," "lawyers," "teachers," and "others." For convenience, these groups could be assigned abbreviated symbols, or codes—for example, "D," "L," "T," and "O," or "1," "2," "3," and "4." In using numeric codes, however, to indicate membership in different occupations, ordinarily a researcher does not mean to imply that an individual in group "4" possesses more of anything than individuals in groups "1" through "3." Nominal variables are defined in *qualitative rather than quantitative* terms, and the order in which categories are listed is arbitrary.

How should the researcher treat occupation and other nominal variables in regression analysis, which presupposes that variables be interval in scale? The answer is to create binary variables, one for each category or attribute identified in the original variable. A binary or dichotomous variable consists of just two values, and these indicate membership and nonmembership in a particular group, possession and nonpossession of a particular trait, or yes and no answers to a particular question. The values, like the coded symbols of the original variable, have no quantitative significance; they are chosen arbitrarily by the researcher. For this reason, dichotomous variables are called *dummy variables.*

Although any two numeric values would do, convention and ease of interpretation induce most researchers to select the values 1 and 0. The nominal variable, occupation, consisting of the four categories identified above, could be recoded as four dummy variables. The recoding is shown in Table 5–2. For example, if an individual is a doctor, that individual is given the code "1" on the first dummy vari-

Table 5–2. Occupational Dummy Variables.

Occupation	Dummy Variables			
	D	L	T	O
Doctor	1	0	0	0
Lawyer	0	1	0	0
Teacher	0	0	1	0
Other	0	0	0	1

able (D) and the code "0" on each of the subsequent dummy variables $(L, T,$ and $O)$.

When the researcher has defined a nominal variable as we have defined occupation so that the categories account for all of the individuals in the data set, then the inclusion of all of the resultant dummy variables in the regression equation would render the equation unsolvable.[14] Instead, the researcher includes *all but one* of the dummy categories in the regression equation. In interpreting the regression results, the excluded category serves as a point of reference for each of the remaining categories.

For example, with occupation the researcher might choose to include the dummy variables D, L, and T in the regression equation, in which case those individuals classified as "others" serve as a *reference group* for those classified as "doctors," "lawyers," and teachers." With the model specified as

$$Y = a + b_1 D + b_2 L + b_3 T \qquad (5-19)$$

the *expected value of Y* for any individual in the research population is given by the regression equation

$$\widetilde{Y}_j = \hat{a} + \hat{b}_1 D_j + \hat{b}_2 L_j + \hat{b}_3 T_j \qquad (5-19')$$

The Y-intercept, $\hat{a}$, is the expected value of Y for an individual classified in the "other" occupational category for whom $D_j = L_j = T_j = 0$. The slope coefficient on the first dummy variable is the *difference* between the expected value of Y for a doctor for whom $D_j = 1$ and $L_j = T_j = 0$ and the expected value of Y for an individual in the reference group. Similar interpretations apply to $\hat{b}_2$ and $\hat{b}_3$. Table 5-3 summarizes the predictions made by the regression model in $(5-19')$.[15]

The use of dummy variables in regression analysis should become clearer as additional examples are encountered in the next few sections of this chapter. Three modes are discussed by which a dummy variable can enter a linear model: (a) as an intercept-shift variable, (b) as a variable in interaction with one or more interval- or ratio-scale variables, and (c) as both.

14. For a technical discussion of this point, see Suits (1957).

15. Because occupation is the only independent variable in the model, the expected value of Y for an individual in any of the four categories is simply the mean value of Y for this category. Readers acquainted with the language of experimentalists may wish to note the correspondence between the regression analysis based on this type of model and *one-way analysis of variance*.

Table 5–3. **Output Predicted by Occupation.**

Occupation	Expected Value of Y
Doctor	$\hat{a} + \hat{b}_1$
Lawyer	$\hat{a} + \hat{b}_2$
Teacher	$\hat{a} + \hat{b}_3$
Other	$\hat{a}$

DUMMY VARIABLES THAT SHIFT THE INTERCEPT TERM

When a dummy variable enters a regression model additively, as do the three dummy variables in (5–19′), the effect of an individual's possessing the attribute indicated by the dummy variable is one of raising or lowering the expected value of the dependent variable by adding to or subtracting from the intercept or constant term, $\hat{a}$. This model consists of dummy explanatory variables only. More frequently, the models we encounter in the study of schooling outcomes will consist of both interval-scale and dummy explanatory variables.

In our model of pupil achievement, for example, we might wish to include a measure of the socioeconomic status (*SES*) of the pupil's family. *SES* serves as a proxy for the quantity and quality of home inputs. Sociologists have constructed continuous measures of *SES*, using indicators of parents' occupation, education, and income. But let us say that we have decided to dichotomize the variable so that the pupils in our sample fall into two categories, which we will label "high" and "low" *SES*.

If we make low *SES* the reference category of the *SES* variable, then the linear model of achievement as a function of class size, teacher's verbal ability, and *SES* may be written

$$A = a + b_1 S + b_2 V + b_3 H \qquad (5-20)$$

in which the dummy variable, H, assumes the values 1 for high *SES* and 0 for low *SES*. It is easier to graph the model in (5–20) if we hold one of the two quantitative inputs constant at its mean value as shown here:

$$A = (a + b_1 \overline{S}) + b_2 V + b_3 H \qquad (5-21)$$

Letting a^* represent the new constant term, $(A + b_1 \overline{S})$, we get

$$A = a^* + b_2 V + b_3 H \qquad (5\text{-}21')$$

It is useful to consider the equation in A, V, and H as *two* equations in A and V, the one for high *SES* pupils $(A = a^* + b_2 V + b_3)$ and the other for low *SES* pupils $(A = a^* + b_2 V)$. The two equations are graphed in Figure 5–5. As depicted, high *SES* pupils score higher on the standardized achievement test (A) than low *SES* pupils, teacher's verbal ability (V) remaining the same. Moreover, the difference in achievement does not vary as teacher's verbal ability varies. The intercept of the equation for low *SES* pupils is a^*, whereas the intercept of the equation for high *SES* pupils is $a^* + b_3$. The difference, b_3, is the vertical distance between the two graphs at each and every point along the V axis. This tells us that the two graphs are parallel (i.e., their slopes are the same), which is to say the effect of teacher's verbal ability on achievement is the same for high and low *SES* pupils. Algebraically, the effect is given by the slope coefficient, b_2.

We might wish to include more than one nominal variable in our model of pupil achievement. To demonstrate how this could be done, let us consider, in addition to *SES*, the pupil's birth rank among his or her siblings. Like *SES*, birth rank is taken to be a proxy for home inputs. As with *SES*, it is conceivable that birth rank be treated as though it were an interval variable. However, we have no

Figure 5–5. High Socioeconomic Status as an Intercept Shift Variable.

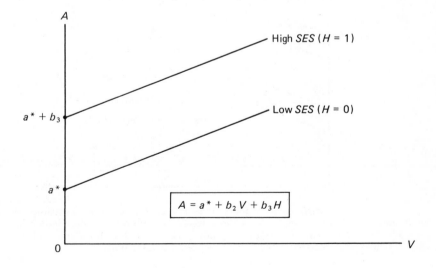

reason to suspect that the relationship between this variable and pupil achievement is linear (i.e., that being second-born is as different from being first-born as being third-born is different from being second-born, etc., for other, adjacent birth positions). Therefore, let us create a dummy variable, call it "F," for which the code "1" indicates that the child is first-born and the code "0" simply the obverse.[16]

The linear model containing the two dummy variables, H (high SES) and F (first-born) is given in (5−22):

$$A = a^* + b_2 V + b_3 H + b_4 F \qquad (5-22)$$

The model, which is represented graphically in Figure 5−6, is an additive model. That is, the effect of SES on achievement is the same for first-born as it is for later-born children. Or stated the other way around, the effect of birth rank on achievement is the same for high SES as it is for low SES children. We may not wish to presume this lack of interaction between SES and birth rank. Indeed, we might

Figure 5−6. High Socioeconomic Status and First-born as Additive Intercept Shift Variables.

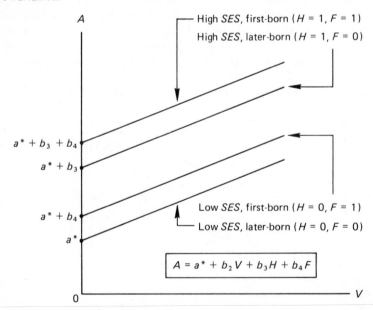

- High SES, first-born ($H = 1, F = 1$)
- High SES, later-born ($H = 1, F = 0$)

$a^* + b_3 + b_4$
$a^* + b_3$

$a^* + b_4$
a^*

Low SES, first-born ($H = 0, F = 1$)
Low SES, later-born ($H = 0, F = 0$)

$A = a^* + b_2 V + b_3 H + b_4 F$

16. To test for *differential* effects of *subsequent* birth-order positions on achievement, we might wish to create a series of dummy variables indicating first-born, second-born, third-born, and so on. However, for this discussion, we shall consider only the two categories, first-born and later-born.

suspect that the effect of birth rank is important in low *SES* homes but "washes out" statistically speaking in high *SES* homes. We might base this suspicion on our having observed that high *SES* parents are able to compensate for the diluting effect of additional children by increasing the overall flow of child-nurturing resources whereas low *SES* parents are not.

To handle this suspicion in mathematical terms, we must add to (5–22) a multiplicative term to capture the interaction between *SES* and birth rank:

$$A = a^* + b_2 V + b_3 H + b_4 F + b_5 HF \qquad (5-23)$$

We have hypothesized that b_5, the coefficient on *HF*, is negative. The revised model is graphed in Figure 5–7.

The reader may have noted that the product of two (or more) dummy variables forms a new dummy variable. In the current example, a "1" code computed for *HF* indicates that the pupil is *both* high *SES and* first-born, whereas a "0" code indicates that the pupil is either later-born or low *SES* or both.

Figure 5–7. High Socioeconomic Status and First-born as Interacting Intercept Shift Variables.

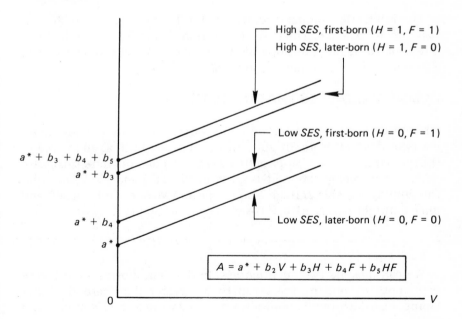

DUMMY VARIABLES THAT INTERACT
WITH INTERVAL-SCALE VARIABLES

The dummy variables encountered in several models thus far have all functioned in the same way. They have acted to shift the linear equation in parallel fashion. Algebraically, the presence of the trait indicated by any of the dummy variables has added to or subtracted from the intercept term (a or a^*). None of the dummy variables has served to alter the *slope* of the linear equation through an interaction with the interval-scale variable, V (teacher's verbal ability). In other words, the effect of teacher's verbal ability on pupil achievement (dA/dV, the slope of A on V) has been assumed, thus far, constant across nominal categories (high *SES*, low *SES*, first-born, later-born).

Sometimes the researcher wishes to test a hypothesis that the effect of an interval-scale input on output is different for different nominal categories. For example, we might suppose that the change in achievement associated with a unit change in teacher's verbal ability is greater (or lesser) in the case of high *SES* pupils than in the case of low *SES* pupils. Stated differently, this hypothesis assumes an interaction between *SES* and teacher's verbal ability:

$$A = a^* + b_2 V + b_3 HV \qquad (5-24)$$

The interaction model is represented in Figure 5-8, in which b_3 is taken to be positive. The two equations in Figure 5-8 have the same intercept (a^*), but the slope of A on $V (dA/dV)$ is greater for high *SES* pupils ($b_2 + b_3$) than for low *SES* pupils (b_2).

DUMMY VARIABLES THAT DO BOTH

Of course, it is possible for a dummy variable to enter a model wearing two hats as it were. In other words, it serves both as an intercept-shift variable and as a slope-shift variable. To demonstrate this possibility, let us merge the models given in (5-21') and (5-24) so that the dummy variable H (high *SES*) appears twice, once by itself, and once multiplicatively with V (teacher's verbal ability):

$$A = a^* + b_2 V + b_3 H + b_4 HV \qquad (5-25)$$

We can imagine two such models. In the first, illustrated in Figure 5-9, both b_3 and b_4 are taken to be greater than zero. In other words, high *SES* pupils tend always to outscore low *SES* pupils, and

Figure 5—8. High Socioeconomic Status in Interaction with Teacher's Verbal Ability.

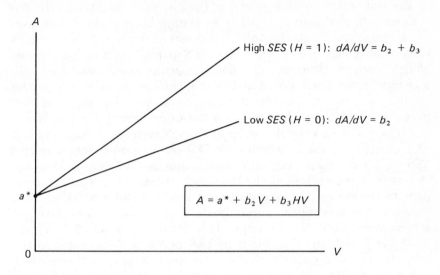

Figure 5—9. High Socioeconomic Status as Intercept Shift Variable and as Variable that Interacts Directly with Teacher's Verbal Ability.

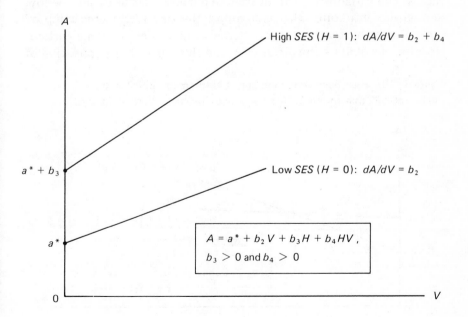

the expected difference in achievement is greater, the higher the teacher's verbal ability.

The only other credible model of the general form given in (5−25) is illustrated in Figure 5−10. Here b_3 is once again positive; however, b_4 is negative. What the model suggests is that high *SES* pupils achieve at a higher level than low *SES* pupils *when taught by low ability teachers*. However, the *change* in achievement associated with a *change* in teacher's verbal ability is smaller in the case of high *SES* pupils. As a result, the two lines intersect, implying that *low SES* pupils are the higher achievers *when taught by high ability teachers*.

Perhaps a more realistic model of the achievement of high and low *SES* children is one in which high *SES* children do better than low *SES* children when classroom instruction is mediocre in quality. However, in this revised model the very best teachers manage to compensate for the relative deprivation of low *SES* children. Thus, these superior teachers elicit approximately the same (high) level of achievement from both groups. This model is sketched in Figure 5−11, in which the line for high *SES* pupils is asymptotic to the curve for low *SES* pupils (i.e., it approaches the curve as V increases).

Unfortunately, the elaboration of a scientific model is often accompanied by a corresponding loss in mathematical simplicity. Nevertheless, the model in Figure 5−11 could be *approximated* by dividing the low *SES* group into several subgroups, defined by intervals on the variable V. For illustrative purposes, let us divide the low *SES* group into only two subgroups, the one (L_{va}) consisting of those taught by teachers whose verbal ability is above some particular level, it could be the mean ($\overline{V}$), and the other (L_{vb}) consisting of

Figure 5−10.   High Socioeconomic Status as Intercept Shift Variable and as Variable that Interacts Negatively with Teacher's Verbal Ability.

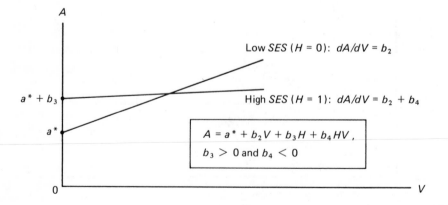

Low *SES* ($H = 0$): $dA/dV = b_2$

High *SES* ($H = 1$): $dA/dV = b_2 + b_4$

$A = a^* + b_2V + b_3H + b_4HV$,
$b_3 > 0$ and $b_4 < 0$

Figure 5—11. Model in which Teacher's Verbal Ability Affects the Achievement of High Socioeconomic Status Children Linearly and that of Low Socioeconomic Status Children Nonlinearly.

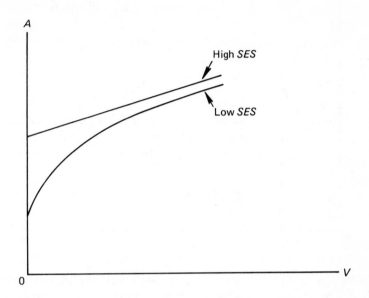

those taught by teachers whose verbal ability is below this level. We now have three subsamples of pupils, labeled H, L_{va}, and L_{vb}. Letting L_{vb} be the excluded category, we can specify the model algebraically as

$$A = a* + b_2 V + b_3 H + b_4 L_{va} + b_5 HV + b_6 L_{vb} V \qquad (5-26)$$

in which

$$\left. \begin{array}{c} b_2 \\ b_3 \\ b_4 \end{array} \right\} \; > \; 0$$

$$\left. \begin{array}{c} b_5 \\ b_6 \end{array} \right\} \; < \; 0$$

$$b_3 \quad \approx \quad b_4$$
$$b_5 \quad \approx \quad b_6$$

Figure 5-12.   Linear Approximation of the Model in Figure 5-11.

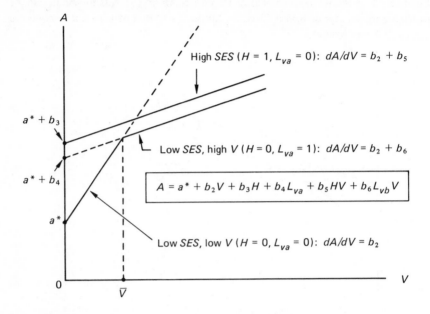

The equation in (5-26) is an approximation of the model sketched in Figure 5-11, and the approximate model can be represented graphically as in Figure 5-12.

PARTITIONING THE POPULATION

Sometimes researchers partition the population and perform separate analyses for each subgroup of the population instead of using dummy variables in a single equation. Race and sex are variables frequently employed as partitioning factors. In running separate regressions for males and females, or whites and blacks, the investigator demonstrates his or her suspicion that the relationship between Y (some dependent variable) and X (one or more independent variables) differs importantly across these categories. Partitioning the data is just one of two, fully equivalent ways of introducing race and sex into the analysis. The alternative to conducting a separate analysis for each subpopulation is to run a single regression equation, fully saturated with race and sex dummy variables.[17]

17. If the researcher cannot predict the effects of race and sex on Y, the appropriate test of significance on each such regression coefficient is a *two-tailed test*. Whereas in a one-tailed test the research hypothesis states the *direction* of the relationship between the dependent and particular independent variables ($b > 0$ or $b < 0$), in a two-tailed test the hypothesis confirmed by rejecting the null hypothesis is simply the *existence* of a relationship ($b \neq 0$).

We can illustrate the equivalence of the two procedures, using a simple model wherein Y is taken to be a linear function of some continuous input, X:

$$Y = a + bX \qquad (5-27)$$

We suspect, however, misspecification in $(5-27)$ in that this model ignores black-white and male-female differences. One way of respecifying the model is as four separate models, one for each subpopulation:

White females:	$Y = e + fX$	$(5-28.1)$
White males:	$Y = g + hX$	$(5-28.2)$
Black females:	$Y = m + nX$	$(5-28.3)$
Black males:	$Y = p + qX$	$(5-28.4)$

The other way is to expand $(5-27)$ so that it allows for a different intercept term and a different slope for each of the four subpopulations. The new equation is

$$Y = b_0 + b_1 M + b_2 B + b_3 MB + b_4 X + b_5 MX + b_6 BX + b_7 MBX$$

$$(5-29)$$

in which M and B are dummy variables indicating male and black, respectively, and white females ($M = B = 0$) constitute the reference group.

The equivalence of the two procedures for handling nominal variables is systematized in Table $5-4$. Take the second category, white males ($M = 1$ and $B = 0$), as an example. The value of Y predicted by

Table 5—4. Model in which Population Partitioned by Race and Sex.

	Category	Equation (5-28)	Equation (5-29)
	White females	e	b_0
Intercept Terms	White males	g	$b_0 + b_1$
	Black females	m	$b_0 + b_2$
	Black males	p	$b_0 + b_1 + b_2 + b_3$
Slope Coefficients of Y on X (dY/dX)	White females	f	b_4
	White males	h	$b_4 + b_5$
	Black females	n	$b_4 + b_6$
	Black males	q	$b_4 + b_5 + b_6 + b_7$

the model when X falls to zero (i.e., the Y-intercept) appears as the sum of b_0 and b_1 in (5−29) or, alternatively, as g in (5−28). Similarly, the change in Y brought about by a one-unit change in X (dY/dX) is given by the sum of b_4 and b_5 in (5−29) and by h in (5−28).

THE PROBLEM OF MULTICOLLINEARITY

Another name for linear correlation is *collinearity*. When the correlation coefficient between two variables is close to 1 (or −1),[18] the variables are said to be "highly collinear." In multiple regression analysis, *multicollinearity* refers to the situation in which some or all of the explanatory variables are linearly related to one another. Some degree of multicollinearity is the rule and not the exception in survey research—an unfortunate fact since multicollinearity affects adversely the regression estimators.

Take, for example, the model considered earlier in which achievement (A) is posited to be a linear function of class size (S) and teacher's verbal ability (V). If the model were to be tested *experimentally*, the researcher would assign pupils randomly to classes of different sizes and to teachers of different verbal ability levels. In a random assortment, the two variables, class size and teacher's verbal ability, would be independent of one another; in other words, the correlation coefficient between S and V would approximate the value zero ($r_{sv} \approx 0$).

Researchers, however, are politically and morally constrained from conducting experiments that, if the hypotheses hold, will affect momentously the future lives of human subjects participating in the experiments. In these cases the researcher must be content with data generated entirely out of social and political happenstance, and not in accordance with research design. Whereas in experimental research the researcher controls the variation of the independent variables in the model to be tested, in correlational research the investigator can be no more than a passive observer.

In a sample survey reflecting "natural" conditions, we could expect to find a negative correlation between class size and teacher's verbal ability ($r_{sv} < 0$). As stated in the previous chapter, wealthier school districts can afford to hire *more* teachers per pupil (i.e., to maintain smaller classes) than can poorer districts, and the teachers hired by wealthier districts tend to be *abler* teachers on the average than the teachers attracted by poorer districts.

18. The product-moment correlation coefficient (r) was presented in Chapter 4.

If the correlation between S and V were exceedingly high (r_{sv} were very close to -1), then either independent variable would serve almost as well as both of them together to "explain" the observed variation in the dependent variable, A. In other words, the coefficients of multiple determination would not differ much among three different estimating equations:

$$\widetilde{A}_j = \hat{a} + \hat{b}_1 S_j + \hat{b}_2 V_j \qquad (5-30.1)$$

which is based on the original model;

$$\widetilde{A}_j = \hat{a} + \hat{b}_1 S_j \qquad (5-30.2)$$

from which teacher's verbal ability has been omitted; and

$$\widetilde{A}_j = \hat{a} + \hat{b}_2 V_j \qquad (5-30.3)$$

from which class size has been omitted.[19] If the researcher's sole objective were to account for variation in the dependent variable, then the presence of multicollinearity among the independent variables would be a matter of small concern.

The multicollinearity "problem" relates to the investigator's desire to estimate the *ceteris paribus* effect on the dependent variable of each of the independent variables. In cases where two (or more) independent variables are highly collinear, the least-squares technique cannot allocate with reliability the explained variation in the dependent variable among the two (or more) independent variables. The separate effects, $\hat{b}_1$ and $\hat{b}_2$ in our example, cannot be sorted out statistically. In such cases the regression coefficients are unstable, which is to say that they are highly sensitive to different specifications of the model, for example, as between (5-30.1) and (5-30.2) or between (5-30.1) and (5-30.3).

This fact is reflected in large standard errors attached to the regression coefficients when both (or all, if there are more than two) of the

---

19. Recall that R^2 is used to denote the coefficient of multiple determination. To avoid confusion in situations where we are considering more than one estimating equation, we can indicate the R^2 associated with a particular equation by appending appropriate subscripts. For example, to represent the coefficient of determination for the equation in (5-30.1), where A is regressed on S and V, we can write $R^2_{a \cdot sv}$, distinguishing it from the coefficients for (5-30.2) and (5-30.3), $R^2_{a \cdot s}$ and $R^2_{a \cdot v}$, respectively. Certainly, too, since the relationships described in (5-30.2) and (5-30.3) are bivariate rather than multivariate, we could replace the capital Rs with lowercase rs (r^2_{as} and r^2_{av}).

linearly related explanatory variables appear together in an estimating equation, as in (5–30.1). Thus, assuming S and V to be very collinear, it would be possible that neither $\hat{b}_1$ nor $\hat{b}_2$ in (5–30.1) were significantly different from zero even if the equation as a whole explained much of the variation in A—that is, in other words, if $R^2_{a \cdot sv}$ were significantly positive. The separate effects, which presumably exist, cannot be disentangled through multiple regression analysis because of multicollinearity in the data set.

When there are just two explanatory variables, the detection of multicollinearity is straightforward. The researcher simply looks at the degree of correlation between the two.[20] However, when there are more than two explanatory variables, the problem of multicollinearity becomes insidious for multicollinearity may be present to a harmful extent even when the correlation coefficient between each pair of independent variables is small or zero. All that is necessary for the presence of multicollinearity and its damaging effects on the slope estimators is that at least one of the independent variables exist as a linear function of one or more of the remaining independent variables. The fact that one variable is linearly related to two or more others does not mean that the correlation coefficient between any two is necessarily large.[21]

To test for the presence of multicollinearity in multiple regression analysis, researchers are advised by some authorities (e.g., Farrar and Glauber, 1967) to look at the coefficient of multiple determination between each independent variable and the remaining independent variables. Unfortunately, if it is confirmed that multicollinearity ex-

---

20. Even then, however, there is no agreement among statisticians as to the precise size at which the correlation between independent variables begins to constitute a "serious" problem for estimation purposes. Certainly, correlation coefficients ranging as far from zero as (plus or minus) 0.5 or 0.6 are commonplace in survey research and seem to cause most researchers no great discomfort.

21. Take, for example, the four-variable model.

$$Y = a + b_1 X_1 + b_2 X_2 + b_3 X_3 \qquad (1)$$

It may be in a particular data set that

$$X_{1j} = \hat{c} + \hat{d}_2 X_{2j} + \hat{d}_3 X_{3j} + u_j \qquad (2)$$

such that Σu_j^2 is small or, in other words, such that $R^2_{1 \cdot 23}$ is large. In this case, there is multicollinearity in the estimation of Equation (1), and the slopes (b_1, b_2, and b_3) will be estimated unreliably, that is, the standard errors (SE_i) of the regression coefficients ($\hat{b}_i$) will be large. However, the fact that $R^2_{1 \cdot 23}$ is large does not imply that each or any of the simple correlation coefficients (r_{12}, r_{13}, or r_{23}) must be large.

ists to a serious degree, the problem of unstable slope estimators is intrinsic to the particular data set, and no ready solution exists. The only way out of the dilemma may be to find independent estimates of some of the slope parameters in the model (Johnston, 1972, pp. 164–65) or to collect additional data in which the degree of multicollinearity is sufficiently reduced to make possible the estimation of all the desired parameters (Kmenta, 1971, p. 391).

THE EFFECT OF AN OMITTED
EXPLANATORY VARIABLE

As discussed in Chapter 4, scientific models are seldom "realistic." They are simplifications of the real world. By imposing order on human behavior or natural occurrences, models enable us to make predictions. As scientists or as the users of scientific research, we should be tolerant of simplification in a model, provided that the model leads consistently to predictions that are "good enough" for whatever purpose we have in mind (cf. Friedman, 1953). On the other hand, when the assumptions of a model are so far afield that our use of the model leads repeatedly to erroneous conclusions, then we should reject the model as inadequate. In technical terms, it is "misspecified."

In survey research (where the researcher has no control over the variation observed in the independent variables affecting outcomes),[22] perhaps the most likely type of *specification error* is the failure to include in an estimating equation one or more inputs that are important to the particular output under investigation.[23] The reason for the omission of a variable may be that this variable has not occurred to the investigator as an important element in the model, or it may be that no measure of the variable is available despite awareness of its importance. The effect of the omission, however, will be

---

22. No control, that is, other than that achieved through stratified random sampling. For discussions of survey sampling methods, including stratified sampling, see Cochran (1963), Kish (1965), or Sudman (1976).

23. Kmenta (1971, pp. 391–402) lists and considers five types of specification error:
1. Omission of a relevant explanatory variable.
2. Disregard of a qualitative change in one of the explanatory variables.
3. Inclusion of an irrelevant explanatory variable.
4. Incorrect mathematical form of the regression equation.
5. Incorrect specification of the way in which the disturbance [i.e., the error term] enters the regression equation.

Although with the exception of the third type, they all lead to biased least-squares estimators, only the first (and an example of the fourth that, as we shall see, actually amounts to a variation of the first) will be considered here.

the same whether the cause is limited vision on the part of the investigator or data deficiency.

Suppose that the true relationship between a dependent variable (Y) and two explanatory variables (X_1 and X_2) is as follows:

$$Y = a + b_1 X_1 + b_2 X_2 \qquad (5\text{--}31)$$

However, the investigator ignores the contribution of X_2 and estimates the simple model,

$$Y = a + b_1 X_1 \qquad (5\text{--}32)$$

What we wish to determine is how the omission of X_2 from (5–32) affects $\hat{b}_1$, the estimator of the slope of Y on the included explanatory variable.

The answer to this question depends on the degree of correlation between X_1 and X_2. If the two are uncorrelated ($r_{12} = 0$), then the estimator $\hat{b}_1$ is unbiased; however, its standard error, SE_1, is inflated so that the test of the null hypothesis that b_1 equals zero tends to result in excessively conservative conclusions.[24] The problem becomes even more serious when X_1 and X_2 are correlated.

To demonstrate the effect of an omitted explanatory variable on the estimated slope of an included variable when the two variables are correlated, let us return to our concrete example in which the dependent variable is pupil achievement (A). Recall (5–20),

$$A = a + b_1 S + b_2 V + b_3 H \qquad (5\text{--}20)$$

in which S and V represent class size and teacher's verbal ability, respectively, and H is a dummy variable for which the value 1 indicates that the pupil comes from a high *SES* background and the value 0 from a low *SES* background. Assuming that these are the important determinants of pupil achievement and that the algebraic specification is a close reflection of the real world, then the correct estimating equation would be

$$\widetilde{A}_j = \hat{a} + \hat{b}_1 S_j + \hat{b}_2 V_j + \hat{b}_3 H_j \qquad (5\text{--}33)$$

in which $\hat{b}_1$, $\hat{b}_2$, and $\hat{b}_3$ are unbiased estimators of the effects of the three independent variables on achievement.

---

24. For proof of the unbiasedness of $\hat{b}_1$ and the upward bias of SE_1, see Kmenta (1971, pp. 392–395).

Suppose, however, that the researcher has no measure of *SES* or fails to recognize it as a determinant of achievement and therefore estimates b_1 and b_2 according to this specificiation:

$$\widetilde{\widetilde{A}}_j = \hat{\hat{a}} + \hat{\hat{b}}_1 S_j + \hat{\hat{b}}_2 V_j \tag{5-34}$$

If $\hat{\hat{b}}_1$ and $\hat{\hat{b}}_2$ in (5-34) are equal to $\hat{b}_1$ and $\hat{b}_2$ in (5-33), then they too are unbiased estimators of the effects of class size and teacher's verbal ability on output. But are they equal to $\hat{b}_1$ and $\hat{b}_2$? The answer, assuming that H is correlated with S and V, is no, and this can be demonstrated diagrammatically.

Suppose that the correlation between H and S is negative (the higher one's status, the smaller one's class tends to be), that the correlation between H and V is positive (the higher one's status, the abler one's teacher tends to be), and that the independent effects of H, S, and V on achievement are positive, negative, and positive, respectively. The relationships are graphed in Figure 5-13, in which triangles are used to represent high *SES* observations and circles to represent low *SES* observations. *HH*, *LL*, *JJ*, and *KK* are the least-squares regression lines based on the correctly specified model (5-20). *HH* and *JJ* are for the high *SES* pupils in the sample; *LL* and *KK* are for the low *SES* pupils.

$$HH: \quad \widetilde{A}_j = (\hat{a} + \hat{b}_1 \overline{S} + \hat{b}_3) + \hat{b}_2 V_j \tag{5-33.1}$$

$$LL: \quad \widetilde{A}_j = (\hat{a} + \hat{b}_1 \overline{S}) + \hat{b}_2 V_j \tag{5-33.2}$$

$$JJ: \quad \widetilde{A}_j = (\hat{a} + \hat{b}_2 \overline{V} + \hat{b}_3) + \hat{b}_1 S_j \tag{5-33.3}$$

$$KK: \quad \widetilde{A}_j = (\hat{a} + \hat{b}_2 \overline{V}) + \hat{b}_1 S_j \tag{5-33.4}$$

BB and *QQ* are the least-squares regression lines based on the alternative model, misspecified owing to the omission of socioeconomic status:

$$BB: \quad \widetilde{\widetilde{A}}_j = (\hat{\hat{a}} + \hat{\hat{b}}_1 \overline{S}) + \hat{\hat{b}}_2 V_j \tag{5-34.1}$$

$$QQ: \quad \widetilde{\widetilde{A}}_j = (\hat{\hat{a}} + \hat{\hat{b}}_2 \overline{V}) + \hat{\hat{b}}_1 S_j \tag{5-34.2}$$

Figure 5—13. Biased Estimates Owing to Omission of Socioeconomic Status Variable.

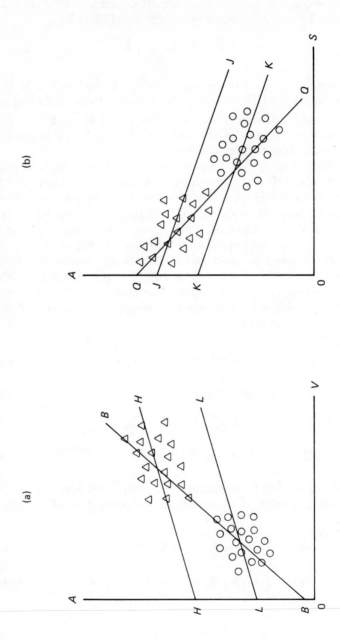

Figure 5–13 makes it clear that $\hat{\hat{b}}_2$ and $\hat{\hat{b}}_1$ are biased estimates:

$$\hat{\hat{b}}_2 > \hat{b}_2 \qquad\qquad (5\text{--}35.1)$$

$$\hat{\hat{b}}_1 < \hat{b}_1 \qquad\qquad (5\text{--}35.2)$$

In general, the omission of a relevant independent variable biases the slope estimator of any included independent variable with which it is correlated. The direction of the bias depends on the direction of the effect of the omitted variable on output and on the direction of the correlation between the omitted and the included explanatory variables. If both are positive, as in Figure 5–13(a), or if both are negative, the slope estimator is based upward. If one is positive and the other negative, as in Figure 5–13(b), the slope estimator is biased downward.

A closely related specification error is the *linear* estimation of a *nonlinear* relationship. Suppose data were collected on pupil achievement (A) and class size (S) that produced the pattern of observations when plotted as seen in Figure 5–14. Clearly, the pattern is not linear. A reasonable approximation would be a quadratic equation

Figure 5–14. Linear Estimation of Quadratic Relationship between Achievement and Class Size.

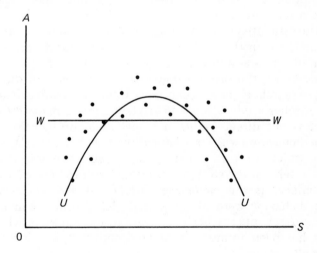

with a *positive* first-degree term and a *negative* second-degree term (a specification considered earlier in this chapter):

$$A = a + b_1 S - b_2 S^2 \qquad (5-36)$$

UU in Figure 5–14 is an equation of this form.

Suppose, however, the researcher failed to recognize the curvilinearity and estimated the linear equation:

$$\widetilde{A}_j = \hat{a} + \hat{b}_1 S_j \qquad (5-37)$$

The "best" linear fit (i.e., the equation that minimizes the sum of the squared error terms) would be WW, a flat line (which implies that Equation 5–37 accounts for little or none of the variance in achievement). We see that the estimation of a linear equation in this situation is tantamount to the omission of a relevant explanatory variable (S^2). Because S^2 is positively correlated with S and negatively correlated with A, its omission biases the b_1 estimator in a negative direction. In sum, the linear estimation of a nonlinear relationship is simply a special case of the kind of specification error that we have been discussing in this section.

The effect of an omitted explanatory variable, treated in this chapter as a statistical problem, was discussed earlier in this book as a conceptual issue—in Chapter 2 under the heading, "The Proxy Problem." Whether a researcher intends it or not, the consequence whenever a relevant explanatory variable is omitted is to inflate (or deflate) the estimated effect on output of any correlated explanatory variable included in the analysis; to the extent that it does so, the included input serves as a proxy for the excluded input.

In some cases, the proxy variable is a *prior cause* of output. For example, researchers have sometimes found a positive relationship between teacher's education and student achievement. Presumably, the effect is not direct; rather it is *mediated* through the teacher's classroom behavior (teacher's education affects teacher's classroom behavior, which in turn affects student achievement). Classroom behavior, rarely observed by educational researchers of the input-output variety, is the *mediating variable*. If a direct measure of classroom behavior were obtained and included in the analysis, the statistical effect of teacher's education on student achievement (where it has been found) would be diminished, and it might even disappear altogether.

In other cases, the statistical relationship between an output and a proxy variable is *spurious* and not in any sense causal. For example, as noted in Chapter 2, the Equality of Educational Opportunity (EEO) researchers found that children whose families possessed vacuum cleaners scored higher on standardized achievement tests than children whose families did not. But it would be very naive to conclude from this that vacuum cleaners cause learning. Instead, there is some prior variable (call it family socioeconomic status) responsible for both outcomes—vacuum cleaner possession *and* higher student achievement. In the absence of any direct measure of this prior variable, vacuum cleaner possession serves as a crude proxy. Once again, the statistical effect of the proxy variable depends on the absence of its correlate. If the EEO researchers had obtained precise information on family socioeconomic status (e.g., a measure of family income) and included this information in their analysis, it is doubtful that they would have found any relationship between vacuum cleaners and achievement.

In general, the interpretation of statistical effects must flow from theory. Often, especially in the early stages of investigating a problem, what passes for theory is little more than common sense. Everyone "knows" that children do not learn very much about reading and arithmetic from exposure to vacuum cleaners. The justification for including this variable in the analysis, therefore, must be that it serves as a proxy for socioeconomic status (*SES*). It is included to control for the impact of *SES*, which common sense tells us *is* related to achievement. If no such control were included in the analysis (or if the vacuum cleaner control were inadequate), the estimated effects of other variables that are correlated with *SES* would tend to be biased.

SUMMARY

In this chapter we have extended our discussion of linear regression analysis, demonstrating its potential application to several types of nonlinear relationships, and introduced the reader to two problems commonly encountered when researchers use regression analysis in correlational (nonexperimental) research.

The first of the problems considered here has been the problem of multicollinearity. When the sampling of cases in the population results in the situation whereby two or more explanatory variables are related to one another in a linear (or near linear) fashion, we are unable through the use of linear regression analysis to sort out the separate effects of these inputs on output. In this situation, the least-squares regression coefficients tend to be very unstable.

The second problem discussed in this chapter concerned omitted explanatory variables, referred to in other contexts as the problem of proxy variables. When a relevant input is omitted from an input-output analysis, its omission tends to bias the estimated effect on the output of any other input with which it happens to be correlated. In this situation, the included variable serves at least in part as a proxy for the omitted variable.

Chapter 6

Estimating Effects
in Educational
Production Functions

The preceding two chapters described the statistical procedure normally used to estimate the parameters of an educational production function. Multiple linear regression analysis is a general method that enables one to examine the impact of a particular input while controlling statistically for other inputs into the educational process. With only a few exceptions, researchers examining the educational production process have used regression analysis, or *ordinary least-squares* (OLS) analysis as it is also called.

One of the advantages of regression analysis is that it produces statistics that are easily interpreted. Accordingly, the partial regression coefficient ($\hat{b}_i$) indicates the amount of predicted change in the dependent variable associated with a one-unit change in the independent variable, *ceteris paribus*. The beta coefficient (β_i) indicates the anticipated change in the dependent variable associated with a one-standard-deviation change in the independent variable, *ceteris paribus*. The beta coefficient, also called the standardized regression coefficient, can be used to compare the statistical effects of multiple independent variables measured on different scales.

Though regression coefficients are easy to interpret, some researchers have chosen to use other regression statistics to estimate the impact of an independent variable, or the impact of a block of independent variables, on educational achievement. The coefficient of determination (R^2), which was described in Chapter 4, estimates the proportion of variance in the dependent variable associated with or "explained by" all of the independent variables in the regression equation. Some researchers have attempted to partition this explained variance into parts that can be attributed to the various independent variables. In other words, they describe the impact of an independent variable as the estimated proportion of variance in the dependent variable that is associated uniquely with this independent variable.

This statistic, which we shall refer to as the *unique variance explained*,[1] differs from the partial regression coefficient in a variety of important ways that will be examined in some detail in this chapter. It should be remembered, however, that the unique variance explained by an input and the input's partial regression coefficient both derive from multiple regression analysis, and hence they are closely related to each other. This can be seen most easily by noting that the significance test for a regression coefficient is equivalent to the significance test for the unique variance explained statistic. Inferential tests of the two yield identical conclusions. Nevertheless, the two statistics reflect different theoretical assumptions about the educational production process. Despite the identity of their inferential or test statistics, they can lead to different conclusions because of these different assumptions.

The assumptions underlying the use of each of these statistics as well as the implications of relying upon one or the other are looked at in this chapter (cf. Pedhazur, 1975). Using results from studies reviewed in more detail elsewhere in this book, we will illustrate the relative advantages and disadvantages of each statistic, and we will explain our own preference for using regression coefficients to estimate the effects of inputs. We conclude the chapter with a discussion of statistics derived not from OLS analysis, but from a closely related analytic method, *two-stage least-squares* (2SLS) analysis, which supersedes OLS analysis as the appropriate method in certain situations.

THE UNIQUE VARIANCE EXPLAINED STATISTIC

When a dependent variable is regressed upon a set of independent variables, the variance in the dependent variable is divided automatically into two components. Some proportion (R^2) of the total variance is "explained" by the independent variables. The remaining proportion ($1 - R^2$) is left unexplained. Beyond this, it is useful analytically to consider the first component—the variance in the dependent variable explained by the independent variables—as con-

---

1. The square root of this statistic is sometimes called the *part correlation coefficient*, or the *semipartial correlation coefficient* (e.g., Cohen and Cohen, 1975; Kenny, 1979).

sisting in general of two parts: (a) the variance that is associated uniquely with each of the independent variables in turn, and (b) the variance that is shared with two or more of the independent variables at the same time.[2] The partitioning of variance into these three major components is shown in Figure 6-1(a), in which U is the "unique" component of explained variance, C is the shared, or "common," component of explained variance, and $1 - R^2$ is the proportion of variance left unexplained. The three parts sum to unity, which is the total variance in the dependent variable.

When a dependent variable is regressed on just two independent variables, the variance in the dependent variable consists conceptually of four parts: that associated *uniquely* with the first, that associated *uniquely* with the second, that associated with the two *in common*, and finally that which is not accounted for by the regression analysis. The variance partitioning in this situation is illustrated in Figure 6-1(b). When we move from two to three independent variables, the number of conceptually distinct components doubles—see Figure 6-1(c)—as there are four common elements (all combinations of variables 1, 2, and 3) in addition to three unique elements. It should be clear that as the number of independent variables (or blocks of independent variables) in the analysis increases, the number of components that must be computed and interpreted increases exponentially.[3] This in itself is a drawback of the variance partitioning approach because the analysis quickly becomes cumbersome.

To see how the various unique and common elements of the variance in the dependent variable are computed, we will concentrate on the relatively simple two-input case. In the situation of three or more inputs, the principles remain the same, but there are more terms involved and the algebra becomes more complicated.

The unique variance explained by an input is defined operationally as the addition to the coefficient of multiple determination when this input is entered into the multiple regression analysis in a final step. Thus, when there are two inputs only,

$$U(1) = R^2_{y \cdot 12} - R^2_{y \cdot 2} \qquad (6-1)$$

$$U(2) = R^2_{y \cdot 12} - R^2_{y \cdot 1} \qquad (6-2)$$

2. Note that this final component can assume negative values under certain, rare conditions. Technically, therefore, it cannot be called a part of the dependent variable's variance since variance is always positive. Heuristically, however, it is useful to conceive of it as a part of variance.

3. In the general case of k independent variables, the number of conceptually distinct components of the *explained* variance in the dependent variable is $(2^k - 1)$.

Figure 6–1. Illustration of Variance Partitioning.

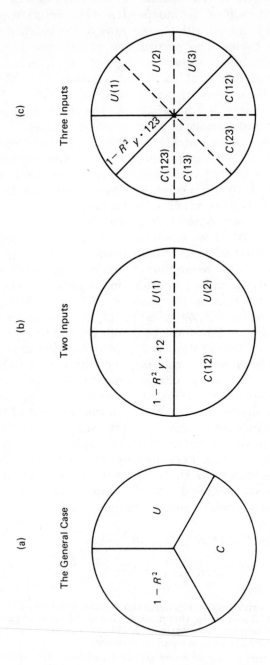

These equations may be rewritten to show that the second coefficient of "multiple" determination in each is nothing more than the squared *simple* correlation coefficient between the dependent variable and one of the independent variables:

$$U(1) = R^2_{y.12} - r^2_{y2} \qquad\qquad (6\text{-}1')$$

$$U(2) = R^2_{y.12} - r^2_{y1} \qquad\qquad (6\text{-}2')$$

The common variance explained, that is, the variance explained jointly by all inputs in the analysis, is equal to the total variance explained (R^2) less the sum of unique variance explained by all inputs. In the two-input case,

$$C(12) = R^2_{y.12} - U(1) - U(2) \qquad\qquad (6\text{-}3)$$

$$= R^2_{y.12} - (R^2_{y.12} - r^2_{y2}) - (R^2_{y.12} - r^2_{y1})$$

$$= r^2_{y2} + r^2_{y1} - R^2_{y.12}$$

The squared simple correlation coefficient between the dependent variable and any input is larger than the unique variance explained by this input by an amount equal to the variance explained in common with other inputs:

$$r^2_{y1} = U(1) + C(12) \qquad\qquad (6\text{-}4)$$

$$r^2_{y2} = U(2) + C(12) \qquad\qquad (6\text{-}5)$$

Because the variance explained in common with other independent variables is subtracted out of an input's simple correlation with the dependent variable, the unique variance explained can be interpreted as a measure of the effect of the input when other inputs are controlled for. Studies that use the variance partitioning strategy (e.g., Coleman et al., 1966; Mayeske et al., 1972 and 1973a) report the proportion of variance uniquely explained by an independent variable controlling for (i.e., subtracting out) the variance explained in common with other independent variables.

The use of the unique variance explained statistic grows out of an analysis strategy widely used in experimental research. Typically when researchers manipulate an independent variable experimentally, they conduct what is known as an *analysis of variance* (ANOVA) to determine the proportion of variance in the dependent variable that is explained by the manipulation of the independent factor. When there is more than one independent variable, the several variables may be manipulated in what is called a *fully crossed factorial design*, in which every level of each factor is paired with every level of all other factors according to some random procedure that ensures that the factors are uncorrelated. So long as the intercorrelation among independent variables is zero, the "*C*" elements in Figure 6–1 must all be zero. There can be no "common variance explained" if the several independent variables share no variance. In this situation, the total variance explained (R^2) is equal to the sum of the unique variance explained statistics. Thus, in experimental research the unique variance explained statistic is a reasonably unambiguous measure of any input's effect on output.

In nonexperimental research, on the other hand, the independent variables are not manipulated, and hence they may be intercorrelated. When independent variables are intercorrelated, variance partitioning produces results that are difficult to interpret as we shall see shortly.

The "Coleman Report," officially entitled Equality of Educational Opportunity (EEO), is probably the best known of the studies that have used a variance partitioning strategy to estimate the effects of inputs into the educational production process. The numerous critics of the EEO report (e.g., Bowles and Levin, 1968; Cain and Watts, 1970) underscored the serious problems that are inherent in this approach to the study of education. First of all, variance partitioning provides scant guidance to policymakers who wish to produce higher achievement scores by altering school inputs. Reporting the variance uniquely explained tells us nothing about the *direction* of an effect, that is, about whether increasing the flow of an input increases or decreases predicted achievement. This estimate also indicates nothing about the *size* of the effect in units that are interpretable. For example, to report that the number of days in the school year uniquely explains 1 percent of the variance in achievement does not tell us what to expect if we were to lengthen the school calendar by one week. Because of this problem of interpretation, we believe that the variance-partitioning strategy is of little use to practitioners who seek to use research results in forming policy.

In nonexperimental situations, in which independent variables may be intercorrelated, researchers following the variance-partitioning approach face a troublesome dilemma. This has to do with the *order* in which independent variables are entered into the analysis. If we have two inputs, X_1 and X_2, affecting output, Y, and we define the effect of X_1 to be the unique variance in Y explained by X_1, we seem to imply that none of the variance in Y explained jointly by X_1 and X_2 is attributable to X_1. In essence, when we control for other inputs (X_2 in this case) by entering them first into the regression equation, we indicate implicitly that the variance in the dependent variable explained in common by the independent variable of interest and by the controls is attributable to the controls alone. In short, the independent variables that enter the equation first "get credit" for the variance that is explained jointly by these variables and others that have not yet entered the equation. This may be appropriate when there are clear theoretical grounds for believing that the control variables are *causally prior* to the input whose effect is being examined. But in the absence of compelling theory, the exclusive assignment of the common variance explained to control variables is arbitrary and may result in the underestimation of effects.

This problem can be illustrated with findings from the EEO study. Table 6–1 reproduces from the 1966 publication the reported proportion of variance in verbal achievement uniquely accounted for by a set of eleven school inputs controlling for six measures of student background.[4] The reader will note that the unique variance explained by school factors is small for every one of the twelve samples. In no case is it greater than 9 percent. The reported contribution of school inputs is limited by the fact that they were entered second into the analysis after background factors, and thus all of the common variance explained by the two input blocks is attributed to background factors alone. This follows from an assumption made by the EEO team, that is, that background factors are causally prior to school inputs.

Table 6–1. Proportion of Variance in Verbal Achievement Uniquely Accounted for by Ten School Inputs Controlling for Six Individual Background Variables and Per Capita Expenditures *(Coleman et al., 1966, p. 306).*

	6th Grade	*9th Grade*	*12th Grade*
Blacks in South	0.0490	0.0752	0.0864
Blacks in North	0.0077	0.0145	0.0314
Whites in South	0.0057	0.0160	0.0316
Whites in North	0.0032	0.0073	0.0187

4. This statistic is presented for four racial/geographic groups at each of three grade levels. The eleven school inputs and six individual background variables used by the EEO team are described in the next chapter.

It seems just as reasonable, however, to argue that school inputs are causally prior to the background characteristics of individual students. They *are* causally prior to the extent that better equipped schools attract families that are economically advantaged. Presumably, only wealthy families can afford to consider the quality of schools in moving from one area to another. In this case, at least some of the variance in achievement explained by background factors and school inputs in common should be attributed to the school inputs. Controlling for background variables and looking only at any additional variance in achievement uniquely explained by school inputs almost certainly underestimates the true effect of the school inputs.

The problem with the arbitrary assignment of common variance explained to control variables becomes even more apparent when we look at the reported effects of particular variables within a set of highly related variables. In addition to the findings presented in Table 6–1, the authors of the EEO study reported (for all of the samples) the unique variance explained by *each* of the eleven school inputs when it was added to the regression equation already containing the background factors and the ten *other* school inputs. The unique variance explained by each of the eleven school inputs, controlling for background factors and other school inputs, was very small in every case, usually less than half of 1 percent of the total variance in achievement. This was to be expected, of course, since school inputs tend to be very much intercorrelated. For example, schools with well-equipped laboratories tend also to have large libraries. Because of the intercorrelation, the variance jointly explained by the eleven inputs is large relative to the variance uniquely explained by any one of them, and it is large even compared to the sum of these unique components.

This being the case, it makes little sense to assign the common variance explained entirely to other school inputs when the effect of a particular input is being examined. When this assignment is made for each of the school inputs in turn, the variance explained in common by the full set of inputs is omitted altogether from the conclusions of the analysis. In other words, that part of the variance explained in common by all of the inputs never gets assigned to any of them. In the extreme, this analytic approach may result in a researcher's reporting a relatively large "effect" for a particular input, not because this input does in fact have a large effect, but because it is minimally correlated with other inputs in the analysis—because relatively little of its zero-order association with the dependent variable is shared with other inputs.

In sum, there are substantial problems in interpreting the results of variance-partitioning studies. First, the estimates of effects are of little use to policymakers, and secondly, the estimates may be systematically biased due to the arbitrary assignment of jointly explained variance in the dependent variable to some inputs (i.e., to the first inputs entered into the equation) and not to others. The original EEO study exhibited both of these defects. A reanalysis of the EEO data set (Mayeske et al., 1972 and 1973a) used a somewhat different variance-partitioning strategy that eliminates the second problem though not the first.

Mayeske and his colleagues in the U.S. Office of Education used what they called a *commonality analysis* to partition the variance in achievement into uniquely explained, jointly explained, and unexplained components as described in the text above and illustrated in Figure 6–1. Unlike the earlier researchers, they do not attribute the jointly explained variance to any particular independent variable or block of variables. They find, for example, that 10 percent of the *explained* variance in achievement[5] is associated uniquely with a set of school inputs (which consists of student body and school personnel measures), 48 percent associated uniquely with a set of family background inputs, and 42 percent associated with the two sets in common. This final component—four-tenths of the total explained variance—they attribute neither to the one set nor to the other (Mayeske et al., 1973a, p. 47).

If a variance-partitioning approach is to be followed, clearly a commonality analysis is preferable to the strategy employed by the authors of the original EEO study unless one is convinced of the causal sequence of inputs into the production process. Reporting the common variance explained as a separate component eliminates a major dilemma encountered by the authors of the original study. It does not, however, eliminate all of the problems associated with variance partitioning. The results remain not particularly useful to policymakers for reasons already enumerated, and in addition, jointly explained variance is now dissociated from all independent variables. The reader may still be left with the impression that the effect of an input is measured by its unique variance explained statistic when in fact the effect is larger than this, though by an amount that is statistically indeterminate.

---

5. Note that the Mayeske team does not define the total variance in output to be unity as we have done thus far but instead defines R^2 (that part of the total variance explained by the inputs in the analysis) to be 100 percent.

THE PARTIAL REGRESSION COEFFICIENT

The reader is by now quite familiar with the OLS partial regression coefficient and with its interpretation. It measures the amount of change in the dependent variable associated with a unit change in an independent variable, *ceteris paribus.* Many social scientists who have examined educational production have reported OLS regression coefficients as estimates of the statistical effects of the independent variables in their models. Thus, for example, in Table 6−2 we reproduce Bowles's analysis of verbal achievement test scores for 1,000 black male twelfth-grade students who were part of the EEO sample. Achievement is regressed on eight independent variables. The t-statistics may be used to determine the statistical significance of the reported regression coefficients ($\hat{b}_i$).

A principal advantage of using the regression coefficient rather than using the unique variance explained statistic to measure the relationship between an input and output is that the intercorrelation among inputs does not result in problems of interpretation. The regression coefficient may be interpreted as an estimate of an input's statistical effect on output regardless of the intercorrelation that may exist between this input and the remaining independent variables. There is no equivalent here to the "common variance explained problem," which was discussed in connection with the unique variance explained statistic.[6]

Table 6−2. Regression Coefficients ($\hat{b}_i$) When Verbal Achievements Is Regressed on Eight Independent Variables, Sample of 1,000 Black Twelfth Graders *(Bowles, 1970, p. 44).*

Independent Variables	$\hat{b}_i$	t-values
1. Reading material in home	1.658	2.22
2. Number of siblings	−1.758	−4.13
3. Parents' education	2.452	4.46
4. Family stability	0.834	1.72
5. Teacher's verbal ability	1.042	5.56
6. Science lab facilities	0.037	1.88
7. Average time spent in guidance	1.480	2.37
8. Days in session	0.203	1.92

6. As was discussed in Chapter 5, very high correlations among independent variables (multicollinearity) can result in large standard errors of the regression coefficients, which result in unduly conservative tests of statistical significance.

However, the reporting of regression coefficients may raise another problem. Mood (1972) and others have argued that what may be only a statistical relationship is all too easily misread to be a causal relationship, and to avoid the possibility of misleading policymakers, researchers should not report regression coefficients. Although their recommendation is extreme, and we would argue that the opponents of the regression coefficient may be throwing out the baby with the bathwater, their fear is not unfounded. Especially in education, it is often difficult to distinguish between the actual causes of achievement and variables that are merely correlates of, or proxies for, these true causes. Quite frequently in studies of educational production we are likely to encounter proxy variables with statistically significant regression coefficients. Of course, these coefficients should not be interpreted as estimates of causal effects.

Let us use the findings in Table 6-2 to illustrate the possibility of misreading regression coefficients, although the author of the study reproduced in the table was quite aware of the proxy problem and was in fact himself using this analysis for illustrative purposes only. Take the partial regression coefficient for the variable, which is the average time spent in guidance. If school decisionmakers were to take this finding literally and manipulate the average time that students spend in consultation with guidance counselors in hopes of raising verbal achievement 1.48 points for each unit increase in the input, they would almost certainly be disappointed. Though it may contribute to the production of achievement, in addition, time in guidance is probably a proxy for many other causal factors, including the wealth of the school district and the amount of attention the student receives from all sources, both at home and in school. If so, the manipulation of this variable alone, without changing the other, unmeasured causes of achievement, would produce a much smaller change in achievement than the regression coefficient might seem to indicate.

Although proxy variables may pose a problem for those who want to apply the results of regression analyses to improving school practices, the problem can be diminished, or even eliminated, if a sufficient number of carefully selected control variables is included in these analyses. For example, if Bowles's equation had included measures of language instruction time and family wealth, the interpretation of the regression coefficient for the average time in guidance would be more straightforward. Several recent studies have included extensive lists of independent variables in an attempt to cover all of the theoretically relevant causes of achievement and thereby mitigate the problem of biased regression coefficients.

In Chapter 8 when we summarize the estimated effects of inputs into the educational production process across a variety of studies that have reported partial regression coefficients, our conclusions must necessarily be tentative due to the problem of proxy variables. We will acknowledge this problem frequently, speculating at times about likely causes of achievement that were omitted from the analyses. In reporting the results for any one input, we will pay close attention to the controls that were used. If most of the hypothetical "true causes" seem to be included in someone's analysis, then we can be more confident than otherwise that any particular input is not merely a proxy for something else.

TWO-STAGE LEAST-SQUARES REGRESSION ANALYSIS

An OLS regression coefficient is an estimate of an input's *causal* effect on output if and only if both of two conditions are met: (1) the input is uncorrelated with all of the unmeasured causes of output and (2) causality is unidirectional, that is, the "input" and the "output" do not affect one another reciprocally. If the first condition is not met, the input serves as a proxy for the unmeasured causes, and the regression coefficient, as discussed in the previous section, is biased to the extent that it incorporates their effects on output. Unidirectional causality is the assumption of a *recursive model*. Unfortunately, *nonrecursiveness* (two-way causality) is undoubtedly more common in the real world than researchers who use OLS regression techniques would care to admit. If either of the above conditions is not met, the OLS regression coefficient does not measure an input's effect except in a purely statistical sense, and we must look for other techniques to estimate a variable's *causal* effect on output.

One such technique is two-stage least-squares (2SLS) regression analysis. This method enables us to estimate the causal effect of an input on output though the input is correlated with other, unmeasured cause(s) as in Figure 6-2.[7] In this particular model, X_1 is assumed to be a proxy for r, which is unmeasured. A 2SLS analysis, as its name suggests, involves two steps. In this case, the first step is to generate predicted values for X_1 through an OLS regression of X_1 on its correlates, X_2 and X_3. Because the new variable ($\tilde{X}_1$, using the

7. As is customary in the diagramming of causal models, a causal effect is indicated by a straight line with the arrow head indicating the direction of causality. A curved line with two arrow heads indicates correlation only; the determination of the correlated variables is outside the scope of the particular model.

Figure 6–2. A Model in Which X_1 is a Proxy for r in the Production of Achievement.

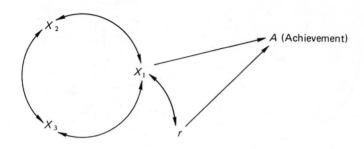

tilde symbol introduced in Chapter 4) is a linear combination of X_2 and X_3 —which according to the model are uncorrelated with r, the unmeasured cause(s) of achievement—$\widetilde{X}_1$ is also uncorrelated with r. In other words, the purpose of the first stage of this two-stage procedure has been to purge X_1 of its correlation with r. At the second stage, A is regressed on $\widetilde{X}_1$. Now, since $\widetilde{X}_1$ is uncorrelated with r, the OLS regression coefficient is an unbiased estimate of the effect of this input on achievement.[8]

The 2SLS technique also enables us to estimate causal effects in nonrecursive models, such as the model presented in Figure 6–3. In this model, a student's attitude is viewed as both a cause and an effect of achievement, and as such the causal effects in the model cannot be derived from an OLS analysis. The problem is that A_2 will tend to be correlated with r_1, the unmeasured cause(s) of A_1; and, similarly, A_1 with r_2. Thus, the problem known as *simultaneous equation bias* is very closely related to the proxy problem, discussed with reference to Figure 6–2.

It is necessary at this point to introduce some new terminology. Until now in describing the variables in a model, the terms "input" and "output" (or "independent variable" and "dependent variable") have sufficed as unambiguous labels. In the model considered here, however, achievement is not just an "output"; it is also an "input" in the production of attitude. To distinguish between the A_i and the X_i in Figure 6–3, we need the terms "endogenous" and "exogenous." The *endogenous* variables in a model are those whose values

8. For a complete discussion of the steps involved in a 2SLS analysis see, for example, Johnston (1972) or Wonnacott and Wonnacott (1970).

Figure 6–3.   A Nonrecursive Model of Educational Production.

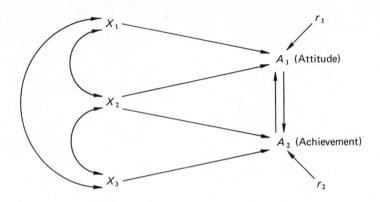

are explained by the model. In this case, A_1 and A_2 are endogenous variables. *Exogenous* variables are those whose values are determined outside the model. In our model, the X_i are exogenous variables. (Of course, in someone else's model any or all of the X_i could be treated as endogenous variables, in which case other exogenous variables would need to be specified.)

Algebraically, the model presented in Figure 6–3 consists of two *structural equations*, so called because they describe the structure of the model:

$$A_1 = a + b_1 X_1 + b_2 X_2 + b_3 A_2 \qquad (6–6)$$

$$A_2 = c + d_1 X_2 + d_2 X_3 + d_3 A_1 \qquad (6–7)$$

As stated above, a 2SLS procedure can be used to estimate the parameters of a model such as this one. In the first step, each of the endogenous variables is regressed on all of the exogenous variables, using the OLS regression procedure:

$$\widetilde{A}_{1j} = \hat{e} + \hat{f}_1 X_{1j} + \hat{f}_2 X_{2j} + \hat{f}_3 X_{3j} \qquad (6–8)$$

$$\widetilde{A}_{2j} = \hat{g} + \hat{h}_1 X_{1j} + \hat{h}_2 X_{2j} + \hat{h}_3 X_{3j} \qquad (6–9)$$

These equations, which exclude endogenous variables from the right-hand side, are called *reduced-form equations*. Each of the regression coefficients indicates the change in an endogenous variable expected as the result of a one-unit change in a particular exogenous variable. This change may represent a direct causal effect, an indirect effect, or the sum of direct and indirect effects. Using (6–8) for illustration,

$\hat{f}_1$ is an estimate of the direct effect of X_1 on A_1; $\hat{f}_3$, of the indirect effect of X_3 on A_1 via A_2; and $\hat{f}_2$, of the direct effect of X_2 on A_1 plus the indirect effect of X_2 on A_1 via A_2.

The second step of the two-step procedure consists of estimating the structural equations, again by OLS regression analysis. In these regressions, however, the observed values for the endogenous inputs are replaced by the values predicted at the first stage of the analysis:

$$\widetilde{\widetilde{A}}_{1j} = \hat{a} + \hat{b}_1 X_{1j} + \hat{b}_2 X_{2j} + \hat{b}_3 \widetilde{A}_{2j} \qquad (6-6')$$

$$\widetilde{\widetilde{A}}_{2j} = \hat{c} + \hat{d}_1 X_{2j} + \hat{d}_2 X_{3j} + \hat{d}_3 \widetilde{A}_{1j} \qquad (6-7')$$

Because $\widetilde{A}_2$ is uncorrelated with r_1, the unmeasured cause(s) of A_1, and $\widetilde{A}_1$ is uncorrelated with r_2, the unmeasured cause(s) of A_2, the regression coefficients in $(6-6')$ and $(6-7')$ are unbiased estimates of the structural parameters.

Only a few researchers in education have used 2SLS regression analysis to estimate effects. Given that the two assumptions underlying the causal interpretation of OLS regression coefficients tend to be quite dubious assumptions in most models of educational production, the reader may well wonder why 2SLS analysis has not been used more often. There are at least two reasons for the reliance to date on OLS analysis in educational research. The first is that until recently very few social scientists other than economists were acquainted with 2SLS analysis. With the publication recently of books on causal models and their estimation intended for sociologists and psychologists (e.g., Kerlinger and Pedhazur, 1973; Duncan, 1975; Heise, 1975; Kenny, 1979), this situation is beginning to change. The second reason for the reliance on OLS analysis is that 2SLS analysis involves assumptions not involved in OLS analysis, and these may raise new problems.

The primary assumption underlying 2SLS analysis is that inputs can be identified that serve as *instrumental variables.* In Figure 6−2, the instrumental variables (X_2 and X_3) are correlated with an input that is correlated with the unmeasured cause(s) of achievement, but they are not themselves correlated with the unmeasured cause(s). In Figure 6−3, each of the instrumental variables (X_1 and X_3) has a direct causal effect upon one but not both of the dependent variables. In the appendix some studies that use 2SLS regression analysis (Levin, 1970; Michelson, 1970; Cohn and Millman, 1975) are reviewed. The authors of all such studies must assume the existence of instrumental variables. For example, Michelson assumes that teachers' attitudes directly affect students' attitudes but not their achievement, whereas teachers' experience directly affects achievement but not attitudes. Unfortunately, assumptions like these, which are necessary if we are to conduct 2SLS analyses, may not be tenable.

Despite difficulties, nevertheless, we expect that future researchers will lean increasingly toward models of the kind suggested by Michelson and others. Clearly, in education recursive models seem less realistic than models that incorporate reciprocal causation, and it is difficult to assume that any list of inputs is entirely free of proxy variables. Educational production is such a complex matter (many variables affect achievement which, in turn, has many effects) that simple recursive models are difficult to defend theoretically.

SUMMARY

In the remainder of this book, we examine the effects of inputs into the educational process as these effects have been reported in various studies, and based on what we have learned from these studies, we make a number of recommendations about the directions in which we believe future research should be headed.

Most of the studies of educational production to date have relied upon OLS regression analysis to estimate the effects of inputs. In a few cases, more complex models have been posited that have required the use of 2SLS regression analysis. The usefulness of 2SLS analysis has been discussed in this chapter. We applaud the few pioneering researchers who have tried to apply this procedure to the study of education.

In Chapter 7, we look only at a particular subset of the studies that use OLS regression analysis to analyze educational production. These are the studies that report the unique variance explained statistic in lieu of the regression coefficient as their estimate of an input's effect on output. The most important of these studies, in terms of having stimulated other research on the determinants of educational outcomes, are the Equality of Educational Opportunity (EEO) study by Coleman et al. (1966) and the reanalyses of the EEO data set by Mayeske et al. (1972; 1973a). As stressed in this chapter, we have serious reservations about the variance-partitioning approach. First, the results of this approach are not easily translated into policy recommendations, and second, any variance in the dependent variable jointly explained by more than one independent variable either is assigned to the first independent variable entered into the analysis (as by Coleman et al.) or is left unassigned to any of the independent variables (as by Mayeske et al.).

✳ *Chapter 7*

Variance Partitioning
in the Analysis of
Educational Achievement

The major studies of educational achievement that have used variance-partitioning procedures to estimate the effects of inputs are reviewed in this chapter. While we believe that the results of these studies are suspect, because of the problems discussed in the previous chapter, it is important that the reader be familiar with the variance-partitioning approach and the classic studies that have used this approach.

For four reasons, our discussion of variance-partitioning studies focuses primarily upon the survey conducted by James S. Coleman, Ernest Q. Campbell, C.F. Hobson, James McPartland, Alexander Mood, Frederic D. Weinfeld, and Robert L. York for the U.S. Office of Education and reported in 1966 under the title *Equality of Educational Opportunity*. First, this report was the first major input-output analysis in education, although a number of other studies predated the EEO report.[1] Second, the EEO survey was a massive undertaking, and because of its size and the fact that it was mandated by Congress, the report received widespread attention among both social scientists and the general public. Third, in many instances the conclusions of the EEO report were radical departures from common educational lore; this stimulated rethinking of some common assumptions about schooling in America. Finally, the EEO report stimulated economists and sociologists[2] to reanalyze the EEO data

---

1. See, for example, Mollenkopf and Melville (1956).
2. See, for example, Bowles (1970), Mayeske et al. (1972, 1973a, 1973b, 1975), and Smith (1972).

and to undertake many other less massive surveys in order to test the report's findings.[3] Thus we start with the EEO report because of its size, the attention it received, the radical nature of the conclusions it reached, and the subsequent research it stimulated.

After familiarizing the reader with the EEO report, we will discuss subsequent reanalyses of the EEO data that have been conducted by George Mayeske and his colleagues (1972, 1973a, 1973b, 1975). Mayeske's group overcame one objection to the variance-partitioning strategy by using a *commonality analysis* to interpret the results. This chapter concludes with a brief overview of the U.S. portion of the International Educational Achievement Project (IEA), which is another large-scale applications of the variance-partitioning approach. The IEA Project is a coordinated effort to document and understand the causes of school achievement in twenty-two countries. Part of this project examined five kinds of achievement in the United States, and these national findings are reported in *Achievement in America* by Richard M. Wolf (1977).

Our treatment of each variance-partitioning study is organized as follows. First, we describe the samples, measures, and analytic methods that were used. Next, the major conclusions of the study are reviewed; and finally, we discuss the major criticisms of the study.

THE EQUALITY OF EDUCATIONAL OPPORTUNITY REPORT

Section 402 of the Civil Rights Act of 1964 authorized the U.S. Office of Education to undertake a massive national survey to assess the "lack of availability of equal educational opportunities for individuals by reason of race, color, religion, or national origin in public education institutions at all levels in the United States." In response to this mandate, the U.S. Commissioner of Education, Francis Keppel, assembled a staff, headed by sociologist James S. Coleman, then of Johns Hopkins University, to conduct the required research. The survey instruments were formulated, sampling designs were prepared, and the data collected and analyzed in only one year. The EEO report was produced with remarkable speed, given the magnitude of the sample and the amount of data that was collected.

Samples
A total of 1,170 public high schools were randomly selected throughout the country according to a stratified random sampling

---

3. See Chapter 8.

design.[4] At the same time, more than 3,200 elementary schools were selected by taking every elementary school in which over 90 percent of the graduates went to one of the selected high schools. Survey questionnaires and achievement tests were administered to all students in grades 1, 3, 6, 9, and 12 of the selected schools. In addition, questionnaires were sent to the teachers and principals in the selected schools, and additional data were collected from the district superintendents in charge of the selected schools.

A large number of people—some 645,000 students and 60,000 teachers—participated in the study, but unfortunately, only 689 of the close to 1,200 high schools furnished complete student and school personnel data. Therefore, the absence of complete data raises severe problems of data analysis and interpretation.

Measures

The sampled students completed a battery of achievement tests including a test of *verbal ability*, which was essentially a vocabulary test, a *reading comprehension* test, a *mathematics* test, and a test of *general information*. Naturally, different test forms were administered to different grade levels, and not all subtests were used in each grade. In the educational production analysis, only the verbal ability test scores were used as a dependent variable. In addition to these tests, questionnaires were administered to the students to measure academic motivation, educational aspirations, attitudes toward life, and perceptions about their home environment. These questionnaires also provided information about each student's family background.

Teachers completed questionnaires that asked about their training, teaching experience, family background, and attitudes. In addition, each teacher completed a self-administered verbal abilities test. Information about the characteristics of the school and student body was gleaned from the school principal's and district superintendent's questionnaires.

Table 7—1 lists the independent variables that were used in the input-output analysis. These variables represent five categories: (a) individual student's characteristics, (b) student's family background characteristics, (c) student body characteristics, (d) teachers' characteristics, and (e) school characteristics. Table 7—1 also indicates the level of aggregation for each variable. Note that the production function section of the EEO report (Section 3) did not use all of the variables that were measured, and thus the variables in Table 7—1 do not represent all of the measures that were gathered in the EEO survey.

4. For a description of the statistical theory underlying stratified random sampling, see Cochran (1963), Kish (1965), or Jessen (1978).

Table 7-1. Independent Variables Used in the Production Function
Analysis of the EEO Report.

Variables

A. Student's Individual Characteristics   All individual level data

1. Race/Ethnicity

2. Interest in school (based on questions about the student's interest in
    school and pursuit of reading outside school)

3. Self-concept (based on questions about how bright students thought
    they were, about how easily students thought they learned, and about
    whether teachers go too fast; some items missing for 6th grade)

4. Locus of control (based on questions about importance of luck versus
    hard work for achieving success, about perceived interferences with
    efforts to "get ahead" and about perceived "chance to be successful
    in life"; last two questions omitted for 6th grade)

B. Student's Family Background Characteristics   All family level data

1. Urbanism of background (Grades 9 and 12 only) (based on questions
    about community in which self and mother grew up)

2. Migration (Grade 6 only) (based on questions about own and mother's
    birthplace)

3. Parents' education (based on both mother's and father's education)

4. Structural integrity of the home (based on questions about the presence
    of mother and father or both in the home)

5. Smallness of family (number of brothers and sisters, in a negative
    direction)

6. Items in home (based on questions about the presence of TV, telephone,
    record player, refrigerator, automobile, and vacuum cleaner)

7. Reading material in home (based on questions about the presence of
    dictionary, encyclopedia, newspaper, magazines, and books; last two
    items missing for the 6th grade)

8. Parents' interests (based on questions about whether parents talked with
    students about school and whether students were read to when small)

9. Parents' educational desires (based on questions about how good a
    student they thought their parents wanted them to be and how far in
    school they thought their parents wanted them to go; last question not
    asked in 6th grade)

C. Peer Group Characteristics   All school level data

1. Educational background (based on proportion of students in school
    reporting encyclopedias in home)

C. Peer Group Characteristics (*continued*)

   2. Educational aspirations (based on proportion having definite plans to go to college; grades 9 and 12 only)

   3. Mobility (based on principal's report of percent of students who were transfers in or out during last year)

   4. Student attendance (based on principal's report of attendance rates)

   5. Average hours of homework (based on students' reports; grades 9 and 12 only)

   6. Student body quality (based on teachers' perceptions; grade 6 only)

   7. Proportion white in school

D. Teacher Characteristics   All school level data

   1. Average education of teachers' families (based on questions about teachers' mothers' education)

   2. Average years of experience in teaching

   3. Localism of teachers (based on questions about whether teachers had gone to high school or college in the area and whether they had lived in area most of their lives)

   4. Average level of education of teachers

   5. Average score on self-administered verbal ability (vocabulary) test

   6. Teachers' stated preferences for teaching middle-class, white-collar students

   7. Proportion of teachers in the school who were white

E. School Characteristics   Some school level data
                                                          Some district level data

   1. Per pupil expenditures (based on school superintendent's budget for school district)

   2. Pupil to teacher ratio

   3. Volumes per student in school library

   4. Science laboratory facilities (9th and 12th grades only)

   5. Presence or absence of an accelerated curriculum (based on principals' responses)

   6. Number of extracurricular activities (9th and 12th grades only)

Table 7−1. continued

E.   School Characteristics (*continued*)

7.   Comprehensiveness of curriculum (based on principals' assessment; 9th and 12th grades only)

8.   Strictness in promotion of slow learners (based on principals' responses; 6th grade only)

9.   Use of grouping or tracking (9th and 12th grades only)

10.   Presence and amount of movement between tracks (9th and 12th grades only)

11.   School size

12.   Number of guidance counselors (9th and 12th grades only)

13.   Urbanism of school's location (rural versus urban)

14.   Geographical location of school (North versus South)

Methods of Analysis

The EEO survey measured more than 400 variables, and the researchers' first task was to reduce this number to a meaningful and useable subset of input and output measures. To do this, zero-order correlations were computed between all variables,[5] and, by and large, these correlations were used to select independent variables for inclusion in the regression analyses. The purpose was to find inputs that were highly correlated with the achievement outcome measures. It is important to note here that most of the independent variables were included in the analysis, not because of their theoretical importance but because of their strong zero-order correlations with the outcome measures.[6]

Verbal achievement, the dependent variable in the regression analyses, was chosen over other achievement and attitude measures for two reasons. First, scores on this test showed greater variation between schools and less within schools than other output measures did. Given that the analyses were intended to find out how differences between schools affected achievement, it makes sense to pick an outcome measure with maximum between-school variance. Sec-

5. See *Equality of Educational Opportunity, Supplementary Appendix*, for these correlation matrices.
6. There were a few exceptions to this rule. For instance, pupil to teacher ratios were included in the analysis even though they showed little correlation with academic achievement.

ond, preliminary regression equations that were computed for each of the outcome measures showed that school inputs accounted for more variance in verbal achievement than any other outcome measure, and hence verbal achievement was selected over other outcomes because it appeared to say more about the effects of differences *between* schools. Again, note that statistical, not theoretical, criteria were used to select variables for inclusion in the regression analyses.

Once the independent and dependent variables had been chosen, regression equations were computed for subgroups stratified by grade, region, and race/ethnicity. That is, separate regression analyses were computed for subgroups defined by grade (1, 3, 6, 9, and 12), geographical region (North vs. South), and race/ethnicity (white, black, Mexican-American, Puerto Rican, Indian American, and Oriental-American). The geographical factor was included only in the analyses for whites and blacks because of the restricted sample sizes for the remaining racial/ethnic groups.[7]

A series of regressions were computed for each of the subgroups, and as the analysis proceeded, blocks of inputs were systematically added to or subtracted from the regression equations used to "explain" verbal achievement scores. Only two statistics were reported: the *total variance in verbal achievement explained by the blocks of inputs in the regression* (i.e., R^2) and the *variance uniquely explained by each block of inputs*. The latter statistic corresponds to the increase in explained variance that occurs when a new block of variables enters the equation. Generally speaking, the blocks of variables were entered in the following order. First, family background variables were entered; then student body variables, teacher variables, school variables, and student attitude variables were entered, in that order.

Results of the EEO Survey

The authors of *Equality of Educational Opportunity* examined the degree to which variations in achievement scores were due to differences between schools versus differences within schools; they then looked at the effects of family background characteristics, student body characteristics, teacher characteristics, and school characteristics. Separate analyses were computed for a large number of student subgroups (strata), but the most important findings, and the ones

7. The sample size was roughly 600,000 students, but the effective sample size in the regression analyses, looking only at between-school variance, is the number of schools, that is, approximately 2,400. When this sample of schools is stratified by race and region, some of the strata contain very small numbers of units.

that we shall concentrate on in this section, concerned the results for Northern and Southern whites and blacks in grades 6, 9, and 12.

Between-school Variance vs. Within-school Variance. If there are in fact large differences between schools but these differences have little impact on student achievement, it makes little sense to ask how we can improve the school system. The EEO analysis of this issue is summarized in Table 7−2, which shows the percentage of variance in verbal achievement that was accounted for by between-school differences.

These data suggest two conclusions. First, for all subgroups (including the strata not reported here) most of the variance in verbal achievement scores was *not* accounted for by between-school differences. In other words, most of the variation in student achievement scores was due to differences among students within schools rather than differences between schools. Second, between-school differences seemed to account for more of the variance in scores in the South than in the North, and more for blacks than for whites. That is, it can be inferred that on the average school factors have more of an impact on blacks than whites and more impact in the South than in the North.

Family Background Characteristics. In the EEO analysis, family background factors were considered before other blocks of inputs "because these background differences are prior to school influence, and shape the child before he reaches school" (p. 298). In subsequent analyses, these family background variables served as controls when the effects of teacher and school inputs were tested. Table 7−3 presents the percentage of variance in verbal achievement that was accounted for by the nine family background variables labeled B−1 through B−9 in Table 7−1. These data make it clear that family background factors accounted for a substantial amount of the vari-

Table 7−2. Percentage of Total Variance in Individual Achievement Scores Accounted for by Between-School Differences.

	Grade		
	12	*9*	*6*
Black South	22.54	20.17	22.64
Black North	10.92	12.67	13.89
White South	10.11	9.13	11.05
White North	7.84	8.69	10.32

Table 7−3. Percentage of Variance in Verbal Achievement Accounted for by Eight Family Background Factors (B−1 to B−9).

	Grade		
	12	*9*	*6*
Black South	15.79	15.69	15.44
Black North	10.96	11.41	10.25
White South	20.13	23.12	19.91
White North	24.56	22.78	15.57

ance in verbal achievement for all subgroups. Interestingly, however, family background characteristics made more of a difference in whites' test scores than in blacks' scores.

As a group, the family background inputs made a large difference in achievement, but it is important to examine the effects of the particular inputs that were used to define "family background." The first distinction that can be made is between "objective characteristics of the home environment" (represented by variables B−1 through B−7) and "subjective characteristics of the home environment" (namely, students' views of their parents' interests and educational aspirations, B−8 and B−9, respectively). The amount of variance accounted for by the so-called objective family variables *decreased* from grade 6 to grade 12, and this decline was especially apparent among minority strata, including Mexican-Americans, Puerto Ricans, and Oriental-Americans. When the two so-called subjective family background variables were entered in the regression, with the objective characteristics already in the equation, the amount of additional explained variance *increased* from grade 6 to grade 12. That is, measures of objective family characteristics appear to be less important explanations of verbal achievement as children grow older.

When the individual family background variables were examined, it appeared that reports of items in the home (B−6) uniquely explained more variance in the achievement of minority sixth graders than any other variable, but for white sixth graders, parents' education uniquely explained more variance in verbal achievement than any other family background characteristic. In grades 9 and 12, parents' education had more impact on verbal achievement than any other family background factor, and this was true for all subgroups.

Student Body Characteristics. Once family background factors are statistically controlled for, the question then becomes how much of the variation in verbal achievement can be accounted for by blocks of inputs representing between-school differences, that is, student body characteristics, teacher characteristics, and school characteristics. The general finding was that the attributes of a student's peers (variables C−1 through C−6 in Table 7−1)[8] explained more of the unique variance in verbal achievement than did school facilities and somewhat more than teachers' characteristics did.

Table 7−4 shows the percentage of variance uniquely explained by student body characteristics when this block of six inputs was added to the regression of verbal achievement on family background variables. The data suggest that the verbal achievement of black students in Southern schools may be particularly susceptible to peer group influences.

The effects of particular student body characteristics can be summarized as follows:[9]

- The larger the proportion of whites in a school, the more members of all racial/ethnic groups achieve on the average; this relationship increases over time and is particularly strong in grades 9 and 12.

- It appears that the effects of racial composition of the school are not due to differences in the school facilities available to whites and blacks. The racial composition of the student body has a much smaller apparent effect when other student body variables are controlled for, and this suggests that the effects of racial composition are not due to race as such. The effects are due it seems

Table 7−4. Percentage of Variance in Verbal Achievement Uniquely Explained by Peer Group Characteristics (C−1 to C−6), Controlling for Family Background Variables.

	Grade		
	12	9	6
Black South	8.07	5.35	6.12
Black North	3.67	1.66	3.69
White South	2.34	1.78	2.11
White North	1.31	1.10	4.31

8. Variable C-7, racial composition of the student body, is not included at this point but will be discussed as a separate case.

9. These conclusions deal only with the unique variance explained by specific student body factors, while family background variables *and all other student body variables* are simultaneously controlled for.

to the fact that students in predominantly white schools tend to have better educational backgrounds (B−1) and higher educational aspirations (B−2) in their families.

- The educational background of fellow students (C−1) and the educational aspirations of fellow students (C−2) are highly correlated; in the South, however, the former variable explains more of the unique variance in verbal achievement, whereas in the North, the opposite is true.

- For all groups, the attendance rate of the student body (C−4) is slightly related to verbal achievement.

- In the North, higher mobility (C−3) results in lower achievement, whereas in the South, the direction of the relationship is reversed. One possible explanation for this interaction is that in the South, mobility may indicate rising aspirations, whereas in the North mobility may be associated with family disruptions.

Teachers' Characteristics. The teachers in America's schools are a diverse lot, but there are some very clear patterns underlying this diversity. The authors of the EEO report summarized these patterns: "Most Negroes are taught by Negro teachers, whites are almost always taught by whites; teachers of Negroes tend to have more positive attitudes toward school integration, and less often express a preference for teaching middle-class, white-collar workers' children. Teachers of Negroes scored lower on the vocabulary test taken by teachers: and there were other differences as well . . ." (p. 316). Do these differences in teachers make a difference in student achievement?

Table 7−5 shows the percentage of unique variance in verbal achievement explained by adding a block of seven teacher inputs

Table 7−5. Percentage of Variance in Verbal Achievement Uniquely Explained by Teacher Characteristics (D−1 to D−7), Controlling for Family Background Variables.

	Grade		
	12	*9*	*6*
Black South	9.97	7.72	5.29
Black North	4.35	1.58	2.19
White South	2.07	2.49	1.12
White North	1.89	1.02	1.67

(D−1 through D−7) to a regression of achievement on family background variables.

These data suggest four major conclusions, to wit:

- Teachers' characteristics account for more variance in achievement than all of the school facilities and curriculum factors combined but less than the student body inputs.

- The importance of teachers' influence appears to be cumulative and increases over the years of schooling.

- Teachers' characteristics tend to have more impact on Southern blacks than Northern blacks, and whites tend to be the least influenced by teachers' characteristics. Coleman and his colleagues note that "This result is an extremely important one, for it suggests that good teachers matter more for children from minority groups which have educationally deficient backgrounds. It suggests as well that for any groups whether minority or not, the effect of good teachers is greatest upon the children who suffer most educational disadvantage in their background, and that a given investment in upgrading teacher quality will have most effect on achievement in underprivileged areas" (p. 317).

- Individual teacher variables (D−1 through D−7) have no impact on white students, but among blacks, the most important teacher variable is the family background of the teacher (specifically, the education of the teacher's mother, D−1). The next most important individual factors are the teacher's years of education (D−4) and the teacher's verbal ability score (D−5). Teaching experience (D−5) has only a very small effect on student achievement among blacks.

School Characteristics: Facilities and Curriculum.   Earlier we saw that differences between schools accounted for relatively little variance in achievement, and it follows that school factors, such as facilities and programs, cannot be very potent determinants of test scores. The data presented in Table 7−6 show the percentage of unique variance in verbal achievement explained by ten school factors, controlling for student background and per capita expenditures. The results are just as one would expect. The amount of unique variance explained by school factors ranges from a low of 0.3 percent for Northern white sixth graders to a high of 8.64 percent for Southern black twelfth graders. In all regions of the country and in all racial/ethnic groups, school inputs become more important as the child progresses through the grades. In addition, in every region and grade, school

Table 7−6. Percentage of Variance in Verbal Achievement Uniquely Explained by Ten Selected School Factors, Controlling for Student Background and Per Capita Expenditures.

	Grade		
	12	9	6
Black South	8.64	7.52	4.90
Black North	3.14	1.45	0.77
White South	3.16	1.60	0.57
White North	1.87	0.73	0.32

facilities and curriculum have more impact on blacks than whites. These assertions describe the impact of all measured school inputs taken together, but the effects of individual school inputs are of more immediate importance to policymakers. The specific effects of these inputs can be summarized as follows:

- For Southern blacks, but for no other racial/ethnic group, achievement increases as per capita expenditures (E−1) increase. That is, for black students in the South, low per capita expenditures are associated with low achievement. The expenditures variable, however, may simply be a proxy for unmeasured student body characteristics, and controlling for these characteristics would eliminate the apparent relationship between school spending and achievement among Southern blacks. In short, how much a school spends does not appear to have a significant effect on student achievement.

- Tracking (E−9) and pupil to teacher ratios (E−2) show no relationship to verbal achievement in any of the subgroups surveyed.

- The number of library volumes per pupil (E−3) and the comprehensiveness of the curriculum (E−7) are only weakly and inconsistently related to verbal achievement.

- The number of extracurricular activities available to students (E−6) and the number of science labs in the school (E−4) have moderate, but consistent, effects on verbal achievement.

- In grades 9 and 12, school size (E−11) is positively related to achievement, probably because larger schools provide more facilities and opportunities than smaller schools. But the precise effects of school size are difficult to detect because size is confounded with urban-suburban-rural location and geographical region. On the average, it appears that small rural schools produce lower achievement than larger urban schools, although very large metropolitan schools may also have a negative impact.

The authors of the EEO report summarized their findings about the impact of school inputs with this generalization: "Differences in school facilities and curriculum, which are the major variables by which attempts are made to improve schools, are so little related to differences in achievement levels of students that, with few exceptions, their effects fail to appear even in a survey of this magnitude" (p. 316). For most readers, this was an unexpected and highly disturbing conclusion.

Student Characteristics. Three kinds of student attitudes were measured in the EEO survey. These included the student's (a) sense of control over the environment, (b) self-concept, and (c) academic motivation. The impact of these student attitudes was very large relative to other sources of variation in achievement. As Coleman and others summarized the findings, "Of all the variables measured in the survey, including all measures of family background and all school variables, these attitudes showed the strongest relation to achievement, at all three grade levels" (p. 319).

Table 7−7 shows the percentage of unique variance in verbal achievement accounted for by each of the three student attitudes, and these data suggest the following conclusions:

- The importance of "academic motivation," which here refers to the student's stated interest in school and frequency of outside reading, declines as students move through the grades; by grade 12, interest in school contributes almost nothing to black students' verbal achievement and only 1.5 to 2 percent of the variance in white students' verbal achievement.

- Self-concept tends to contribute more to verbal achievement scores as students move through the grades; in every grade, region, and racial/ethnic group, the higher the self-concept, the better the student's performance on the average.

- An internal locus of control orientation, that is, a feeling of control over the environment, is associated with higher achievement in all subgroups, especially in ninth grade relative to other grades and among blacks relative to whites.

- In searching for school factors that would explain variations in student attitudes, the EEO researchers found one variable that was consistently related to attitudes. As the proportion of white

Table 7−7. Percentage of Variance in Verbal Achievement Uniquely Explained by Student's Academic Motivation (A−2), Self-concept (A−3), and Locus of Control Orientation (A−4).

			Grade		
Race/Ethnicity	*Region*	*Input*	*12*	*9*	*6*
Black	South	Motivation	0.05	0.07	1.79
		Self-concept	3.06	0.87	1.00
		Locus of Control	5.76	9.68	5.41
Black	North	Motivation	0.03	0.01	1.19
		Self-concept	3.72	1.95	1.23
		Locus of Control	5.07	7.96	4.89
White	South	Motivation	1.60	1.52	1.96
		Self-concept	7.67	3.62	3.17
		Locus of Control	0.69	4.84	2.92
White	North	Motivation	1.37	1.82	1.79
		Self-concept	5.02	3.36	4.40
		Locus of Control	1.55	3.42	3.52

students in the school increases, students' feelings of control over the environment *increase* and their self-concept scores *decrease*. Family background factors, especially the parents' educational aspirations for their children, seem to have a strong impact on both self-concept and locus of control; higher aspirations are associated with a more positive self-concept and a more internal locus of control orientation.

Summary of Findings. The authors of the EEO report summarized their analyses of the educational production function with the following conclusions:

- Family background has a great impact on achievement.
- The importance of family background factors does not diminish as the child progresses through the grades.
- Most of the variance in achievement is due to differences within schools rather than differences between schools, and most of the

between-school variance is accounted for by individual student attitudes.

- School facilities and curriculum account for very little of the between-school variance in academic achievement.

- Although neither teacher nor school inputs account for much variance in achievement, teacher factors are somewhat more important sources of variance than school factors.

- Student body characteristics account for more variance in achievement than either school or teacher characteristics do.

- Certain student attitudes, notably self-concept and sense of control over the environment, are highly related to academic achievement.

These conclusions were considered quite revolutionary when the EEO report was published, and indeed they continue to challenge widely held assumptions about the way schools affect learning. One interpretation of the EEO results holds that schools merely perpetuate the inequalities between children that accrue from differences in family background factors long before children enter school, and despite our good intentions, the inequalities that exist between children cannot be offset by better schooling. Understandably, *Equality of Educational Opportunity* generated substantial controversy, which in turn evoked detailed critiques of the report's data collection and analysis methods.

Criticisms of the EEO Report[10]
Three kinds of questions have been raised about the EEO report. First, there are questions about the adequacy of the data base, including questions about the representativeness of the completed sample and the quality of the data that were collected from students, teachers, principals, and superintendents. Second, there are questions about the way the data were aggregated during the analysis stage of the study. Finally, there are questions about the wisdom of using a variance-partitioning procedure to estimate the effects of various inputs. The third set of questions was treated extensively in Chapter 6 and will not be repeated here. The other two kinds of methodological questions are discussed below.

10. This section relies heavily upon critiques of the EEO report that were prepared by earlier writers, including Bowles and Levin (1968). Cain and Watts (1970), Smith (1972), Jencks (1972), and Hanushek and Kain (1972).

Data Problems. The EEO data base can be criticized on at least three grounds: (a) many selected schools did not participate in the survey or returned only incomplete data, and hence the data base does not accurately represent the U.S. public school population; (b) the validity of many of the measures is suspect; and (c) the study was cross-sectional, not longitudinal, and hence it represents a "snapshot" at one point in time and does not document how previous experiences affect current aspirations, attitudes, and achievement. Each of these problems is discussed in turn.

The EEO survey was designed to produce results that could be generalized to all public school students in the United States, and hence a stratified random sampling plan was used with geographical region, grade, and race ethnicity defining the strata. Unfortunately, there was a large difference between the intended sample and the sample that actually completed the survey instruments and achievement tests. The key problem was that the participating schools were very different from the schools that failed to participate. In statistical terms, the pattern of nonresponse was nonrandom, and therefore nonresponse biases crept into the EEO data base.[11]

Of the 1,170 high schools selected for the EEO survey, 689, or 59 percent, participated. The remaining 41 percent of the schools either returned incomplete data or no data at all. An analysis by Bowles and Levin (1968) demonstrated that large metropolitan school districts were disproportionately represented among nonresponding schools, and hence the EEO data set probably underrepresents large urban school districts and their student populations. Moreover, Jencks (1972) demonstrated that while the percentage of white students in Northern metropolitan schools is known to average 73.2 percent, the Northern metropolitan schools that failed to respond to the EEO survey had an average of 60.3 percent white students. It is reasonable to conclude, therefore, that the EEO data set underrepresents nonwhite and lower socioeconomic status urban populations. This is a serious shortcoming, given that the EEO study was intended to improve the lot of educationally disadvantaged populations.

Nonresponse bias occurred when schools failed to participate in the EEO survey, but this was not the only source of nonresponse bias. In many cases, students, teachers, principals, and superintendents failed to answer specific questions, and hence item nonresponse occurred. Jencks (1972) illustrates the problem with some particularly blatant examples of nonresponse on individual items.

---

11. Methods for detecting and adjusting for nonresponse bias in mail surveys are described in Bridge (1974).

For example, about one-third of the students were unable or unwilling to indicate their parents' educational background; 31 percent did not know their mother's education, and 36 percent did not know their father's education. This item nonresponse cumulates with the initial nonresponse biases. For example, if we assume that about 59 percent of the sampled sixth graders returned completed questionnaires, but only 64 percent of these respondents indicated their father's education, it follows that the statistical tests of the relationship between father's education and student achievement are based on only 38 percent of the intended sample of U.S. sixth graders. The important point is that this group of respondents is not a random sample of U.S. public school students.

A second problem with the EEO data set is that the validity of many of the input measures is unknown. It is unclear what some of the variables measure and how well the conceptual variables of interest were operationalized. For example, the EEO measures of family background, particularly the measures of socioeconomic status (SES), have been challenged. Traditionally, SES has been viewed as a weighted combination of education, occupation, and sometimes income; in the EEO analysis, however, parents' education was used as a proxy for the socioeconomic status of the family. While education, occupation, and income are highly correlated, it is also true that the magnitude of these correlations varies systematically with race. As a result, it may be wrong to assume that parents' education is an adequate index of SES for all racial/ethnic groups in the United States.

Bowles and Levin (1969) make a convincing argument that the EEO survey's inadequate measures of family background variables may have inflated the amount of variance in achievement attributed to peer group characteristics. Children tend to go to school with others who are highly similar in socioeconomic status, and to the extent that the individual student's SES was inadequately measured, the peer group variables may have served as proxies for the individual's own background. Thus, the variance that should have been attributed to individual student characteristics was mistakenly attributed to peer group inputs.[12]

The general problem, which the SES proxy problem illustrates, is that inputs were included in the EEO analysis because of their demonstrated correlation with the achievement test measures rather than on the strength of their theoretical relevance. Without a well-articulated theory of causal processes, it is unclear when a variable is oper-

---

12. A footnote on page 305 of the EEO report acknowledges this problem and explains the authors' attempts to deal with the problem.

ating as a proxy for underlying but unmeasured causal variables and when it is a cause of achievement in and of itself. The authors of the EEO report frequently assumed that the variables in their regressions were merely proxies for other unmeasured causal variables. Thus, the presence of science labs in high schools and the number of volumes in school libraries were meant to represent the general level of physical facilities in the school. Unfortunately, the EEO survey provided no evidence that these measures captured the whole range of school facilities available to students; on balance, it seems highly unlikely that these two measures adequately reflected all of the physical facilities and instructional aids that may have an impact on student achievement. It is not unreasonable to assume, therefore, that the two facilities proxies produced a spuriously low estimate of the impact of school facilities on achievement. Moreover, Hanushek and Kain (1972) point out that these two facilities proxies were not very good measures of science labs or libraries because they tell us nothing about the *quality* of these facilities or how much or how effectively they were used by students.

A third problem, which has been noted by Bowles and Levin (1968) and Hanushek and Kain (1972), is that the EEO data are cross-sectional rather than longitudinal. That is, comparisons of students in different grades (a cross-sectional analysis) may lead to very different conclusions from a study of cohorts of students as they move through the grades (a longitudinal study). No historical data were collected; the data represent only students' current conceptions of their home environments, current teacher attitudes, and current school inputs. Yet current student achievement is a product of more than the immediately present inputs; achievement reflects the cumulation of past and present inputs.

In general, measures of current family background characteristics probably reflect past family conditions (e.g., parents' education) better than current teacher and school measures reflect past teacher and school inputs that the students receive. If family background measures capture historical data more reliably than other kinds of input measures do, it is very likely that the amount of variance attributed to family factors is overestimated at the expense of teacher and school factors.

Data Aggregation Problems.   In Chapter 4, we discussed the dangers of using averages (based on classrooms, schools, districts, or even states) to assess the relationships between independent variables and achievement. The case of per pupil expenditures provides a salient example. If a measure of expenditure per pupil is averaged at the district level while the dependent variable measures are not averaged, all variation within the district in expenditure per pupil will be lost, and the strength of the relationship between expenditure and achievement will be underestimated. This is precisely what happened in the EEO report; data on per pupil expenditures were gathered at the district level, and therefore all within-district variance in expenditure was lost. The same type of aggregation problem occurred in most of the teacher and school measures, although for most of these variables the school rather than the district was the unit of aggregation.

The net effect of using school and district averages, rather than individual level measures, is that ignoring within-school variation in inputs reduces the unique variance in achievement explained by these inputs. For example, it seems misleading to conclude, as the EEO report did, that teacher characteristics account for only 1 to 10 percent of the unique variance in achievement when within-school variations in teacher quality were ignored (because all of the teacher variables were aggregated at the school level). This mythical "average teacher" masks wide variations in actual teacher characteristics within a school. The important point to remember is that aggregating input measures at the school or district level, while maintaining individual level outcome measures, results in underestimation of the effects of school and teacher inputs. This was a severe problem in the EEO study, and the same problem plagues many other input-output studies of educational achievement.

REANALYSES OF THE EEO DATA BY MAYESKE AND COWORKERS

The EEO survey was a tremendous undertaking, and the analysis was done under severe time pressures. The EEO data set represented a large investment, and the U.S. Department of Education thought that these data deserved more refined analyses. A team headed by George W. Mayeske was commissioned to reanalyze the EEO data, and their work resulted in four detailed volumes (1972, 1973a, 1973b, 1975).[13] Our brief review of these four volumes is divided into two parts, methods of analysis and major results.

Methods of Analysis

The analytic techniques that the Coleman and Mayeske teams used differed in three important ways. In the Mayeske analysis (a) com-

13. Other members of the Mayeske group included Albert Beaton, Jr., who participated in all four studies; Tetsuo Okada, who participated in the first three studies; Wallace Cohen and Carl Wisler, who participated in two of the four studies; and John Proshek, Kenneth Tabler, and Frederic Weinfeld.

monality analysis was used to partition the effects of inputs into unique and joint (common) variance components; (b) independent variables were combined to form input indices; and (c) in some of the analyses, the achievement measures were aggregated at the school level and the population was stratified differently than in the EEO analysis. The significance of each of these differences is discussed below.

Commonaltiy analysis, which was described in Chapter 6, partitions explained variance into unique effects and joint effects of inputs. This is in contrast to the method used in the EEO report, in which joint effects were assigned to sets of independent variables (in most cases the family background variables). The Mayeske group's use of commonality analysis was a major advance over the earlier Coleman group's methodology.

The second difference between the EEO and Mayeske analyses involves the way inputs were treated in the regressions. In the EEO analysis, the validity of many of the input measures was questionable; moreover, many of the measures were highly intercorrelated, and the theoretical distinctions between different inputs were often abstruse. Recognizing these problems, Mayeske and his coworkers factor analyzed the original 400 EEO survey variables and formed indices by combining those input measures that seemed to measure the same underlying dimension. Table 7-8 identifies the major indices that the Mayeske group formed.

The Coleman and Mayeske analyses also differed in the way the dependent variables were aggregated and the way in which the sample was stratified during the analysis. Mayeske and his coworkers tried a variety of aggregation and stratification strategies. The first of their four volumes did not stratify the population at all. That is, no separate commonality analyses were reported for different races or regions of the country. This volume aggregated the dependent variable at the school level, thus eliminating the distinction between individual background variables and peer group characteristics. The second and fourth volumes stratified the analysis by sex, race/ethnicity, geographical region, and other variables at times. These volumes analyzed unaggregated student outcomes; thus there were separate measures of individual and peer group characteristics. The third volume examined school outcomes other than achievement, and hence is not reviewed in detail here.

Results

The first volume (1972) examined the impact of two clusters of inputs—student social background and school characteristics. The

Table 7–8. Indices of Independent Variables Used by the Mayeske Group.[14]

	Index Abbreviation	Index Name	Examples of Variables Included	Aggregation Level
1.	SES	Socioeconomic Status	Parents' Occupation Parents' Education Family Possessions	Family
2.	FSS	Family Structure and Stability	Family Mobility Real or Surrogate Parents	Family
3.	RETH	Racial/Ethnic Group		Individual
4.	HB	Home Background	SES + FSS	Family
5.	PRCS	Family Process	Parents' expectations Study Habits Attitudes	Individual Family
6.	FB	Family Background	HB + PRCS	Family
7.	SBB	Student Body Background	Same as HB	School
8.	SO	School Outcomes	Student Body Attitudes Student Body Achievement	School
9.	PPE	Personnel and Personnel Expenditures	Teacher Characteristics Principal Characteristics	School
10.	SF	School Facilities	School Plant Characteristics Instructional Facilities Pupil to Teacher Ratio	School

11.	PPP	Pupil Programs and Policies	Tracking Pupil Transfers Remedial Programs	School
12.	SCHL	School Characteristics	PPE + SF + PPP	School
13.	SCHT	School Total	SCHL + SO	School

14. Note that many of the indices are actually composites of other primary indices. For example, HB (home background) is made up of SES (socioeconomic status), FSS (family structure and stability), and RETH (race and ethnicity). Note too that some indices differ only in the level of aggregation. For example, HB and SBB (student body background) consist of the same input variables, but HB is unaggregated whereas SBB is aggregated at the school level to represent peer group characteristics.

school was used as the unit of analysis, and thus no comparisons were made between subgroups within schools. The results of the commonality analyses can be summarized as follows:

- It is virtually impossible to separate the influences of student background from the influences of school inputs. The authors describe the relationship in these terms:

  > The schools, as they are currently constituted, produce more learning and foster greater motivation in students who:
  >
  > (i) Come from higher socioeconomic strata rather than from the lower socioeconomic strata;
  >
  > (ii) Have both parents in the home rather than only one or neither parent in the home;
  >
  > (iii) Are white or Oriental-American rather than Mexican-American, Indian-American, Puerto Rican, or Negro (p. 2).

- Schools that produced high achievement test scores tend to produce high scores on other outcome measures, such as attitudes toward school and academic motivation.

- Before grade 12, the unique variance in achievement due to student background factors is somewhat larger than the unique variance due to school characteristics. However, the variance jointly explained by these kinds of inputs is always larger than the two unique variance components alone, and the joint variance component becomes increasingly larger in the higher grades.

The second volume in the series (1973a) used the individual student rather than the school as the basic unit of analysis. The analyses were stratified by race/ethnicity, sex, and geographical region (North, South, metropolitan, nonmetropolitan). Both student achievement and affective outcomes were examined, and the inputs were assigned to two major groups: Family background (consisting of home background and family process clusters) and school characteristics (consisting of indices of facilities, pupil programs, and personnel factors). As in all of the Mayeske group's work, commonality analysis was used to separate unique variance due to particular inputs from the variance jointly explained by combinations of inputs. Briefly summarized, the major results are:

- Family disruptions resulting in only one or neither parent being in the home have less impact on whites and blacks than on other racial/ethnic groups.

- When all racial/ethnic groups are combined, 47 percent of the explained variance in achievement can be attributed to family background alone, 21 percent to school characteristics alone, and 32 percent to the joint effects of family and school inputs. When race/ethnicity is considered in the regressions, the importance of family factors remains stable while the importance of school factors falls and is taken up by the joint effects of race/ethnicity and school characteristics. It is very difficult to differentiate the effects of school inputs and race/ethnicity given the attendance patterns in American schools.

- It appears that the impact of school characteristics depends, at least in part, upon the race/ethnicity of the student, and the authors of *A Study of the Achievement of Our Nation's Students* posited the following model to explain the results: "(a) students of similar family background tend to go to school together; (b) schools vary widely in achievement levels of their entering students; (c) the achievement mix of entering students sets a 'going rate' that, once established, affects each student independently of his family background. In the South, family background played a greater role in determining which school the student attended and so in the level of achievement he was likely to reach" (p. 13).

- Motivational aspects of the family—whether or not they had high aspirations for their children and the interactions they engaged in to foster these aspirations—have more impact on student achievement than either the objective socioeconomic status of the family or the presence or absence of key family members in the household. In short, how a family thinks and acts toward their children has more impact on student achievement than how much the family has in material terms.

This last finding stimulated Mayeske and his colleagues to examine the way families and schools contribute to certain student attitudes, which included: (a) expectations of excellence in school, (b) educational plans and desires, and (c) "attitudes toward life." This latter variable, which is central in the analysis, taps students' locus of control beliefs and is the chief dependent variable discussed in the third volume, *A Study of the Attitudes Toward Life of Our Nation's Students* (1973b).

The fourth and final volume in the series (1975) refines earlier analyses and concentrates on the effects of race/ethnicity, geographical region, and male-female differences in the production of educational outcomes. Whereas the three earlier volumes concentrate on ninth graders and consider only four regional groupings, the final volume reports data for seven geographical regions and grades 1, 3, 6, 9, and 12. The results of these special studies suggest that:

- Student sex is not a major source of variation in achievement scores.

- The family's socioeconomic status plays a significant role in student achievement, and this is true irrespective of region.

- Attitudes and motivation are more important determinants of achievement than are social class factors.

- For all students, family background factors contribute more to achievement than school factors do.

- To the extent that school factors make a difference in achievement, minority students seem to be more affected by school inputs than majority students are.

- Race/ethnicity accounts for 20 to 24 percent of the variance in achievement when social background factors are left uncontrolled. But when these background factors are controlled for, race/ethnicity accounts for only 1 percent of the variance in achievement. In other words, ethnicity as such makes little difference in achievement; the social background factors that are correlated with race/ethnicity actually make the difference in the test scores.

- A single production function seems adequate to describe all students' achievement test scores; separate functions are not required for different sexes, racial/ethnic groups, or geographical regions of the country if the proper statistical controls are instituted.

Only the briefest highlights of the extensive work of Mayeske and his colleagues have been presented here, but even this cursory overview should make two points clear. First, commonality analysis, which Mayeske and his coworkers used, is not without problems,[15] but it is clearly a major methodological improvement over the EEO analysis, although both the original EEO analysis and the reanalysis of the EEO data are limited by the weaknesses of the variance-partitioning approach. Second, the conclusions that the Mayeske group reached after ten years of analysis are much more detailed than the findings of the EEO report, but they are not markedly different.

---

15. See, for example, Alexander Mood's foreword to Mayeske et al. (1973a).

INTERNATIONAL EDUCATIONAL ACHIEVEMENT PROJECT: U.S. FINDINGS

One of the most recent studies of educational outcomes in America was sponsored by the International Educational Achievement (IEA) Project, a consortium of twenty-two nations that conducts multinational studies of achievement. These studies were designed for maximum comparability, and hence similar input and output measures, comparable national samples, and nearly identical analytic methods were used in each country. The following brief discussion summarizes the methods and results of the part of the U.S. study that was reported by Wolf (1977) in *Achievement in America.*

Samples
The IEA Project used a multistage stratified random sampling design to select a sample of American public and parochial schools. A total of twenty-nine strata were used with strata defined by community size, socioeconomic status of the community, and type of school (public vs. parochial). As in the EEO survey, many of the selected schools failed to participate, and hence the validity of the IEA results may be constrained by problems of nonresponse bias. Specifically, the final sample seems to have underrepresented lower social class and inner-city schools.

Three different age cohorts were surveyed: students age 10 years to 10 years, 11 months; students age 14 years to 14 years, 11 months; and students in the last year of high school. In most analyses, the sample of ten year olds consisted of 5,550 students in 272 schools, the sample of fourteen year olds consisted of 3,530 students in 160 schools, and the senior high school sample consisted of 2,700 students in 127 schools.

Measures
The achievement tests, which served as the dependent variables in the regression analyses, were constructed especially for the IEA studies and were similar for all twenty-two countries that participated. A detailed discussion of the development and content of these achievement measures may be found in Peaker (1975). American students were tested in up to five different areas of achievement: science, reading comprehension, literature, French as a foreign language, and civic education.

Questionnaires administered to students, teachers, and principals provided measures of the independent variables. Three categories of inputs were examined. Block I consisted of student and family background variables, including parents' education and occupation, and student sex and age. Block II consisted of measures of school program characteristics. Block III included measures of what we have previously called school and teacher variables, and all of these were measured as school averages rather than as individual level data.

Methods of Analysis

Separate regression analyses were carried out for each age cohort and each achievement measure. The variance-partitioning strategy used reported the R^2 for achievement regressed onto the Block I variables, and then it reported additions to R^2 that resulted from adding each of the remaining blocks in order with previous blocks of variables still in the equations. Within each block, the variance uniquely explained by each input variable was calculated, controlling for all previous blocks and all other variables in the block.

Results

The first set of regressions that Wolf (1977) presents uses school averages of reading comprehension, science, and literature as the dependent variables. In all regression equations, a composite index of student body socioeconomic status, included in Block I, explains considerable variation in achievement. Other measures from Blocks I and II have less consistent effects across samples and dependent variables. The contribution of Block III variables to explained variance depends upon the type of achievement being measured. For reading comprehension, the school and teacher variables (Block III) explain very little unique variance; but for science and especially for literature, the unique contribution to R^2 is somewhat higher.

Even though some school effects are important for literature and science achievement, few inputs in Block III show consistent, unique contributions to R^2. Only a measure of hours of homework per week consistently explains unique variance in all kinds of achievement. Other than that, the effects of individual variables are inconsistent. As Wolf (p. 143) notes:

> Educators who are seriously concerned about the identification of potent instructional variables will find the results rather unsatisfying. No single variable can be recommended to the reader for his consideration in any subject at any population level.

The second set of regression equations uses individual achievement scores rather than school aggregates as the dependent variables. Regressions are calculated for all achievement measures: reading comprehension, science, literature, civic education, and French. While the total variance explained by these equations is considerably less than that explained in the aggregate analysis, the conclusions are about the same. Block I variables tend to explain most of the variance in achievement, and measures of student socioeconomic background are the most important individual variables. The effects of Block III variables depend upon the dependent variable under consideration. School and teacher characteristics explain little unique variance in either reading comprehension or civic education, but for science and literature, the picture is brighter. For French achievement, Block III variables are very important, explaining about 7 to 18 percent of the unique variance. Again, though, no single input or set of inputs consistently explains student achievement.

Wolf notes that the total uniquely explained variance in most of the regression equations is less than one-half of the total variance explained (R^2). This observation reinforces the Mayeske group's argument that most of the variance in achievement is jointly explained, and this again underscores the pitfalls of the variance-partitioning approach. Because the variables in Blocks I and III are highly correlated, the effects of the Block III school and teacher variables are probably systematically underestimated in the IEA analysis.

SUMMARY

This chapter reviewed three large-scale analyses of educational production that used the variance-partitioning strategy to estimate the effects of inputs. These studies are important because of their size, their historical position in the development of input-output studies in education, and their often unexpected findings. In general, all of these studies have concluded that, relative to student and family background factors, school and teacher inputs have little impact on educational achievement.

All of the studies suffer, in varying degrees, from the shortcomings inherent in the variance-partitioning approach. The chief problem with this approach is that any variance in the dependent variable that is jointly explained by two or more inputs is assigned to the first input to enter the regression (as in the Coleman et al. and Wolf studies) or is left unassigned to any of the independent variables (as in the Mayesek et al. study). The other important problem with this approach is that the findings are not easily translated into policy recommendations.

Despite these shortcomings of the variance-partitioning approach, we cannot reject the findings of the studies that used this approach without first comparing the conclusions of these studies with the findings of studies that did not use the variance-partitioning approach. The next chapter summarizes the results of a number of studies that have tested partial regression coefficients to determine the effects of inputs, and this provides an opportunity to assess the validity of the conclusions from the EEO, Mayeske and IEA studies.

Chapter 8

Propositions About the
Effects of Inputs

This chapter attempts the difficult task of synthesizing what we know about the effects of different inputs on achievement test scores. Our purpose here is to discover the *direction* of effects, where effects exist, and we make no claims about the *magnitude* of effects. We are trying to identify which inputs have consistently positive effects, which have consistently negative effects, and which seem not to affect achievement at all.

Altogether the separate and combined effects of thirty-five different inputs are considered in this chapter. These are grouped into the five categories that were introduced in Chapter 2, namely: (1) individual student characteristics, (2) family characteristics, (3) peer group (student body) characteristics, (4) teacher characteristics, and (5) school characteristics. From the standpoint of public policy, the teacher and school inputs are the most interesting since they are the most tractable.

The findings are assembled from the twenty-eight major input-output studies that are identified in Table 8–1. The table describes the sample, the inputs, the output(s), and any special features of each study. Fuller synopses of these studies are provided in the appendix.

Studies that partition variance instead of reporting regression coefficients are not discussed in this chapter.[1] In addition, four studies

---

1. See Chapter 6 for a description and comparison of these two approaches, and see Chapter 7 for a review of the major variance partitioning studies of U.S. education.

Table 8−1. Summary of Input-Output Studies Reviewed in Chapter 8.

Author(s)/ Publication Date	Description of Sample/ Data Source(s)[a]	Abbreviation	Outputs
Bidwell & Kasarda (1975)	104 of 178 high school districts in Colorado, 1969–70 (district records and 1970 Census).	B&K	Reading and mathematics (district median percentile scores).
Bowles (1969)	Approximately 100 black male 12th graders, 1960 (Project Talent).	B1	Reading, mathematics, and general academic ability (individual scores).
Bowles (1970)	1,000 black male 12th graders, 1965 (EEO).	B2	Verbal (individual score).
Burkhead, Fox, & Holland (1967)	39 of 52 high schools in Chicago, 1961–62 (district records and 1960 Census).	BFH1	IQ (index relating IQ scores of 11th graders in school to IQ scores of 11th graders citywide; residual, in regression of 11th grade index on 9th grade index, same year); reading (two measures, as for IQ); 11th grade dropout rate; 11th grade college aspiration rate.
	22 of 24 high schools in Atlanta, 1961 (district records and 1960 Census).	BFH2	Verbal (school median; residual, in regression of 10th grade median on 8th grade median, same year); male dropout rate; post high school continuation rate.
	181 high schools in small communities, pop. 2,500 to 25,000, 1960 (Project Talent).	BFH3	Reading (12th grade mean; residual, in regression of 12th grade mean on 10th grade mean, same year); dropout rate; post high school continuation rate.
Cohn (1968)	All 377 high school districts in Iowa, of which 372 were single school districts, early 1960's (Iowa State Dept. of Instruction records).	C	Composite achievement (mean 12th grade score in 1963 minus mean 10th grade score in 1961); expenditure per pupil.

Table 8–1. continued

	Inputs		
Category[b]	Number[c]	Level of Aggregation	Special Features of the Study
F	2	District	Bidwell and Kasarda estimate indirect
T	1	District	effects on outputs of "environmental
S1	2	District	variables" (F and S1), as well as direct
S2	3	District	effects. In their recursive model, the indirect effects of F and S1 are mediated through district "organizational attributes" (T and S2).
F	2–3	Family	
PG	0–1	School	
T	1	School	
S	2–4	School	
I	(2)	Individual	The two individual-type inputs are attitudinal variables, "sense of control of
F	4	Family	environment" and "self-concept."
T	1	School	Bowles treats these two as endogenous
S	1–3	School	variables, omitting them from "reduced-form" equations.
F	1	School	
T	2	School	
S	7	School	
F	1	School	
S	7	School	
F	1	School	
T	1	School	
S	6	School	
T	2	School	Cohn provides estimates for a multiplicative
S	6	School	model, as well as linear estimates.

Table 8-1. continued

Author(s)/ Publication Date	Description of Sample/ Data Source(s)[a]	Abbreviation	Outputs
Cohn & Millman (1975)	The 11th grades of 53 high schools in Pennsylvania, 1971 (Pa. Dept. of Educ.; supplementary data collected by Penn. St. Univ. graduate student).	C&M	Self-concept, understanding others, verbal skills, math skills, interest in school, citizenship, health habits, creativity potential, creativity output, vocational development, appreciation of human accomplishments, preparation for change (school averages).
Hanushek (1972, Chpts. 4 and 5)	471 schools of white 6th graders in metropolitan areas of New England, Mid-Atlantic, and Great Lakes regions, 1965 (EEO).	H1a	Verbal and mathematics (school means).
	242 schools of black 6th graders in metropolitan areas of New England, Mid-Atlantic, and Great Lakes regions, 1965 (EEO).	H1b	Verbal and mathematics (school means).
Hanushek (1972, Chpt. 3)	515 Anglo-American 3rd graders from blue-collar homes, a large California School district, 1968–69 (school records).	H2a	Reading (individual raw scores).
	323 Anglo-American 3rd graders from white-collar homes, same large California school district, 1968–69 (school records).	H2b	Reading (individual raw scores).
Katzman (1971)	All 56 elementary school districts in Boston, 1964–65 (district records).	K	"Holding power" (attendance rate and continuation rate); reading (dist. median 6th grade score minus dist. median 2nd grade score, same year); mathematics (dist. median 5th grade score); "academic aspiration" (percentage of 6th graders who take Boston Latin School exam); "academic achievement" (percentage of 6th graders who pass Boston Latin School exam).

Table 8-1. continued

Category[b]	Inputs Number[c]	Level of Aggregation	Special Features of the Study
I/F	(4 factors)	School	Simultaneous equation model, with 12
T	(15)	School	interdependent outputs. Each of the 12
S	(16)	School	structural equations in the model consists of one output (on the left-hand side) and a subset of the endogenous and exogenous variables (on the right-hand side). The authors use a two-stage least-squares (2SLS) procedure to estimate the structural coefficients. These estimates are presented, together with reduced form estimates and ordinary least-squares (OLS) estimates. If the simultaneous equation model is correctly specified, the OLS estimates are subject to bias.
I	3	School	Unlike Coleman et al. and most others
F	4	School	using the EEO data set (e.g., B2, L, MI),
PG	1-2	School	Hanushek aggregates *all* variables at the
T	3	School	school level. Hanushek chooses a multiplicative specification and estimates his equations using a weighted regression procedure.
I	2	School	
F	4	School	
PG	1	School	
T	2-3	School	
I	3	Individual	These are longitudinal data sets: Hanu-
T	5	Classroom	shek has obtained achievement data on each child over three years (1st-3rd grades), and information on a child's teachers in both 2nd and 3rd grades. A third sample, consisting of Mexican-American 3rd grad-
I	1	Individual	ers, is excluded from the analysis of teacher
F	1	Family	characteristics after the set of teacher
T	4	Classroom	dummy variables is found not to contribute significantly to R^2.
F	1	District	Katzman estimates both linear and
T	1-3	District	multiplicative models for each of his
S	1-5	District	six output measures.

Table 8-1. continued

Author(s)/ Publication Date	Description of Sample/ Data Source(s)[a]	Abbreviation	Outputs
Kiesling (1969)	97 of 1,400 New York State school districts, late 1950s (NYS Dept. of Educ. data set).	KI1	Composite achievement and arithmetic (dist. mean 6th grade score; dist. mean 6th grade score minus dist. mean 4th grade score, two years earlier).
Kiesling (1970)	86 of 801 New York State school districts mid 1960's (district records, 1964–65, for test scores and family information; NYS Basic Educational Data System, for other information).	KI2	Language, mathematics, and composite (dist. mean 5th and 8th grade scores).
Levin (1970)	597 white 6th graders, a large Eastern city, 1965 (EEO).	L	Verbal achievement (individual raw score); student's sense of personal efficacy (index value based on 8 questions in EEO questionnaire); student's educational aspiration (grade indi. wishes to complete); parents' educational expectation (index value based on 3 questions in EEO questionnaire).
Michelson (1970)	597 white 6th graders, a large Eastern city, 1965 (EEO-same sample as Levin's).	MI1	Verbal achievement (individual raw score); student's sense of control over life; student's educational aspiration.
	458 black 6th graders, same large Eastern city, 1965 (EEO).	MI2	
Murnane (1975)	Approximately 440 black 2nd graders, New Haven, 1970–71 (school records and 1970 Census).	MU1	Reading and mathematics (individual scores).
	Same cohort in 3rd grade, 1971–72 (see MU1).	MU2	
	Approximately 440 black 3rd graders, New Haven, 1970–71 (see MU1).	MU3	Reading, mathematics, and spelling (individual scores).

Table 8 -1. continued

	Inputs		
Category[b]	Number[c]	Level of Aggregation	Special Features of the Study
I F S	0-1 1 5	District District District	When the dependent variable is the mean 6th grade score instead of the *change* in mean scores between the 4th and 6th grades, Kiesling introduces the mean 4th grade score as an explanatory variable. In addition to districtwide analysis, the four output measures are computed separately for students in each of six SES groups, as defined by father's occupation, and separate analyses are conducted.
F T S	1 2-3 3-4	District District District	Unlike KI1, the KI2 sample contains no longitudinal information. In lieu of districtwide analysis, the six output measures are computed separately for students in each of 7 groups defined by father's educational level and 7 groups defined by father's occupational level, and separate analyses are conducted.
I F PG T S	(3) (6) (1) (5) (2)	Individual Family School School School	A simultaneous equation model, with 3 interdependent outputs (though parents' expectation is specified as endogenous too, the causal flow is thought to be uni-directional—from parents' expectation to the other 3 outputs). Levin uses a 2SLS procedure to estimate the structural coefficients. Together with these results, he presents reduced form estimates and ordinary least-squares estimates.
I F T S	(3) (6) (4) (2)	Individual Family School School	A simultaneous equation model, with 3 interdependent outputs. Michelson's analysis parallels Levin's (see above). In addition, Michelson conducts single equation analysis on verbal achievement, mathematics achievement, and reading ability, using a set of independent variables that is larger but devoid of student attitudes.
I F PG T S	3 (2 (1 3 1-6 1 (class size)	Individual Census block Family Classroom Classroom Classroom	These are longitudinal data sets: Murnane has collected achievement data on each child at the end of two successive school years.

Table 8-1. continued

Author(s)/ Publication Date	Description of Sample/ Data Source(s)[a]	Abbreviation	Outputs
Perl (1973)	3,265 male 12th graders, 1959–60 (Project Talent).	P	Verbal ability and abstract reasoning (individual scores).
Summers & Wolfe (1974)	627 6th graders in Philadelphia, early 1970's (school and district files, and 1970 Census).	S&W1	Composite achievement (individual grade equivalent scores, difference between 3rd and 6th grades).
	553 8th graders in Philadelphia, early 1970's (see S&W1).	S&W2	Composite achievement (individual grade equivaient scores, difference between 6th and 8th grades).
	716 12th graders in Philadelphia, early 1970's (see S&W1).	S&W3	Composite achievement (individual national percentile rankings, difference between 9th and 12th grades).
Wiley (1976)	2,519 6th graders, Detroit Metropolitan Area Sample (EEO).	WY	Verbal, mathematics, and reading (individual scores).
Winkler (1975)	388 black 8th graders, a large urban school district in California, 1964–65 (district records, and questionnaires completed by students.	W1	Reading (individual 6th and 8th grade percentile rankings).
	385 white 8th graders, same large urban school district in California, 1964–65 (see W1).	W2	Reading (individual 8th grade percentile ranking).

[a]EEO refers to the U.S. Office of Education Equality of Educational Opportunity data set (see Coleman et al., 1966), which is described in Chapter 7.

[b]I = individual student inputs, F = family inputs, PG = peer group or student body inputs, T = teacher inputs, and S = school inputs.

[c]Each figure refers to the number of input variables of a particular type included in the regression equation(s). When the figure is enclosed in parentheses, or when a range of figures is given, this indicates that the number of input variables of this type varies from equation to equation. The number of variables reported here reflects the number of variables found in the *published* regression results though the original set of variables available to the researcher(s) may have been larger than this and reduced by some sort of stepwise procedure.

Table 8-1. continued

	Inputs		
Category[b]	Number[c]	Level of Aggregation	Special Features of the Study
F	2	Individual	In part of his analysis, Perl stratifies the
PG	2	School	sample by family income of the student.
T	6	School	
S	8	School	
I	6	Individual	Summers and Wolfe search for interactions
F	1 (income)	Census block	between student-body/teacher/school
PG	2	School	inputs and a student's (a) family income,
T	3	Classroom	(b) race, and (c) "initial ability," i.e.,
S	{ 1 (class size)	Classroom	earlier test scores.
	{ 3	School	
			The authors have obtained achievement
I	8	Individual	test scores for 6th graders in 1st, 3rd,
F	1 (income)	Census block	and 6th grades; for 8th graders in 3rd, 6th,
PG	1	School	and 8th grades; and for 12th graders in 7th,
T	6	Classroom	9th, and 12th grades. Although several
S	{ 1 (class size)	Classroom	years of classroom information are available
	{ 4	School	for each student, only current-year classroom
			inputs are retained in the final regression
I	5	Individual	equations.
PG	2	School	
T	1	Classroom	
S	{ 1 (class size)	Classroom	
	{ 1 (sch. size)	School	
I	3	Individual	The effective hours of schooling variable
I	1 (effective hrs of schooling)	School	is defined as the number of days in the school year, times the number of hours in the school day, times the average daily percentage of students in attendance.
I	1	Individual	Winkler has obtained achievement test
F	3	Family	scores for all students in 1st, 6th, and 8th
PG	1–3	School	grades. All input measures are longitudinal
T	0–1	Track	(except for individual and family inputs).
S	{ 2	Track	
	{ 1	School	

that do estimate the effects of particular inputs (KI2, S&W1, S&W2, and S&W3 in Table 8—1) are excluded from the synthesis attempted in this chapter because of methodological unwieldiness or inadequacies.[2]

For the most part, the findings reported here are highly tentative. Our conclusions should be viewed as propositions for future research rather than bases for policy action. Obviously, none of the studies reviewed here is totally free of defects. Usually in formulating propositions, however, we are able to draw upon several studies, each suffering from a different set of technical defects. This permits us to triangulate on the probable effect of a particular input. When studies that do not share the same weak points show essentially the same results, our conclusions can be accepted with some confidence.

The findings about an input can assume any of the following patterns: (a) the input has a significant positive effect in study after study; (b) the input has a significant negative effect in study after study; (c) the results are mixed, with some studies showing a positive effect and others a negative effect, or some a statistically significant effect and others a nonsignificant effect; and finally (d) the input appears consistently to have no effect on output. We have the most confidence in our conclusions when an input shows a consistently positive or consistently negative effect. When the findings are mixed, we try to integrate the results theoretically. That is, we try to understand what differences in the studies would explain contrary findings about an input.

When a study produces a statistically nonsignificant effect there are at least two different interpretations. On the one hand, the input may affect the output, but the researcher has misspecified the rest of the model and/or failed to measure the components of the model accurately so that the true relationship cannot be detected statistically. On the other hand, the input may in truth have no impact at all. In this case, the null result accurately reflects reality. It is difficult, however, to distinguish the one from the other. This is not the only problem we face in interpreting these disparate studies.

Although all of the twenty-eight studies listed in Table 8—1 are prominent examples of the input-output approach, the studies differ widely in a number of important respects. They employ different

2. Kiesling (1970) stratifies his sample in so many ways that the results are difficult to summarize. The three studies by Summers and Wolfe (1974) show some inconsistencies between statistical results and the authors' interpretations of these results so that these studies are excluded as well. For descriptions of Kiesling (1970) and Summers and Wolfe (1974) refer to the appropriate sections of the appendix.

samples, which may reflect different student populations. In addition, these samples frequently differ in the unit of analysis employed. By the unit of analysis, we mean the level at which the outcome measures are gathered, for example, the individual level or the average level of a classroom, school, or district. Strictly speaking, hypotheses about the process by which *individuals* learn cannot be tested with data collected at some higher level.

Some studies have attempted to explain the achievement of individual students (i.e., have taken the individual to be the unit of analysis) while measuring at least some of the inputs (most often, school and teacher inputs) at the level of the school. The reason for this inconsistency is clear. Inputs at the level of the individual are often expensive or inconvenient to measure. The problem with this shortcut in data collection is that it introduces measurement error, the extent of which depends on the amount of input variation *within* schools. For example, we would not expect the verbal ability of all teachers within a school to be equal. Thus, we may overestimate or underestimate the verbal ability of any individual student's teacher when we take the mean verbal ability of all teachers in the school as our measure.

A related methodological problem is that many of the input measures used are merely proxies for the real causal factors, as we have emphasized in earlier chapters. There are two models, the distinction between which is important and should be kept in mind in the course of reading this chapter. Let us explicate the two models in terms of three variables: A, B, and C. In both cases A and C are measured; B is not.

In the first model, A causes B, which in turn causes C. Using A as a proxy for B results in an underestimation of the effect of B on C. For example, teacher's education may be one cause of teacher's classroom behavior, which in turn affects achievement.

In the second model, A and B are simply correlated (perhaps both are caused by some prior variable), and B causes C. Again, using A as a proxy for B results in the underestimation of the effect of B on C, and in this case it also leads to problems of interpretation since in no way does A cause C. For example, a student's race may be inappropriately inferred to have a causal impact on achievement when in fact it is merely correlated with other variables (e.g., socioeconomic status) that are the true causes of achievement.

In both models, the measured effect of A on C is diminished as more direct measures of B are included in the analysis. In interpreting these studies, therefore, it is important to examine the entire set of independent variables included in the analysis and to relate the included variables to a theoretical model of educational production.

In addition, there is the problem of attenuated variance in either input or output measures. It is impossible to detect the impact of different levels of a resource if all children receive the same or very similar amounts of the resource. Similarly, it is impossible to identify the effects of different resources if all children have identical or very similar outcome scores (perhaps due to "bottoming out" on tests that are too difficult). Attenuated variance in any measure limits our ability to detect relationships between that variable and any other variable.

Finally, we must acknowledge the inadequacy of using standardized achievement test scores as the sole outcome of education. Achievement test scores have been by far the most frequently used output measure to date. As we saw in Chapter 3, Table 3−1, most input-output studies have taken one or another measure of *verbal achievement* as the operational definition of outputs. Math achievement is the second most widely used measure. Our concentration on standardized test scores, especially verbal achievement scores, reflects the reality of current educational evaluation.

Summarizing extremely diverse studies is a perilous intellectual undertaking, but one which must be attempted if input-output studies are to produce cumulative results and the technology is to mature and advance. We view the propositions that follow as tentative guides to future research. For supplementary reviews of the educational input-output literature, the reader is referred to the surveys by Averch, Carroll, Donaldson, Kiesling, and Pincus (1974), by Cohn and Millman (1975, ch. 4), by Jamison, Suppes, and Wells (1974), and by Simmons and Alexander (1975).

1.0 INDIVIDUAL STUDENT INPUTS

Children within the same family may differ widely in achievement, and of course they also differ in their personal characteristics, including birth order, sex, age, intellectual ability, and unique experiences. Input-output researchers have paid little attention to these characteristics in the past. There may be at least two reasons for this reluctance to consider individual student inputs. First, most I-O researchers are oriented toward policy, and student inputs tend not to be amenable to manipulation by policymakers. A second reason is that most of the I-O research has been associated with the disciplines of economics and sociology. Despite the widespread advocacy of interdisciplinary work, it is difficult to be proficient in one discipline, let alone two or three. Hence, most economists and sociologists stay within their disciplinary boundaries and leave to psychologists the study of the effects of individual differences on achievement. This gap will probably be eliminated as the I-O field matures. More attention should be paid to the likely interactions between individual characteristics and the teacher-school inputs. So-called "learning style" variables have not been used in any input-output study we know of, and yet experimental research suggests that learning style and teaching style interact to affect achievement (e.g., Cronbach and Snow, 1977; Hunt, 1975, and 1974).

The individual student characteristics, the effects of which we review in this section, are (1) sex, (2) preschool experience, (3) age, (4) affective inputs, which here consist of internal-external control expectancies, self-concept, and grade aspirations (a measure of academic motivation), and (5) school attendance. Each of the propositions in Chapter 8 is identified by three numbers. The first number refers to the basic input cluster (1 = individual student characteristics, 2 = family characteristics, 3 = peer group (student body) characteristics, 4 = teacher characteristics, and 5 = school characteristics). The second number refers to a particular type of input within a cluster, for example, sex, age, or preschool experience. And the last number serves to give each proposition a unique identifier.

1.1 Sex

1.1.1 Reading achievement tends to be greater for females than for males. This finding holds true for both blacks and whites.

1.1.2 The results pertaining to verbal achievement are less clear than those pertaining to reading achievement, but here again it appears that females hold some advantage.

1.1.3 The child's sex has the opposite effect on mathematics achievement than it has on verbal achievement and reading ability, at least among white children. Females tend to be at a disadvantage in mathematics.

These propositions are based on the six studies summarized in Table 8−2. Although the results of these studies are mixed, it appears that for one reason or another being female contributes to verbal achievement and reading ability and detracts from mathematics achievement. This probably reflects the role training imposed upon boys and girls at a very young age. Almost from birth, girls are expected to be verbal and expressive while it is often assumed that they have little ability (or interest) in technical matters including mathematics (e.g., Lewis, 1976).

Table 8–2. Sex of Child.[a]

Study	Input Measure	Input Level of Aggregation	Output Measure	Output Level of Aggregation	Direction of Effect[b]	Sample/Other Comments
L	Sex dummy variable (female = 1, male = 0)	Individual	Verbal	Individual	Nonsignificant (positive)	597 urban white 6th graders (EEO); 2SLS estimates in addition to OLS
MI1	Sex dummy variable (female = 1, male = 0)	Individual	Verbal / Reading / Math	Individual / Individual / Individual	Nonsignificant (mixed) / POSITIVE / NEGATIVE	597 urban white 6th graders (EEO); 2SLS estimates in addition to OLS
MI2	Sex dummy variable (female = 1, male = 0)	Individual / Individual	Verbal / Reading / Math	Individual / Individual / Individual	Nonsignificant (mixed) / Nonsignificant (positive) / Nonsignificant (negative)	458 urban black 6th graders (EEO); 2SLS estimates in addition to OLS
MU1	Sex dummy variable (female = 1, male = 0)[c]	Individual	Reading / Math	Individual / Individual	Nonsignificant (positive) / Nonsignificant (negative)	440 black 2nd graders, New Haven; fall score entered as independent variable
MU2	Sex dummy variable (female = 1, male = 0)[c]	Individual	Reading / Math	Individual / Individual	Nonsignificant (positive) / Nonsignificant (negative)	440 black 3rd graders, New Haven; score from previous year entered as independent variable
MU3	Sex dummy variable (female = 1, male = 0)[c]	Individual	Reading / Math / Spelling	Individual / Individual / Individual	Nonsignificant (positive) / Nonsignificant (negative) / POSITIVE	440 black 3rd graders, New Haven; fall score entered as independent variable

[a] The estimated effects reported in this table are partial effects. To ascertain the control variables used in a particular study, the reader is referred to Table 8–1, or to the appropriate section of the appendix.

[b] An effect is declared POSITIVE or NEGATIVE in this table if the null hypothesis can be rejected at the 95% confidence level (i.e., $p \leq .05$) in a two-tailed test. Nonsignificant effects are reported here only when the inputs have been retained in the analysis. In many instances, researchers will have dropped inputs whose coefficients are not significantly different from zero and, in such instances, the "noneffects" are not reported here.

[c] For ease of reading and to maintain consistency in the presentation, the direction of this variable has been reversed from that in the original study.

1.2 Preschool Experience

1.2.1 Kindergarten attendance contributes to verbal, mathematics, and reading achievement, and the effects appear to last through at least the sixth grade.

Kindergarten attendance seems to have a lasting impact on both verbal and mathematics achievement and on reading skills. This conclusion is based on three different studies (see Table 8–3). All three used the EEO data set so that the degree of apparent consistency between the studies is not surprising. The analyses, however, incorporated adequate individual measures of family socioeconomic status, and thus it is unlikely that kindergarten attendance is merely a proxy for social class. Kindergarten does make a difference.

1.3 Age

1.3.1 The older a child is relative to his or her classmates, the less well that child tends to do on verbal and mathematics achievement tests.

Obviously, a child's achievement increases with age, but here we are concerned with a different issue, namely, *within a given grade*, what is the relationship between age and achievement? The results in Table 8–4 indicate that age is negatively related to achievement. Age in these studies is probably a proxy for ability or previous learning. Children are held back because they failed to master the material the first time around. This may be common sense, but it is somewhat surprising that the studies found any relationship at all, given the relatively small number of repeaters in any class.

1.4 Affective Variables

1.4.1 A feeling of control over the environment (i.e., internal control) contributes positively to verbal achievement.

1.4.2 A positive self-concept contributes positively to verbal achievement.

1.4.3 The greater a child's academic motivation, as measured by grade aspirations, the greater the child's verbal achievement.

We consider evidence on three kinds of affective inputs here—internal-external (I-E) control beliefs, self-concept, and academic motivation. These concepts were described earlier (see Chapter 3). The findings reported in the input-output research suggest quite clearly that the more internally oriented students are, the better their self-concept, or the higher their academic motivation, the better they

Table 8–3. Kindergarten Attendance.[a]

Study	Input Measure	Input Level of Aggregation	Output Measure	Output Level of Aggregation	Direction of Effect[b]	Sample/Other Comments
L	Kindergarten dummy	Individual	Verbal	Individual	Nonsignificant (positive)	597 urban white 6th graders (EEO); 2SLS estimates in addition to OLS
MI1	Kindergarten dummy	Individual	Verbal Math	Individual Individual	POSITIVE POSITIVE	597 urban white 6th graders (EEO); 2SLS estimates in addition to OLS
MI2	Kindergarten dummy	Individual	Reading	Individual	POSITIVE	458 urban black 6th graders (EEO); 2SLS estimates in addition to OLS

[a] The estimated effects reported in this table are partial effects. To ascertain the control variables used in a particular study, the reader is referred to Table 8-1, or to the appropriate section of the appendix.

[b] An effect is declared POSITIVE or NEGATIVE in this table if the null hypothesis can be rejected at the 95% confidence level (i.e., $p \leqslant .05$) in a two-tailed test. Nonsignificant effects are reported here only when the inputs have been retained in the analysis. In many instances, researchers will have dropped inputs whose coefficients are not significantly different from zero and, in such instances, the "noneffects" are not reported here.

Table 8-4. Age of Child.[a]

	Input		Output			
Study	Measure	Level of Aggregation	Measure	Level of Aggregation	Direction of Effect[b]	Sample/Other Comments
L	12 years or over dummy	Individual	Verbal	Individual	NEGATIVE	597 urban white 6th graders (EEO); 2SLS estimates in addition to OLS
MI1	12 years or over dummy	Individual	Verbal Reading Math	Individual Individual Individual	NEGATIVE NEGATIVE NEGATIVE	597 urban white 6th graders (EEO); 2SLS estimates in addition to OLS
MI2	12 years or over dummy	Individual	Verbal Reading Math	Individual Individual Individual	NEGATIVE NEGATIVE NEGATIVE	458 urban black 6th graders (EEO); 2SLS estimates in addition to OLS

[a] The estimated effects reported in this table are partial effects. To ascertain the control variables used in a particular study, the reader is referred to Table 8-1, or to the appropriate section of the appendix.

[b] An effect is declared POSITIVE or NEGATIVE in this table if the null hypothesis can be rejected at the 95% confidence level (i.e., $p \leq .05$) in a two-tailed test. Nonsignificant effects are reported here only when the inputs have been retained in the analysis. In many instances, researchers will have dropped inputs whose coefficients are not significantly different from zero and, in such instances, the "noneffects" are not reported here.

do on standardized tests of verbal achievement. Because four of the studies in Table 8−5 used the EEO data set, or some portion of that data set, we should expect consistency in the results. Althought these results are predictable a priori, there is considerable supplementary evidence supporting the conclusion that affective variables contribute to achievement.

The strength of the relationship between I−E control beliefs and achievement is noteworthy, especially for black students. The study by Coleman et al., described in the last chapter, reports data indicating that relatively "internal" children (those with a sense of personal efficacy) score higher in verbal achievement than do "externals." This finding is consistent across all ethnic groups and geographic regions (Coleman et al., 1966).

Whereas the relationship between affective variables and scholastic achievement has been clearly established, the nature of that relationship is likely to be more complicated than others we have considered in this section. Presumably, affective variables influence achievement. But they are in turn influenced by achievement. Cognitive achievement and affective characteristics are both outputs of the educational process. They are related to one another in a bidirectional manner, and both are affected by other inputs, including early family inputs to the child's personality formation. In fact, some evidence suggests that stable internal-external control beliefs are formed by the age of three (Mischel et al., 1974).

Of the authors in Table 8−5, only Levin, Michelson, and Cohn and Millman look for a bidirectional relationship between cognitive and affective variables. To do this, they posit models in which cognitive achievement and affective characteristics serve as dependent variables in different equations. Statistically, this set of equations is estimated simultaneously via a two-stage least-squares (2SLS) procedure, as contrasted with the ordinary least-squares (OLS) procedure used in most input-output studies. This approach is a move in the right direction because it acknowledges that (a) schools produce more than one output at a time, (b) different production functions may be necessary to explain different outputs, and (c) inputs and outputs have reciprocal effects over time. While the objectives of the Levin, Michelson, and Cohn and Millman studies were admirable, the results may have little external validity because of small regional samples.

Figure 8–1 illustrates the model that Levin uses. This model involves four equations:[3]

(1) Verbal achievement = f(locus of control, academic motivation, parents' attitudes, and "other inputs")

(2) Locus of control = f(verbal achievement, parents' attitudes, and "other inputs")

(3) Academic motivation = f(verbal achievement, parents' attitudes, and "other inputs")

(4) Parents' attitudes = f("other inputs")

Figure 8–1. Interrelationships between Parents' Attitudes, Student's Locus of Control, Academic Motivation, and Verbal Achievement, as Tested by Levin (1970, p. 72).

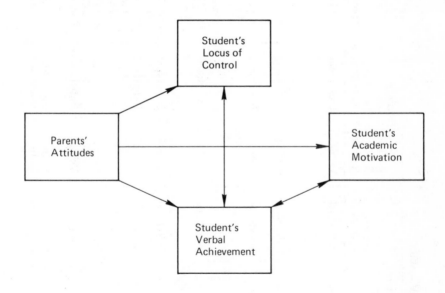

3. The set of "other inputs" in each of the equations consists of the child's age, sex, a kindergarten attendance dummy, a family possessions index, family size, identity of mother, identity of father, mother's employment, percent of students white in school, teacher turnover, father's education, teacher's verbal score, teacher's parents' income, teacher's experience, teacher's undergraduate institution, teacher's satisfaction with present job, and library volumes per student.

Table 8–5. Affective Variables.[a]

Study	Input Measure	Input Level of Aggregation	Output Measure	Output Level of Aggregation	Direction of Effect[b]	Sample/Other Comments
B2	Control of environment (internal control)	Individual	Verbal	Individual	POSITIVE	1,000 black male 12th graders (EEO)
	Self-concept	Individual	Verbal	Individual	POSITIVE	
L	Efficacy (internal control) index	Individual	Verbal	Individual	POSITIVE under OLS[c]	597 urban white 6th graders (EEO); 2SLS estimates in addition to OLS
	Grade aspiration (motivation)	Individual	Verbal	Individual	POSITIVE under OLS[c]	
MI1	Efficacy	Individual	Verbal	Individual	POSITIVE under OLS[c]	597 urban white 6th graders (EEO); 2SLS estimates in addition to OLS
	Grade aspiration	Individual	Verbal	Individual	POSITIVE under OLS[c]	
MI2	Efficacy	Individual	Verbal	Individual	POSITIVE under 2SLS	458 urban black 6th graders (EEO); 2SLS estimates in addition to OLS
	Grade aspiration	Individual	Verbal	Individual	Nonsignificant (pos.)	
C&M	Self-concept	Individual	Verbal	Individual	Nonsignificant (pos.)	53 schools of 11th graders, Pennsylvania; 2SLS estimates in addition to OLS
		Individual	Math	Individual	Nonsignificant (pos.)	

Understanding others	Individual Individual	Verbal Math	Individual Individual	Nonsignificant (pos.) Nonsignificant (pos.)
Vocational development	Individual	Verbal	Individual	Nonsignificant (neg.)

[a] The estimated effects reported in this table are partial effects. To ascertain the control variables used in a particular study, the reader is referred to Table 8–1, or to the appropriate section of the appendix.

[b] An effect is declared POSITIVE or NEGATIVE in this table if the null hypothesis can be rejected at the 95% confidence level (i.e., $p \leq .05$) in a two-tailed test. Nonsignificant effects are reported here only when the inputs have been retained in the analysis. In many instances, researchers will have dropped inputs whose coefficients are not significantly different from zero and, in such instances, the "noneffects" are not reported here.

[c] Positive but not significant under 2SLS.

The 2SLS procedure Levin used to estimate the coefficients in these equations produced the following results:

- Verbal achievement was positively related to an internal locus of control orientation, to teacher's experience, and to the prestige of the teacher's undergraduate institution.[4]

- An internal locus of control was related to a child's verbal achievement score, sex (females were more internal than males in this sample), family size (smaller families produced more internal children), father's education (the more educated the father, the more internal the children), and teacher turnover (the lower the turnover, the more internal the children).

- The grade aspirations that a child reported were used to measure "academic motivation." Verbal achievement was positively related to motivation, as were teacher's experience and the quality of the teacher's undergraduate institution. Age was negatively related to motivation. Older sixth graders had lower grade aspirations.

Together, these results lend some credence to the model that Levin set out to test. The results indicate that affective outcomes (e.g., locus of control) and cognitive outcomes (e.g., verbal achievement) are reciprocally related. This is an important point that has not been recognized explicitly in the majority of input-output studies done to date.

Michelson's model was similar to Levin's but excluded parents' attitudes as an input. Michelson's results for white sixth graders were comparable to Levin's since he used the same sample as Levin and similar methods of analysis. Unlike Levin, however, Michelson tested the model on a sample of black sixth graders as well, and his results suggest that the educational production functions for blacks and whites are quite different. For example, the signs of the coefficients differed for whites and blacks on the following inputs: age, possessions, kindergarten attendance, identity of person serving as father, and mother's employment. The important thing that Michelson's research teaches us is that there is more than one production function and that researchers (and policymakers) should adjust their strategies accordingly.

4. The 2SLS and OLS solutions produced markedly different results. In the OLS solution, aspirations were positive contributors to verbal achievement, but this was not the case in the 2SLS solution. This suggests that a child's grade aspirations have only an indirect effect on achievement, that is, the effect is mediated through other inputs.

1.5 School Attendance

1.5.1 Reading comprehension, verbal achievement, and mathematics achievement benefit significantly from time spent in school.

Evidence for this commonsense finding can be found in two places—Murnane's studies of black elementary school students in New Haven and Wiley's reanalysis of the EEO survey data collected from sixth graders in the Detroit Metropolitan Area. Table 8–6 summarizes the relevant data. Both studies suggest the same conclusion; that is, the more time spent in school, the better children do in mathematics, reading comprehension, and verbal achievement. Of course, attendance might be a proxy for other family background factors, and some people might argue that these background factors—not exposure to school—account for the variations in achievement. But Murnane's analyses in particular are based on individual-level input and output measures, and adequate controls were used; therefore the proposition that time in school increases achievement is easy to accept on both empirical and intuitive grounds.

Wiley's analysis gives us some idea of the magnitude of the impact of attendance on achievement. His results suggest that an increase in class time of 11 percent is required to get a one point increase in reading comprehension or verbal achievement, and an increase of 28 percent is required to get a one point increase in mathematics achievement.

In addition to the studies reviewed here, other interesting discussions of the relationship between time and achievement may be found in Bloom (1974), Carroll (1963), Garner (1973), Karweit (1976), and Wiley and Harnischfeger (1974).

2.0 FAMILY INPUTS

One of the most consistent findings in the various input-output studies has been that family background seems to make a large difference in achievement outcomes. In fact, part of the reason that the EEO report drew so much attention was because of its findings that the effect of home and family background variables as a group was so much larger than that of either teacher or school characteristics. In this section, we shall try to untangle the effects of individual home and family background variables on achievement.

The following variables are considered in this section: (1) family size, (2) parents' education, (3) family occupational status, (4) family income, (5) family housing arrangements, (6) possessions in the

Table 8-6. Attendance.[a]

Study	Input		Output		Direction of Effect[b]	Sample/Other Comments
	Measure	Level of Aggregation	Measure	Level of Aggregation		
MU1	Days attended	Individual	Reading	Individual	POSITIVE	440 black 2nd graders, New Haven; fall score entered as independent variable
MU2	Days attended	Individual	Reading	Individual	POSITIVE	440 black 3rd graders, New Haven; score from previous year entered as independent variable
MU3	Days attended	Individual	Reading	Individual	POSITIVE	440 black 3rd graders, New Haven; fall score entered as independent variable
WY	Hours of schooling per year	School School School	Reading Verbal Math	Individual Individual Individual	POSITIVE POSITIVE POSITIVE	2,519 sixth graders, Detroit Metropolitan Area sample (EEO)

[a] The estimated effects reported in this table are partial effects. To ascertain the control variables used in a particular study, the reader is referred to Table 8-1, or to the appropriate section of the appendix.

[b] An effect is declared POSITIVE or NEGATIVE in this table if the null hypothesis can be rejected at the 95% confidence level (i.e., $p \leq .05$) in a two-tailed test. Nonsignificant effects are reported here only when the inputs have been retained in the analysis. In many instances, researchers will have dropped inputs whose coefficients are not significantly different from zero and, in such instances, the "noneffects" are not reported here.

home, and (7) the educational environment of the home. As will be apparent, each of these general input categories has been operationalized in a variety of ways, and differences between the findings of studies for any given variable could well be caused by the different specific indicators used within the general category.

Before proceeding to summarize the findings for home and family background variables, one important warning needs to be repeated. We alluded to this problem in general terms in the introductory section of this chapter. Frequently, researchers are not interested in the effects of family variables per se. Instead they simply want to control for family background differences. Their goal is the analysis of *tractable* inputs—those that are purchased and applied within the context of the schools. Hence they may show less care in the selection and measurement of background variables than in the selection and measurement of teacher and school variables. They often seize on readily available measures of background without careful consideration of how these relate theoretically to achievement outcomes. When statistical effects are found interpreting them is problematic, as was indicated above and as we stress throughout this book. Accordingly, our conclusions about these proxy variables should be regarded as highly speculative.

2.1 Family Size

2.1.1 Among both black and white children, verbal and math achievement decline as the number of children in the family or the number of people in the household increases even when other family characteristics remain the same.

2.1.2 The effect of family size upon achievement when social class is controlled for may be an indirect effect, at least among white students. Family size may affect the student's attitudes about himself or herself and thus indirectly influence achievement.

Children from bigger families do less well in school according to the studies reported in Table 8−7. Poor families tend to have more children, but the strong relationship between large families and low achievement holds even when statistical controls for socioeconomic status are introduced.

The second conclusion is based on the studies by Levin and Michelson, who employed two-stage least-squares analyses. Under ordinary least squares, family size showed a negative effect upon achievement. When student's attitude was introduced as a second dependent variable under two-stage least-squares, however, family size was no

Table 8–7. Number of Siblings/Family Size.[a]

Study	Input Measure	Input Level of Aggregation	Output Measure	Output Level of Aggregation	Direction of Effect[b]	Sample/Other Comments
B2	Number of siblings	Individual	Verbal	Individual	NEGATIVE	1,000 black male 12th graders (EEO)
H1a	Family size	School	Verbal Math	School School	NEGATIVE NEGATIVE	471 schools of white 6th graders (EEO)
H1b	Family size	School	Verbal Math	School School	NEGATIVE NEGATIVE	242 schools of black 6th graders (EEO)
L	Family size	Individual	Verbal	Individual	NEGATIVE	597 urban white 6th graders (EEO); 2SLS estimates in addition to OLS
MI1	Number of people at home	Individual	Verbal Math Reading	Individual Individual Individual	NEGATIVE NEGATIVE NEGATIVE	597 urban white 6th graders (EEO); 2SLS estimates in addition to OLS
MI2	Number of people at home	Individual	Verbal Reading	Individual Individual	NEGATIVE NEGATIVE	458 urban black 6th graders (EEO); 2SLS estimates in addition to OLS
W1	Number of siblings	Individual	Verbal	Individual	NEGATIVE	388 black 8th graders, California; 1st grade IQ entered as independent variable
W2	Number of siblings	Individual	Verbal	Individual	Nonsignificant (negative)	385 white 8th graders, California; 1st grade IQ entered as independent variable

[a] The estimated effects reported in this table are partial effects. To ascertain the control variables used in a particular study, the reader is referred to Table 8–1, or to the appropriate section of the appendix.

[b] An effect is declared POSITIVE or NEGATIVE in this table if the null hypothesis can be rejected at the 95% confidence level (i.e., $p \leq .05$) in a two-tailed test. Nonsignificant effects are reported here only when the inputs have been retained in the analysis. In many instances, researchers will have dropped inputs whose coefficients are not significantly different from zero and, in such instances, the "noneffects" are not reported here.

longer significantly related to achievement. Instead it was found primarily to affect student's attitude.

2.2 Parents' Education

2.2.1 Parents' education seems to affect positively the mathematics and verbal achievement of both elementary and high school students even when other measures of family background are controlled for.

2.2.2 Similar to the findings for family size, the effect of parents' education upon achievement may be indirect when other family characteristics are controlled for—via a student's attitude and expectations, which in turn affect achievement.

2.2.3 The relationship between parents' education and student achievement may be somewhat weaker for black students than for white students. However, the less evident effects reported for blacks may be due simply to less variation in parents' education among black families in the samples used.

The first of these conclusions (2.2.1) seems to be well supported by the evidence from the various studies summarized in Table 8—8. There are a few nonsignificant regression coefficients reported; however, these are found generally with black students, which supports our third conclusion (2.2.3).

The second conclusion is based upon those studies using nonrecursive models (Levin and Michelson). Like the effects reported for family size, the effects of parents' education upon achievement seem to be indirect through attitudes.

Our third conclusion must remain especially tentative. It is true that the reported regression coefficients for samples of black students are less often significant than for white students. Nevertheless, this difference may be due only to more variance in the independent measure among white students than among black students. There is no theoretical reason why the size of effects should differ by race of student.

2.3 Parents' Occupational Status

2.3.1 The higher the parents' occupational status, the higher their children's reading, math, and general academic ability.

Occupations vary in prestige, and demographers have created scales that measure the prestige of various occupations. These scales

Table 8–8. Parents' Education.[a]

Study	Input		Output		Direction of Effect[b]	Sample/Other Comments
	Measure	Level of Aggregation	Measure	Level of Aggregation		
B&K	Percent of parents completing high school	District	Reading Math	District District	POSITIVE (indirect through staff qualifications)	104 high school districts, Colorado
B1	Mother's education	Individual	Reading General academic ability Math	Individual Individual Individual	POSITIVE POSITIVE Nonsignificant (positive)	100 black male 12th graders (Project Talent)
B2	Parents' education	Individual	Verbal	Individual	POSITIVE	1,000 black male 12th graders (EEO)
H1a	Father's education	School	Verbal Math	School School	POSITIVE POSITIVE	471 schools of white 6th graders (EEO)
H1b	Father's education	School	Verbal Math	School School	Nonsignificant (positive) Nonsignificant (positive)	242 schools of black 6th graders (EEO)
L	Father's education	Individual	Verbal	Individual	POSITIVE	597 urban white 6th graders (EEO); 2SLS estimates in addition to OLS
MI1	Father's education	Individual	Verbal Reading Math	Individual Individual Individual	POSITIVE POSITIVE POSITIVE	597 urban white 6th graders (EEO); 2SLS estimates in addition to OLS

MI2	Father's education	Individual	Reading Math	Individual Individual	POSITIVE POSITIVE	458 urban black 6th graders (EEO); 2SLS estimates in addition to OLS
	Mother's education	Individual	Verbal	Individual	POSITIVE	
P	Father's education	Individual	Verbal Abstract reasoning	Individual Individual	POSITIVE POSITIVE	3,265 male 12th graders (Project Talent)

[a] The estimated effects reported in this table are partial effects. To ascertain the control variables used in a particular study, the reader is referred to Table 8–1, or to the appropriate section of the appendix.

[b] An effect is declared POSITIVE or NEGATIVE in this table if the null hypothesis can be rejected at the 95% confidence level (i.e., $p \le .05$) in a two-tailed test. Nonsignificant effects are reported here only when the inputs have been retained in the analysis. In many instances, researchers will have dropped inputs whose coefficients are not significantly different from zero and, in such instances, the "noneffects" are not reported here.

range from very sophisticated systems (e.g., Duncan, 1961; Trieman, 1977) to indices that make only gross "blue-collar/white-collar" distinctions. Surprisingly, few input-output studies have included measures of parents' occupational prestige, and this is probably at least in part because of the difficulty of reliably determining parents' occupations and because of the time required to code prestige values. But the available studies, which are summarized in Table 8−9, do seem to show a consistent pattern. The higher the prestige of the parents' occupation(s), the better children do in school.

2.4 Family Income

2.4.1 Family income seems to have a positive effect on both verbal and reading achievement. However, the effect is not found with achievement growth.

The evidence in support of this proposition is contained in Table 8−10. Burkhead, Fox, and Holland consistently report positive effects of family income upon verbal and reading achievement. However, they report nonsignificant effects for a family income measure when the dependent variable is the achievement residual (i.e., the individual error term when achievement is regressed on earlier achievement). In other words, when the dependent variable is the equivalent of achievement change or growth from some earlier level of achievement, the regression coefficients for family income become nonsignificant. Students from more well-to-do backgrounds seem to have an initial advantage in academic achievement, which lasts even through high school. However, in spite of their initial advantage, these students may not learn any faster than students who are more economically deprived.

Perl breaks down his sample into high- and low-income students, and examines the effects of family income for the two groups separately. His results are suggestive. Family income seems to have a greater impact on students from poorer families. This suggests that there may be some threshold below which income makes a difference, but above which increasing amounts of income are not associated with higher levels of achievement.

2.5 Housing Arrangements

2.5.1 Generally, various measures of housing arrangements are not related significantly to achievement.

The series of variables that have been placed into this category, summarized in Table 8−11, are a very diverse group. Any relation-

Table 8-9. Parents' Occupational Status.[a]

Study	Input		Output			Direction of Effect[b]	Sample/Other Comments
	Measure	Level of Aggregation	Measure	Level of Aggregation			
B1	Father's occupation index	Individual	Reading	Individual		POSITIVE	100 black male 12th graders (Project Talent)
			Math	Individual		POSITIVE	
			General academic ability	Individual		POSITIVE	
K	Percent white collar	District	Reading	District		POSITIVE	56 elementary school districts, Boston
			Math	District		POSITIVE	
KI1	Parental occupation index	District	Composite achievement	District		POSITIVE	97 districts of 6th graders, New York State
			Math	District		POSITIVE	
MI2	Father's occupation	Individual	Reading	Individual		Nonsignificant (positive)	458 urban black 6th graders (EEO); 2SLS estimates in addition to OLS
			Math	Individual		POSITIVE	

[a]The estimated effects reported in this table are partial effects. To ascertain the control variables used in a particular study, the reader is referred to Table 8-1, or to the appropriate section of the appendix.

[b]An effect is declared POSITIVE or NEGATIVE in this table if the null hypothesis can be rejected at the 95% confidence level (i.e., $p \leqslant .05$) in a two-tailed test. Nonsignificant effects are reported here only when the inputs have been retained in the analysis. In many instances, researchers will have dropped inputs whose coefficients are not significantly different from zero and, in such instances, the "noneffects" are not reported here.

Table 8–10. Family Income.[a]

Study	Input		Output			Sample/Other Comments
	Measure	Level of Aggregation	Measure	Level of Aggregation	Direction of Effect[b]	
BFH1	Median family income	School	Verbal	School	POSITIVE	39 schools of 11th graders, Chicago
			Reading	School	POSITIVE	
			Verbal residual	School	Nonsignificant (negative)	
			Reading residual	School	Nonsignificant (negative)	
BFH2	Median family income	School	Verbal	School	POSITIVE	22 high schools, Atlanta
			Verbal residual	School	Nonsignificant (positive)	
BFH3	Median family income	School	Reading	School	POSITIVE	181 small community schools of 12th graders
			Reading residual	School	Nonsignificant (positive)	
P	Family income	Individual	Verbal	Individual	Nonsignificant (negative)	1,498 high-income male 12th graders (Project Talent)
			Abstract reasoning	Individual	Nonsignificant (negative)	
			Verbal	Individual	POSITIVE	1,767 low-income male 12th graders (Project Talent)
			Abstract reasoning	Individual	Nonsignificant (positive)	

[a] The estimated effects reported in this table are partial effects. To ascertain the control variables used in a particular study, the reader is referred to Table 8–1, or to the appropriate section of the appendix.

[b] An effect is declared POSITIVE or NEGATIVE in this table if the null hypothesis can be rejected at the 95% confidence level (i.e., $p < .05$) in a two-tailed test. Nonsignificant effects are reported here only when the inputs have been retained in the analysis. In many instances, researchers will have dropped inputs whose coefficients are not significantly different from zero and, in such instances, the "noneffects" are not reported here.

ships that these variables could be expected to have with achievement would likewise be diverse. Murnane, for instance, included a dummy variable for whether or not the student lived in publicly subsidized housing, arguing that among inner-city families such living arrangements reflect greater stability. Such reasoning would not apply to Winkler's home ownership dummy, which should only be related to achievement to the extent that it serves as a measure of economic status.

These variables have been included in input-output studies in general simply to control for unspecified differences that might exist in family backgrounds. It is not surprising that the regression coefficients generally are nonsignificant, given the unclear theoretical links with achievement and given the fact that other socioeconomic measures are generally controlled for.

These measures of housing arrangements seem to have missed an important feature of children's living conditions. The real issue is probably whether or not a child has a quiet place to study, a place to keep possessions safe, and a place to meet with peers. These are the features of housing arrangements that should affect achievement, self-concept, and perhaps feelings of personal efficacy.

2.6 Family Possessions

2.6.1 Indices of possessions in the student's home seem related to measures of achievement, both verbal and mathematical, even when various other measures of family economic status are controlled for.

The studies listed in Table 8−12 support this conclusion with only a couple of exceptions. While both Levin and Michelson report significant coefficients for the possessions index under ordinary least-squares analysis, the effect of this input on achievement becomes nonsignificant when they use a two-stage model. However, unlike parents' education, which was discussed earlier, the possessions index does not emerge as a significant predictor of any of the other dependent measures in the two-stage analysis. Moreover, Michelson fails to find a positive relationship between the possessions index and achievement in mathematics and reading for black students even under ordinary least-squares. It is difficult to explain these differences in results.

Table 8–11. Housing Arrangements.[a]

	Input		Output		Direction of Effect[b]	Sample/Other Comments
Study	Measure	Level of Aggregation	Measure	Level of Aggregation		
MU1	Percent in block in low rental housing	Census block	Reading Math	Individual Individual	Nonsignificant (negative) Nonsignificant (negative)	440 black 2nd graders, New Haven; fall score entered as independent variable
MU2	Percent in block in low rental housing	Census block	Reading Math	Individual Individual	Nonsignificant (negative) Nonsignificant (negative)	440 black 3rd graders, New Haven; score from previous year entered as independent variable
MU3	Percent in block in low rental housing	Census block	Reading Math Spelling	Individual Individual Individual	Nonsignificant (negative) POSITIVE Nonsignificant (negative)	440 black 3rd graders, New Haven; fall score entered as independent variable
MU1	Publicly subsidized housing dummy	Individual	Reading Math	Individual Individual	Nonsignificant (positive) POSITIVE	See above
MU2	Publicly subsidized housing dummy	Individual	Reading Math	Individual Individual	Nonsignificant (positive) Nonsignificant (negative)	See above
MU3	Publicly subsidized housing dummy	Individual	Reading Math Spelling	Individual Individual Individual	Nonsignificant (positive) Nonsignificant (positive) Nonsignificant (negative)	See above
MU1	Percent in block in female headed household	Census block	Reading Math	Individual Individual	Nonsignificant (negative) Nonsignificant (negative)	See above

MU2	Percent in block in female headed household	Census block	Reading Math	Individual Individual	Nonsignificant (positive) POSITIVE	See above
MU3	Percent in block in female headed household	Census block	Reading Math Spelling	Individual Individual Individual	Nonsignificant (negative) NEGATIVE NEGATIVE	See above
W1	Home ownership dummy	Individual	Verbal	Individual	Nonsignificant (negative)	388 black 8th graders, California; 1st grade IQ entered as independent variable
W2	Home ownership dummy	Individual	Verbal	Individual	POSITIVE	385 white 8th graders, California; 1st grade IQ entered as independent variable

[a] The estimated effects reported in this table are partial effects. To ascertain the control variables used in a particular study, the reader is referred to Table 8–1, or to the appropriate section of the appendix.

[b] An effect is declared POSITIVE or NEGATIVE in this table if the null hypothesis can be rejected at the 95% confidence level (i.e., $p \leq .05$) in a two-tailed test. Nonsignificant effects are reported here only when the inputs have been retained in the analysis. In many instances, researchers will have dropped inputs whose coefficients are not significantly different from zero and, in such instances, the "noneffects" are not reported here.

Table 8–12. Possessions in the Home.[a]

Study	Input Measure	Input Level of Aggregation	Output Measure	Output Level of Aggregation	Direction of Effect[b]	Sample/Other Comments
B1	Possessions index	Individual	Reading Math General academic ability	Individual Individual Individual	POSITIVE POSITIVE POSITIVE	100 black male 12th graders (Project Talent)
H1a	Index of goods in home	School	Verbal Math	School School	POSITIVE POSITIVE	471 schools of white 6th graders (EEO)
H1b	Index of goods in home	School	Verbal Math	School School	POSITIVE POSITIVE	242 schools of black 6th graders (EEO)
L	Possessions index	Individual	Verbal Math	Individual Individual	POSITIVE under OLS POSITIVE under OLS	597 urban white 6th graders (EEO); 2SLS estimates in addition to OLS
MI1	Possessions index	Individual	Verbal Math	Individual Individual	POSITIVE under OLS POSITIVE under OLS	597 urban white 6th graders (EEO); 2SLS estimates in addition to OLS
MI2	Possessions index	Individual	Verbal Math Reading comprehension	Individual Individual Individual	POSITIVE Nonsignificant (positive) Nonsignificant (positive)	458 urban black 6th graders (EEO); 2SLS estimates in addition to OLS

[a] The estimated effects reported in this table are partial effects. To ascertain the control variables used in a particular study, the reader is referred to Table 8–1, or to the appropriate section of the appendix.

[b] An effect is declared POSITIVE or NEGATIVE in this table if the null hypothesis can be rejected at the 95% confidence level (i.e., $p \leqslant .05$) in a two-tailed test. Nonsignificant effects are reported here only when the inputs have been retained in the analysis. In many instances, researchers will have dropped inputs whose coefficients are not significantly different from zero and, in such instances, the "noneffects" are not reported here.

2.7 Educational Environment of the Home

2.7.1 In all of the studies reviewed, parental educational expectations for the child and the general educational environment of the home seem to make a positive difference in achievement.

This conclusion is supported by the various studies listed in Table 8—13. It seems that variables in this broad category have significant effects upon achievement even when various other background variables are controlled for. The problem with this broad category is the fact that it *is* so broad. It remains unclear exactly which variables within the category exert the causal effects upon achievement.

Concluding Comment on Family Inputs

The results we have reviewed in this section strongly support a commonsense conclusion; that is, the student's family background makes a substantial difference in educational outcomes. This conclusion should surprise no one. To some extent, researchers have taken the variables in the family background category for granted, precisely because everyone "knows" that families affect children's cognitive development. In addition, researchers have chosen not to focus on these variables because they are not tractable, that is, not subject to manipulation by school administrators.

While this lack of attention is understandable, it is unfortunate. We firmly believe that these variables should be studied, especially to determine how family background interacts with school and teacher characteristics. To hypothesize different effects for school and teacher variables depending on student's background is intuitively plausible and potentially very important. Knowledge of such interactions could be of enormous value in the setting of educational policies.

3.0 PEER GROUP INPUTS

Several researchers have examined the effects exerted upon a student's achievement by those with whom the student goes to school. In this section, we summarize the results relating to four peer group variables: (1) social class composition, (2) racial composition, (3) ability composition, and (4) peer turnover. In part, researchers have looked at the effects of peer group composition because of the efforts of the last twenty years toward school desegregation. There are excellent reviews of the many studies of desegregation and its impact upon student achievement (e.g., see Crain and Mahard, 1977).

Table 8–13. The Educational Environment of the Home and Family Educational Expectations.[a]

Study	Input		Output		Direction of Effect[b]	Sample/Other Comments
	Measure	Level of Aggregation	Measure	Level of Aggregation		
B2	Reading materials index	Individual	Verbal	Individual	POSITIVE	1,000 black male 12th graders (EEO)
L	Parents' educational expectations for child	Individual	Verbal	Individual	POSITIVE under OLS	597 urban white 6th graders (EEO); 2SLS estimates in addition to OLS
W1	Index of cultural items in home	Individual	Verbal	Individual	POSITIVE	388 black 8th graders, California; 1st grade IQ entered as independent variable
W2	Index of cultural items in home	Individual	Verbal	Individual	POSITIVE	385 white 8th graders, California; 1st grade IQ entered as independent variable

[a] The estimated effects reported in this table are partial effects. To ascertain the control variables used in a particular study, the reader is referred to Table 8–1, or the appropriate section of the appendix.

[b] An effect is declared POSITIVE or NEGATIVE in this table if the null hypothesis can be rejected at the 95% confidence level (i.e., $p \leq .05$) in a two-tailed test. Nonsignificant effects are reported here only when the inputs have been retained in the analysis. In many instances, researchers will have dropped inputs whose coefficients are not significantly different from zero and, in such instances, the "noneffects" are not reported here.

In the present discussion, we will confine ourselves to studies that examine peer group effects within the education production function framework.

While research on the importance of peer group characteristics in the educational production process has been fairly abundant, it has not been without its pitfalls. Attempts to estimate the effects of student body composition upon achievement are particularly susceptible to ambiguities due to data aggregation. An example will help make this point.

Consider the variable, student body social class (or economic background). Suppose we are interested in the hypothesis that going to school with relatively well-to-do peers enhances achievement. To test this hypothesis, it is necessary that achievement (output) be measured at the level of the individual student and, ideally, that there be a measure of the student's *own* socioeconomic background on the right-hand side of the equation. If *all* the variables are aggregated (e.g., at the level of the school), the aggregated social class variable becomes conceptually unclear. Its effect cannot be interpreted as a "peer group effect"; nor is it unambiguously a "family effect." With aggregate data, there is no way to distinguish between these two effects.

If we find that higher aggregate achievement is associated with higher aggregate social class, clearly it would be inappropriate to conclude that going to school with economically advantaged peers raises achievement. To reach such a conclusion, we need to control for the individual's own background characteristics.

In light of this problem, we confine our propositions in this section to studies where individual data are available and where the effects of peer group composition are examined controlling for the individual's own background.

3.1 Social Class Composition
3.1.1 Going to school with economically advantaged peers is associated with higher verbal and reading achievement and with higher abstract reasoning ability.

The evidence in support of this proposition is presented in Table 8—14. The two studies that include school social class composition as an input into the production of individual-level achievement outcomes both find that this variable is positively related to achievement. The only qualification we might add is that the coefficient is statistically nonsignificant for Winkler's sample of black students.

Table 8–14. Social Class Composition.[a]

Study	Input		Output			Direction of Effect[b]	Sample/Other Comments
	Measure	Level of Aggregation	Measure	Level of Aggregation			
P	Mean family income	School	Verbal Abstract reasoning	Individual Individual		POSITIVE POSITIVE	3,265 male 12th graders (Project Talent)
	Standard deviation of family income	School	Verbal Abstract reasoning	Individual Individual		Nonsignificant (negative) Nonsignificant (negative)	
W1	Percent low SES	School	Reading	Individual		Nonsignificant (negative)	388 black 8th graders, California; 1st grade IQ entered as independent variable
W2	Percent low SES	School	Reading	Individual		NEGATIVE	385 white 8th graders, California; 1st grade IQ entered as independent variable

[a] The estimated effects reported in this table are partial effects. To ascertain the control variables used in a particular study, the reader is referred to Table 8–1, or to the appropriate section of the appendix.

[b] An effect is declared POSITIVE or NEGATIVE in this table if the null hypothesis can be rejected at the 95% confidence level (i.e., $p \leq .05$) in a two-tailed test. Nonsignificant effects are reported here only when the inputs have been retained in the analysis. In many instances, researchers will have dropped inputs whose coefficients are not significantly different from zero and, in such instances, the "noneffects" are not reported here.

Whether the positive relationship between student achievement and the average social class level of peers is due to social class, or whether it reflects other correlated characteristics of those peers is unclear. It may be that social class here is a proxy for achievement level, motivation, and other peer characteristics.

Interestingly, the dispersion in social class composition seems not to affect a student's achievement. While in Perl's study mean family income is positively related to individual achievement, the standard deviation of family income is not.

3.2 Racial Composition

3.2.1 For black students, a higher proportion of black peers in school seems to be associated with lower verbal and mathematics achievement.

3.2.2 For white students, the racial composition of peers is not clearly related to achievement.

These propositions seem to be supported by the evidence presented in Table 8–15. The reader should note that Hanushek's research is included in this table even though the outcome measures are school aggregates. In this case, however, we can speak of peer group effects despite the aggregated data because Hanushek conducts separate school level analyses for whites (H1a) and for blacks (H1b). Since the output measures in the one study reflect the mean school achievement of whites *alone* (and in the other study of blacks *alone*), the racial composition variable does not confound the race of the students in the analysis with the racial mix of the student body. It unambiguously reflects the latter.

Bowles's and Hanushek's findings are consistent with our propositions; that is, a higher proportion of black peers hurts the achievement of black students and may not affect the achievement of white students (the results for whites in H1a are statistically nonsignificant in three out of four cases). Winkler's results may appear to be inconsistent with our propositions. In fact, they are not when examined in detail. Winkler reports the following regression coefficients for black students: proportion black in grades 1–6, 10.83; proportion black in grades 7–8 minus proportion black in grades 1–6, 29.30. If these variables are labeled (B1–6) and [(B7–8) − (B1–6)], respectively, the results for blacks are 10.83 (B1–6) + 29.30 [(B7–8) − (B1–6)], which can be rewritten as 29.30(B7–8) − 18.47(B1–6). Thus, although Winkler's coding of these variables is confusing, the proportion black in the elementary school has a net negative effect on the achievement of black students. Black students who went to school

Table 8–15.   Racial Composition.[a]

	Input		Output			
Study	Measure	Level of Aggregation	Measure	Level of Aggregation	Direction of Effect[b]	Sample/Other Comments
B1	Percent black	School	Reading Math General academic ability	Individual Individual Individual	Nonsignificant (negative) NEGATIVE NEGATIVE	100 black male 12th graders (Project Talent)
H1a	45–75% black = 1, 0 otherwise	School	Verbal Math	School School	Nonsignificant (negative) Nonsignificant (negative)	471 schools of white 6th graders (EEO)
	75–100% black = 1, 0 otherwise	School	Verbal Math	School School	NEGATIVE Nonsignificant (negative)	
H1b	45–75% black = 1, 0 otherwise	School	Verbal Math	School School	NEGATIVE NEGATIVE	242 schools of black 6th graders (EEO)
	75–100% black = 1, 0 otherwise	School	Verbal Math	School School	NEGATIVE NEGATIVE	
W1	Proportion black in elementary school attended	School	Reading	Individual	Nonsignificant (positive)	388 black 8th graders, California; 1st grade entered as independent variable; N.B., see text for interpretations
	Proportion black in junior high school attended minus percent black in elementary school attended	School	Reading	Individual	POSITIVE	

W2	Percent black in elementary school attended	School	Reading	Individual	POSITIVE	385 white 8th graders, California; 1st grade IQ entered as independent variable; N.B., see text for interpretations
	Percent black in junior high school attended minus percent black in elementary school attended	School	Reading	Individual	Nonsignificant (positive)	

[a] The estimated effects reported in this table are partial effects. To ascertain the control variables used in a particular study, the reader is referred to Table 8–1, or to the appropriate section of the appendix.

[b] An effect is declared POSITIVE or NEGATIVE in this table if the null hypothesis can be rejected at the 95% confidence level (i.e., $p \leqslant .05$) in a two-tailed test. Nonsignificant effects are reported here only when the inputs have been retained in the analysis. In many instances, researchers will have dropped inputs whose coefficients are not significantly different from zero and, in such instances, the "noneffects" are not reported here.

with more black peers do less well. This is not the case for white students.

The positive effect of (B7−8) for blacks is somewhat problematic, but it is explainable when it is noted that many black students were transferred at the end of grade six from highly segregated schools to schools that were much more integrated. The more integrated the junior high school (the higher B7−8), the larger the *change* in racial mix, and this change seems to be associated with lower achievement. Thus, although going to segregated elementary schools seems to hurt the achievement of blacks, transferring to schools dramatically more integrated also seems to have an adverse effect. The implication would seem to be that higher achievement for blacks is obtained in more integrated elementary schools from which the shift to integrated junior high schools is less dramatic.

As we have already mentioned, the effects of school desegregation have been studied extensively in the last few years (e.g., Armor, 1972; Pettigrew and Green, 1976). The reader may wish to examine this literature, most of which is beyond the scope of the present volume.

3.3 Ability Composition
3.3.1 The ability of the peer group may be positively related to a student's own achievement.

Reviewing the evidence in Table 8−16, we are inclined to argue that the ability of peers has a positive effect on achievement, but we must caution the reader that, although all of the significant coefficients are positive in direction, there are too many nonsignificant ones to be content with such a proposition. The evidence is weak at best, and further research clearly is called for.

3.4 Turnover in the Classroom
3.4.1 Whether or not the extent of student turnover in individual classrooms is associated with differences in achievement is unclear.

All of the results relating to student turnover reported in Table 8−17 are from Murnane's New Haven research. Like us, he expected to find a negative effect of turnovers on individual achievement, believing that these disrupt the learning process. Although this hypothesis is highly plausible, once again the data do not cooperate, not consistently at least. More evidence is needed to clarify the picture.

4.0 TEACHER INPUTS

To the makers of public policy, the ultimate purpose of input-output research should be to inform them of the appropriate "buttons to push" and "levers to pull" for bringing about higher achievement outcomes in the educational system. Far more tractable from their point of view than the characteristics of students and their families are the characteristics of teachers and the schools in which they teach.

In this section, we summarize the results relating to the following teacher inputs: (1) amount of education, (2) type of education, (3) recency of education, (4) certification and tenure, (5) teacher's experience, (6) teaching assignments and teacher's time allocation, (7) teacher's verbal achievement, and (8) personal characteristics of teacher (sex, race, and marital status). Largely absent from the list of teacher inputs are measures of the educational *process*—of the internal organization and management of classrooms. The ways in which teachers allocate time to various classroom activities and to various (groups of) students as well as aspects of personality and teaching style are undoubtedly at the heart of the student learning process. However, the collection of data on such matters would normally require long hours of classroom observation, which is costly in researchers' time and cumbersome for classroom continuity. As a result, to date microlevel research has been based usually on quite small samples, and the data collected do not lend themselves to the kind of statistical analysis examined in this book.

4.1 Teacher's Education: Amount

4.1.1 The educational attainment of teachers seems to have a positive effect on reading and verbal achievement when it has an effect. However, this has been shown only with aggregated data where education may be a proxy for student socioeconomic status.

4.1.2 For mathematics at the elementary school level, there appears to be a negative relationship between teacher's educational attainment and student achievement.

Proposition 4.1.1 is based primarily on the study by Bidwell and Kasarda. Their finding, as reported in Table 8–18, is that the percentage of staff possessing at least an M.A. is positively related to reading achievement at the district level. In their equation, however, there is only one explicit measure of student background (percentage

Table 8–16. Ability Composition.[a]

Study	Input		Output		Direction of Effect[b]	Sample/Other Comments
	Measure	Level of Aggregation	Measure	Level of Aggregation		
MI1	Percent of students achieving in upper quartile of nation	School	Reading	Individual	POSITIVE	597 urban white 6th graders (EEO); 2SLS estimates in addition to OLS
			Math	Individual	POSITIVE	
MU1	Mean reading achievement	Class	Reading	Individual	Nonsignificant (negative)	440 black second graders, New Haven; fall score entered as independent variable
	Mean math achievement	Class	Math	Individual	Nonsignificant (negative)	
	Standard deviation of reading scores	Class	Reading	Individual	Nonsignificant (negative)	
	Standard deviation of math scores	Class	Math	Individual	Nonsignificant (positive)	
MU2	Mean reading achievement	Class	Reading	Individual	Nonsignificant (positive)	440 black 3rd graders, New Haven; score from previous year entered as independent variable
	Mean math achievement	Class	Math	Individual	POSITIVE	
	Standard deviation of reading scores	Class	Reading	Individual	Nonsignificant (positive)	
	Standard deviation of math scores	Class	Math	Individual	Nonsignificant (negative)	

MU3					440 black 3rd graders, New Haven; fall score entered as independent variable
Mean reading achievement	Class	Reading	Individual	Nonsignificant (positive)	
Mean math achievement	Class	Math	Individual	Nonsignificant (negative)	
Standard deviation of reading scores	Class	Reading	Individual	POSITIVE	
Standard deviation of math scores	Class	Math	Individual	Nonsignificant (negative)	

a The estimated effects reported in this table are partial effects. To ascertain the control variables used in a particular study, the reader is referred to Table 8–1, or to the appropriate section of the appendix.

b An effect is declared POSITIVE or NEGATIVE in this table if the null hypothesis can be rejected at the 95% confidence level (i.e., $p \leq .05$) in a two-tailed test. Nonsignificant effects are reported here only when the inputs have been retained in the analysis. In many instances, researchers will have dropped inputs whose coefficients are not significantly different from zero and, in such instances, the "noneffects" are not reported here.

Table 8–17. Turnover of Peers.[a]

	Input		Output				
Study	Measure	Level of Aggregation	Measure	Level of Aggregation	Direction of Effect[b]	Sample/Other Comments
MU1	Student turnover, percent of class	Class	Reading Math	Individual Individual	NEGATIVE NEGATIVE	440 black 2nd graders, New Haven; fall score entered as independent variable
MU2	Student turnover, percent of class	Class	Reading Math	Individual Individual	Nonsignificant (negative) NEGATIVE	440 black 3rd graders, New Haven; score from previous year entered as independent variable
MU3	Student turnover, percent of class	Class	Reading Spelling Math	Individual Individual Individual	Nonsignificant (negative) Nonsignificant (positive) POSITIVE	440 black 3rd graders, California; 1st grade IQ entered as independent variable

[a] The estimated effects reported in this table are partial effects. To ascertain the control variables used in a particular study, the reader is referred to Table 8–1, or to the appropriate section of the appendix.

[b] An effect is declared POSITIVE or NEGATIVE in this table if the null hypothesis can be rejected at the 95% confidence level (i.e., $p \leq .05$) in a two-tailed test. Nonsignificant effects are reported here only when the inputs have been retained in the analysis. In many instances, researchers will have dropped inputs whose coefficients are not significantly different from zero and, in such instances, the "noneffects" are not reported here.

of district population classified as nonwhite), and the teacher educational variable can be expected to measure home environment differences that the one variable does not pick up. Bowles finds that students' math achievement and general academic ability are related to teachers' graduate education measured at the level of the school, but Perl finds no such effects.

Proposition 4.1.2 is based primarily on Murnane's research. For two out of three of his samples, teachers with M.A. degrees are associated with smaller gains in mathematics by elementary school pupils. These results are noteworthy because both the input and output are measured at the level of the individual and because of the many control variables included in Murnane's equations. Although Murnane offers no explanation, perhaps personnel policies in the school district he studied resulted in the most highly trained teachers' teaching the lowest achieving students.

Bowles reports a positive relationship between graduate education measured at the level of the high school and individual mathematics achievement, but again the aggregation of data makes it difficult to interpret the result.

4.2 Teacher's Education: Type

4.2.1 There appears to be a negative relationship between a teacher's having majored in education at college and the verbal achievement of students, but this has only been shown where the input is aggregated at the level of the school.

4.2.2 There seems to be a positive relationship between the "prestige" of a teacher's undergraduate institution and the reading achievement of students, but this has only been shown where the input is aggregated at the level of the ability track within a school.

The evidence on the effect of education type is inconclusive to date. To the extent that teachers with more academic and prestigious undergraduate backgrounds are assigned to teach students who come from wealthier homes, the statistically significant relationships reported in Table 8–19 may be largely spurious. It is noteworthy that in Murnane's study, the only one of the three studies based entirely on data at the level of the individual pupil or pupil's classroom, there is no relationship found in any of the samples between a teacher's majoring in education and any measure of pupil achievement.

Table 8–18.   Education: Amount.[a]

Study	Input Measure	Input Level of Aggregation	Output Measure	Output Level of Aggregation	Direction of Effect[b]	Sample/Other Comments
B&K	Percent of certified staff with MA+	District	Reading Math	District District	POSITIVE Nonsignificant (positive)	104 high school districts, Colorado
B1	Number of teachers with graduate training divided by number of classes in school	School	Reading Math General academic ability	Individual Individual Individual	Nonsignificant (positive) POSITIVE POSITIVE	100 black male 12th graders (Project Talent)
BFH1	Percent of teachers with MA+	School	IQ & IQ residual Reading & reading residual	School School	Nonsignificant (negative) Nonsignificant (negative)	39 schools of 11th graders, Chicago
K	Percent of teachers with MA+	District	Reading Math	District District	Nonsignificant (negative) NEGATIVE[c]	56 elementary school districts, Boston
P	Percent of teachers with MA+	School	Verbal Abstract reasoning	Individual Individual	Nonsignificant (positive)[d] Nonsignificant (positive)	3,265 male 12th graders (Project Talent)
	Percent of teachers with Ph.D.	School	Verbal Abstract reasoning	Individual Individual	Nonsignificant (positive) Nonsignificant (positive)[d]	
MU1	MA+	Class	Reading Math	Individual Individual	Nonsignificant (negative) NEGATIVE	440 black 2nd graders, New Haven; fall score entered as independent variable

| MU2 | MA+ | Class | Reading
Math | Individual
Individual | Nonsignificant (positive)
Nonsignificant (positive) | 440 black 3rd graders, New Haven; score from previous year entered as independent variable |
| MU3 | MA+ | Class | Reading
Math
Spelling | Individual
Individual
Individual | Nonsignificant (positive)
NEGATIVE
Nonsignificant (negative) | 440 black 3rd graders, New Haven; fall score entered as independent variable |

[a] The estimated effects reported in this table are partial effects. To ascertain the control variables used in a particular study, the reader is referred to Table 8–1, or to the appropriate section of the appendix.

[b] An effect is declared POSITIVE or NEGATIVE in this table if the null hypothesis can be rejected at the 95% confidence level (i.e., $p \leq .05$) in a two-tailed test. Nonsignificant effects are reported here only when the inputs have been retained in the analysis. In many instances, researchers will have dropped inputs whose coefficients are not significantly different from zero and, in such instances, the "noneffects" are not reported here.

[c] Not significant in multiplicative form.

[d] Significant, high-income students.

Table 8–19. Education: Type. [a]

Study	Input		Output		Direction of Effect [b]	Sample/Other Comments
	Measure	Level of Aggregation	Measure	Level of Aggregation		
L	Mean score on scale where 1 = educational institution and 3 = college or university	School	Verbal	Individual	POSITIVE	597 urban white 6th graders, New York State
MU1, MU2, and MU3	Education major = 1, 0 otherwise	Class	Reading, math, and spelling	Individual	Nonsignificant (mixed)	Black 2nd and 3rd graders, New Haven; prior achievement entered as independent variable
W1	Percent of teachers from "prestigious colleges"	Ability track within school	Reading	Individual	POSITIVE	388 black 8th graders, California; 1st grade IQ entered as independent variable
W2	Percent of teachers from "prestigious colleges"	Ability track within school	Reading	Individual	POSITIVE	385 white 8th graders, California; 1st grade IQ entered as independent variable

[a] The estimated effects reported in this table are partial effects. To ascertain the control variables used in a particular study, the reader is referred to Table 8–1, or to the appropriate section of the appendix.

[b] An effect is declared POSITIVE or NEGATIVE in this table if the null hypothesis can be rejected at the 95% confidence level (i.e., $p \le .05$) in a two-tailed test. Nonsignificant effects are reported here only when the inputs have been retained in the analysis. In many instances, researchers will have dropped inputs whose coefficients are not significantly different from zero and, in such instances, the "noneffects" are not reported here.

4.3 Teacher's Education: Recency

4.3.1 The more recent a teacher's last educational experience, the higher students seem to achieve in reading. In other words, the more recent a teacher's last course or degree, the higher is the expected achievement test score of a student in this teacher's class.

The only researcher to include the recency of teacher's education in his analysis of educational production has been Eric Hanushek, in his California study of English-speaking third graders stratified by father's occupational status. Although the direction of the relationship is the same in four out of four tests, in only one can the null hypothesis be rejected at the 0.05 level (see Table 8−20). Although it is not unreasonable to suppose that a teacher's effectiveness deteriorates as a function of how long it has been since the teacher's most recent educational experience, it is equally possible that this variable is acting as a proxy for something else, for example, for the teacher's motivation and enthusiasm for teaching. It will be interesting to see the effect of this variable in future research that controls more extensively for other factors.

4.4 Certification and Tenure

4.4.1 Apparently no relationship exists between student achievement and a teacher's being certified or tenured.

Although the precise measure differs in each of the three studies reported in Table 8−21, and in all three these are measured at the level of the school or district rather than at the level of the individual student's classroom, the suggested conclusion is clear. The effectiveness of teachers is not well reflected either in their being certified or not or in their being tenured or not. The signs of the coefficients on these variables are usually negative, though only in one case is it significantly negative. This one could be a chance result.

4.5 Teacher's Experience

4.5.1 In general, the teaching experience of a student's teacher is positively related to the student's achievement.

4.5.2 The relationship between teaching experience and student achievement is likely to be curvilinear—steeply positive over the first years of experience and flat (or negative) thereafter.

Table 8–20. Education: Recency.[a]

Study	Input		Output		Direction of Effect[b]	Sample/Other Comments
	Measure	Level of Aggregation	Measure	Level of Aggregation		
H2a	Years since most recent degree or course, present teacher	Class	Reading	Individual	Nonsignificant (negative)	515 blue-collar 3rd graders, California; 1st grade achievement entered as independent variable
	Years since most recent degree or course, last year's teacher	Class	Reading	Individual	NEGATIVE	
H2b	Years since most recent degree or course, present teacher	Class	Reading	Individual	Nonsignificant (negative)	323 white-collar 3rd graders, California; 1st grade achievement entered as independent variable
	Years since most recent degree or course, last year's teacher	Class	Reading	Individual	Nonsignificant (negative)	

[a] The estimated effects reported in this table are partial effects. To ascertain the control variables used in a particular study, the reader is referred to Table 8–1, or to the appropriate section of the appendix.

[b] An effect is declared POSITIVE or NEGATIVE in this table if the null hypothesis can be rejected at the 95% confidence level (i.e., $p \leqslant .05$) in a two-tailed test. Nonsignificant effects are reported here only when the inputs have been retained in the analysis. In many instances, researchers will have dropped inputs whose coefficients are not significantly different from zero and, in such instances, the "noneffects" are not reported here.

Table 8–21. Certification and Tenure.[a]

Study	Input		Output			Sample/Other Comments
	Measure	Level of Aggregation	Measure	Level of Aggregation	Direction of Effect[b]	
K	Percent of teachers accredited	District	Reading Math	District District	Nonsignificant (negative) Nonsignificant (negative)	56 elementary school districts, Boston
P	Percent of teachers certified	School	Verbal Abstract reasoning	Individual Individual	Nonsignificant (positive) Nonsignificant (negative)	3,265 male 12th graders (Project Talent)
MI1	Percent of teachers tenured	School	Reading Math	Individual Individual	Nonsignificant (negative) NEGATIVE	597 urban white 6th graders (EEO); 2SLS estimates in addition to OLS

[a] The estimated effects reported in this table are partial effects. To ascertain the control variables used in a particular study, the reader is referred to Table 8–1, or to the appropriate section of the appendix.

[b] An effect is declared POSITIVE or NEGATIVE in this table if the null hypothesis can be rejected at the 95% confidence level (i.e., $p \leqslant .05$) in a two-tailed test. Nonsignificant effects are reported here only when the inputs have been retained in the analysis. In many instances, researchers will have dropped inputs whose coefficients are not significantly different from zero and, in such instances, the "noneffects" are not reported here.

Table 8–22. Teaching Experience.[a]

	Input		Output			
Study	Measure	Level of Aggregation	Measure	Level of Aggregation	Direction of Effect[b]	Sample/Other Comments
BFH1	Median years	School	Reading	School	Nonsignificant (positive)	39 schools of 11th graders, Chicago
			Reading residual	School	POSITIVE	
			IQ & IQ residual	School	Nonsignificant (positive)	
BFH3	Mean years	School	Reading	School	POSITIVE	181 small community schools of 12th graders
			Reading residual	School	Nonsignificant (positive)	
H1a	Mean years	School	Verbal	School	POSITIVE	471 schools of white 6th graders (EEO)
			Math	School	POSITIVE	
H1b	Mean years	School	Verbal	School	POSITIVE	242 schools of black 6th graders (EEO)
			Math	School	POSITIVE	
H2b	Years teaching this socioeconomic group	Class	Reading	Individual	Nonsignificant (positive)	323 white-collar 3rd graders, California; 1st grade achievement entered as independent variable
K	Percent of permanent teachers with more than 10 years	District	Reading	District	POSITIVE	56 elementary school districts, Boston
			Math	District	Nonsignificant (positive)	
L	Mean years	School	Verbal	Individual	POSITIVE	597 urban white 6th graders (EEO); 2SLS estimates in addition to OLS

MI1	Mean years	School	Verbal Reading	Individual Individual	POSITIVE POSITIVE	597 urban white 6th graders (EEO); 2SLS estimates in addition to OLS
MU1, MU2, and MU3	0–2 years	Class	Reading Math Spelling (MU3 only)	Individual Individual Individual	POSITIVE POSITIVE POSITIVE	Black 2nd and 3rd graders, New Haven; prior achievement entered as independent variable; experience entered as three-piece linear function
	3+ years	Class	Reading, math, and (MU3 only) spelling	Individual	Mixed results—generally, the effect of an additional year not significantly different from zero.	
P	Mean years	School	Verbal Abstract reasoning	Individual Individual	Nonsignificant (positive) Nonsignificant (negative)[c]	3,265 male 12th graders (Project Talent)

[a] The estimated effects reported in this table are partial effects. To ascertain the control variables used in a particular study, the reader is referred to Table 8–1, or to the appropriate section of the appendix.

[b] An effect is declared POSITIVE or NEGATIVE in this table if the null hypothesis can be rejected at the 95% confidence level (i.e., $p \leq .05$) in a two-tailed test. Nonsignificant effects are reported here only when the inputs have been retained in the analysis. In many instances, researchers will have dropped inputs whose coefficients are not significantly different from zero and, in such instances, the "noneffects" are not reported here.

[c] Significant, low income students.

The findings reported in Table 8–22 lend solid support to proposition 4.5.1. Wherever a regression coefficient on teaching experience is significant at the 0.05 level in a two-tailed test, the direction of the coefficient is positive. Only in the Murnane study, however, is teaching experience measured at the level of the individual student's classroom teacher. In all of the remaining studies, experience is aggregated at the level of the school or district, rendering interpretation of the relationship problematic.

In addition, Murnane's study is noteworthy in that it allows for a relationship between teaching experience and student achievement that is other than linear. Murnane divides the experience continuum into three pieces, the first piece spanning the interval from zero to two years, the second from three to five years, and the third from six to the maximum number of years observed. He finds for all samples and all output measures that experience over the first two years positively affects student achievement but that additional years of experience show no relationship to achievement.

One interpretation of this finding is that teachers learn from classroom experience at the beginning of their careers but after two years nothing more is learned that enhances teacher effectiveness. An alternative explanation, which Murnane favors but which cannot with the data at hand be distinguished empirically from the first explanation, is that those teachers who are more effective teachers *to begin with* tend to leave the classroom after a few years (to become school administrators or, in the case of inner-city school systems like New Haven, to teach in surrounding suburbs), whereas the less effective teachers are less likely to move to better jobs because of their ineffectiveness.

In other words, the flat regression slope on experience beyond two years may well be a statistical artifact, reflecting the fact that *pupils* and not *teachers* were sampled for Murnane's analysis. To distinguish between the impact of experience per se on a teacher's effectiveness and the impact of attrition on the average ability of teachers with different levels of experience, it would be necessary to follow a cohort of teachers and observe what happens to them over time.

4.6 Teaching Assignments and Teacher's Time Allocation

4.6.1 The less diversified (more specialized) a teacher's teaching load, the more students achieve.

4.6.2 The smaller the percentage of class time given to discipline, the more students achieve.

An a priori argument for proposition 4.6.1 would stress the maxim that "practice makes perfect"—a specialist is likely to become more skilled in a single area than a generalist can be in each of several areas. On the other hand, "variety is the spice of life"—repetition could lead eventually to a lower performance by a teacher prone to boredom. Findings relevant to proposition 4.6.1 are reported in Table 8–23 from the studies by Cohn, Cohn and Millman, and Perl. Cohn's measure of teacher diversification/specialization is the number of different subjects taught by a teacher (related negatively to student achievement), and Perl's is the percentage of teaching time spent in a teacher's own area of specialization (related positively to student achievement).

In neither study, however, does the measure refer specifically to the teachers of individual students. They are averages in both cases. As such, at least in part they are likely to be proxies for the socio-economic standing of the district or the school. Because they can afford to do so rich communities hire specialists to cover subjects, whereas poor communities may have to rely on generalists. The greater achievement of students in communities where teaching loads are less diversified may, on the one hand, be the result of more effective teaching or, on the other hand, reflect the impact of nonschool inputs for which there are no direct measures in the data set.

Proposition 4.6.2, which has to do with time spent on discipline and its relation to student achievement, is based on Hanushek's sample of blue-collar children. The negative coefficient on the discipline time variable has several interpretations. It may be that disciplinarians make poor teachers. Equally plausible, in classes where there is much misbehavior and hence the need for extraordinary disciplinary procedures on the part of teachers, pupils learn less than in classes without such misbehavior, and more time must be spent on discipline than in classes where students learn more. In sum, it would seem to be true that student behavior and student achievement are two outcomes of the educational process and that their relation to one another would need to be sorted out in a simultaneous equations model.

4.7 Teacher's Verbal Ability

4.7.1 The verbal ability of teachers seems to have a positive effect on the verbal (and perhaps the reading) achievement of students.

The positive relationship between the verbal ability of teachers and student achievement is reported in all of the studies using (all or

Table 8–23. Teaching Assignments and Teacher's Time Allocation.[a]

Study	Input Measure	Input Level of Aggregation	Output Measure	Output Level of Aggregation	Direction of Effect[b]	Sample/Other Comments
C	Number of different subjects per teacher	District	Composite change score	District	NEGATIVE	377 districts of 12th graders, Iowa
C&M	Number of different subjects per teacher	School	Math	School	Nonsignificant (negative)	53 schools of 11th graders, Pennsylvania; 2SLS estimates in addition to OLS
	Mean number of instructional hours per teacher (average teaching load)	School	Verbal Math	School School	Nonsignificant (negative) Nonsignificant (negative)	
H2a	Percent of teacher's time spent on discipline	Class	Reading	Individual	NEGATIVE	515 blue-collar 3rd graders, California; 1st grade achievement entered as independent variable
P	Mean percent of teacher's time in area of specialization	School	Verbal Abstract reasoning	Individual Individual	POSITIVE POSITIVE	3,265 male 12th graders (Project Talent)

[a] The estimated effects reported in this table are partial effects. To ascertain the control variables used in a particular study, the reader is referred to Table 8–1, or to the appropriate section of the appendix.

[b] An effect is declared POSITIVE or NEGATIVE in this table if the null hypothesis can be rejected at the 95% confidence level (i.e., $p \leqslant .05$) in a two-tailed test. Nonsignificant effects are reported here only when the inputs have been retained in the analysis. In many instances, researchers will have dropped inputs whose coefficients are not significantly different from zero and, in such instances, the "noneffects" are not reported here.

parts of) the EEO data set. As measured in the EEO survey, however, this variable is flawed in at least two ways. First, since the examination for testing verbal ability was self-administered by teachers in the sampled schools, the scores of individual teachers may reflect in addition to verbal ability the seriousness with which the teachers regarded the examination, their willingness to spend the full time allotted (or *more* time than the time allotted) in completing it, and the extent to which they collaborated with other teachers who were also completing it. Secondly, since the scores of those who completed the examination were then aggregated to the level of the school, the resulting variable, like many other aggregated inputs that we have discussed, is as much a measure of community socioeconomic status as it is a measure of anything about the individual teacher of an individual student.

This second flaw, however, is avoided in Hanushek's study of third graders in one school district in California. In this study (H2a in Table 8−24), the measure of vocabulary skills remains at the level of the individual teacher. Hanushek's finding confirms, at least for blue-collar children, the conclusion suggested by the studies based on the EEO sample, that there is a positive effect of teacher's verbal ability on the verbal achievement of students.

4.8 Personal Characteristics—Sex, Race, and Marital Status

4.8.1 Men seem more effective than women in teaching black inner-city elementary school children.

4.8.2 Men seem less effective than women in teaching abstract reasoning to low-income high school seniors. This has been shown, however, in only one study (P) where the variable indicating male teacher is aggregated at the level of the school. The relationship may, therefore, reflect the possibility that male teachers are more likely than female teachers to be assigned to low-achievement schools.

4.8.3 Black teachers seem more effective than white teachers in teaching black inner-city children.

4.8.4 Black teachers seem less effective than white teachers in teaching white elementary school children. This has been shown, however, in only one study (H1a) where the variable indicating black teacher is aggregated at the level of the school. The relationship may, therefore, reflect the possibility that black teachers are more likely than white teachers to be assigned to low-achievement schools.

4.8.5 There appears to be no relationship between a teacher's marital status and student achievement.

Table 8–24.   Teacher's Verbal Achievement.[a]

Study	Input		Output		Direction of Effect[b]	Sample/Other Comments
	Measure	Level of Aggregation	Measure	Level of Aggregation		
B2	Verbal score[c]	School	Verbal	Individual	POSITIVE	1,000 black male 12th graders (EEO)
H1a	Verbal score[c]	School	Verbal Math	School School	POSITIVE Nonsignificant (positive)	471 schools of white 6th graders (EEO)
H1b	Verbal score[c]	School	Verbal	School	POSITIVE	242 schools of black 6th graders (EEO)
H2a	Quick Word Test score	Class	Verbal	Individual	POSITIVE	515 blue-collar 3rd graders, California; 1st grade achievement entered as independent variable
L	Verbal score[c]	School	Verbal	Individual	Nonsignificant (positive)	597 urban white 6th graders (EEO); 2SLS estimates in addition to OLS
MI1	Verbal score[c]	School	Verbal Reading	Individual Individual	POSITIVE POSITIVE	597 urban white 6th graders (EEO); 2SLS estimates in addition to OLS
MI2	Verbal score[c]	School	Reading	Individual	Nonsignificant (positive)	458 urban black 6th graders (EEO); 2SLS estimates in addition to OLS

[a] The estimated effects reported in this table are partial effects. To ascertain the control variables used in a particular study, the reader is referred to Table 8–1, or to the appropriate section of the appendix.

[b] An effect is declared POSITIVE or NEGATIVE in this table if the null hypothesis can be rejected at the 95% confidence level (i.e., $p \leqslant .05$) in a two-tailed test. Nonsignificant effects are reported here only when the inputs have been retained in the analysis. In many instances, researchers will have dropped inputs whose coefficients are not significantly different from zero and, in such instances, the "noneffects" are not reported here.

[c] School mean on self-administered vocabulary test, EEO survey.

Propositions 4.8.1, 4.8.3, and 4.8.5 are based on Murnane's findings as reported in Table 8—25. He shows that men are more effective than women in teaching mathematics, and perhaps reading as well, to children included in his three samples of black inner-city pupils.

Murnane also finds that blacks are more effective than whites in teaching these black inner-city children although the strength of this finding varies across samples and school subjects. When Murnane looks only at teachers with less than six years of experience (not reported in Table 8—25) he gets *t*-statistics that are somewhat larger (especially when the output is reading achievement), suggesting that black and white teachers with less than six years of experience are less alike than black and white teachers with more than five years of experience. Murnane attributes the greater effectiveness of black teachers to their greater understanding of the needs and the behavioral patterns of black children. In addition, "black teachers provide a model with which black children can identify" (Murnane, 1975, p. 73).

Propositions 4.8.2 and 4.8.4 are based on findings in the studies of Perl and Hanushek, respectively. The qualifiers contained in these propositions are meant to suggest that male teachers and black teachers may be assigned to "difficult schools" in which achievement levels are low and disciplinary problems abound. They are thought to be more effective in maintaining discipline in such situations than are women and whites. For black teachers, assignment to difficult schools could also reflect racial discrimination by school administrators.

Other Teacher Inputs

The list of teacher inputs considered thus far is by no means exhaustive. Other variables that have been considered in one or another of the studies reviewed here have not been mentioned because they do not fit neatly into any of the above categories.

Michelson (1970) includes in his set of equations for black students (MI2) a measure of teacher's family background. The measure, parents' education, Michelson finds is related positively to cognitive achievement in five ordinary least-squares equations, but the coefficients are significant at the 0.05 level in only two of the five equations.

In addition, Michelson (1970) considers the effect of a teacher's preference for white students in class on the achievement of white students (MI1). The partial relationship is significantly positive in the

Table 8–25.   Personal Characteristics—Sex, Race, and Marital Status.[a]

Study	Input Measure	Input Level of Aggregation	Output Measure	Output Level of Aggregation	Direction of Effect[b]	Sample/Other Comments
MU2	Male teacher = 1, 0 otherwise	Class	Reading Math	Individual Individual	POSITIVE POSITIVE	440 black 3rd graders, New Haven; score from previous year entered as independent variable
MU3	Male teacher = 1, 0 otherwise	Class	Reading Math Spelling	Individual Individual Individual	Nonsignificant (positive) POSITIVE Nonsignificant (negative)	440 black 3rd graders, New Haven; fall score entered as independent variable
P	Percent of teachers male	School	Verbal Abstract reasoning	Individual Individual	Nonsignificant (negative) NEGATIVE[c]	3,265 male 12th graders (Project Talent)
H1a	Percent of sampled pupils having non-white teacher previous year	School	Verbal Math	School School	NEGATIVE NEGATIVE	471 schools of white 6th graders (EEO)
H1b	Percent of sampled pupils having non-white teacher previous year	School	Verbal Math	School School	Nonsignificant (negative) Nonsignificant (negative)	242 schools of black 6th graders (EEO)
MU1	Black teacher = 1, 0 otherwise	Class	Reading Math	Individual Individual	Nonsignificant (positive) Nonsignificant (positive)	440 black 2nd graders, New Haven; fall score entered as independent variable
MU2	Black teacher = 1, 0 otherwise	Class	Reading Math	Individual Individual	POSITIVE POSITIVE	440 black 3rd graders, New Haven; score from previous year entered as independent variable

| MU3 | Black teacher = 1, 0 otherwise | Class | Reading Math Spelling | Individual Individual Individual | Nonsignificant (positive) POSITIVE Nonsignificant (positive) | 440 black 3rd graders, New Haven; fall score entered as independent variable |
| MU1, MU2, and MU3 | Married teacher = 1, 0 otherwise | Class | Reading, math, and (MU3 only) spelling | Individual | Nonsignificant (mixed) | Black 2nd and 3rd graders, New Haven; prior achievement entered as independent variable |

[a] The estimated effects reported in this table are partial effects. To ascertain the control variables used in a particular study, the reader is referred to Table 8-1, or to the appropriate section of the appendix.

[b] An effect is declared POSITIVE or NEGATIVE in this table if the null hypothesis can be rejected at the 95% confidence level (i.e., $p \leq .05$) in a two-tailed test. Nonsignificant effects are reported here only when the inputs have been retained in the analysis. In many instances, researchers will have dropped inputs whose coefficients are not significantly different from zero and, in such instances, the "noneffects" are not reported here.

[c] Not significant, high-income students.

two equations in which tests of the relationship were conducted. A different attitudinal variable is considered in the study by Levin (1970). Levin finds that a teacher's satisfaction with his or her present school is not related significantly to student achievement.

Murnane (1975) finds that a school principal's evaluation of a teacher's performance reflects very well the teacher's actual performance as evidenced by the dependent variable, which is the cognitive achievement of individual students in the teacher's class. There are two, quite different interpretations of this finding. On the one hand, the observed relationship might indicate that the principals in Murnane's New Haven schools were able to distinguish between "good" teachers and "bad" by noting the teachers' background characteristics (those not measured in Murnane's equations) and by observing the teachers' interactions with students; that is, the principals could *predict* achievement outcomes. On the other hand, the principals might have evaluated teachers ex post facto, rating them on the basis of the very scores that their ratings ostensibly predict. If so, then the relationship between the evaluation of a teacher's performance and student achievement is tautological; the "independent" variable is simply an alternative measure of the dependent variable.

The latter argument provides no reason to expect the accuracy of a principal's evaluation to differ across teacher groups. But Murnane finds that the principals, who were predominantly white, were more successful on the average in rating white teachers than in rating black teachers. Perhaps they were better informed about the performance of white teachers than of black. In other words, they may have been less sensitive to variation in the quality of black teachers than they were to variation in the quality of white teachers. Alternatively, they may have used different criteria in evaluating the two groups of teachers. Murnane suggests that in evaluating black teachers the principals may have placed "particularly heavy weight on the success of these teachers in raising the noncognitive skills of their [predominantly black] students, . . . in improving [the students'] self-image and aspirations . . ." (Murnane, 1975, p. 50).

This concludes our discussion of variables that we have characterized as "teacher inputs." In the following section, we shall consider the effects of "school characteristics"—the structure within which students and teachers operate.

5.0 SCHOOL INPUTS

This section summarizes the effects on cognitive achievement of school variables other than those variables that may pertain to an individual teacher.[5] The inputs summarized in this section fall into the following subcategories: (1) expenditure per pupil, (2) ability tracking, (3) enrollment (i.e., school or district size), (4) nonteaching staff, (5) teacher turnover, (6) teachers' salaries, (7) physical plant, (8) age of school building, (9) library and supplies, (10) class size, and (11) the school calendar.

5.1 Expenditure per Pupil

5.1.1 Expenditure (or revenue) per pupil has a positive effect on a student's achievement; however, the effect is indirect.

Do schools make a difference? This question has received much attention, especially since the publication of the EEO report (Coleman et al., 1966), which suggested to many that schools do *not* make a difference. This "finding" of the EEO report may have been predetermined by certain methodological characteristics of the study.[6] More generally, however, we should not expect to find a statistical relationship between school characteristics and achievement to the extent that school characteristics *do not differ* across students.

The importance of water to fish in a tank cannot be observed unless we remove at least some of the fish from the tank. Similarly, we cannot measure the effect of "schooling" on children if all of the children that we look at are in school. We can only measure the effect of "more schooling" vis-à-vis "less schooling," and if differences in the quantity of schooling are small relative to nonschool differences, then most of the *variation* in educational outcomes must be caused by the latter and not the former. We should not conclude from this, however, that schools do not affect achievement. The effect could be very great but, because it encompasses *all* students, we cannot measure it, any more than we can measure the effect of water on fish when they all remain in the water.

Still, despite the fact that all of the children included in the studies of educational production considered here have been in school,

5. The distinction we are making between "teacher characteristics" and "school characteristics" is sometimes quite arbitrary. To give an example, certainly teacher's salary could be measured at the level of the individual teacher, where it would be a reasonable proxy for academic credentials and teaching experience (the two most important factors in the scheduling of salaries for teachers). However, in all of the studies that we review in which salary is included as an independent variable, the variable is measured at the level of the school or district (where its interpretation becomes somewhat ambiguous). Because in practice no researchers have looked at the effect of teacher's salary at the level of the individual on the achievement of classroom students, we have moved this variable from the teacher category to the school category of inputs.

6. The EEO report is described in Chapter 7.

we find that schools do have certain distinguishable characteristics. These can be used to measure the effects of schooling at the margin, that is, to estimate the effects of differences in schooling. An extremely gross measure of school differences is the amount of money spent per pupil, and the results presented in Table 8—26 suggest that even so gross a measure as this explains variation in achievement among children. The effect, however, is not direct. It is mediated by those things in schools that money can buy.

Bidwell and Kasarda employ a recursive model to show that the level of district resources has a positive impact on the ratio of teachers to pupils, which in turn has a positive impact on reading and mathematics achievement. When fiscal resources and the pupil-teacher ratio appear in the same equation, the direct effect of resources on achievement is negligible. This finding seems to be borne out by the two studies of Burkhead, Fox, and Holland in which they test for an effect of expenditure per pupil on achievement. They find no effect, as we would predict since they include several, more direct measures of teacher and school inputs in their equations. Curiously, in Perl's study, the direct effect of expenditure per pupil does not "wash out" even though his equations include average class size, number of days in the school year, age of the school building, number of books in the library, and five measures of the average characteristics of teachers.

5.2 Ability Grouping (Tracking)
5.2.1 Tracking seems to have a negative effect on verbal and mathematics achievement among blacks and whites alike.

Current data on the prevalence of homogeneous ability grouping in American schools are scarce, but one nationwide survey conducted during the 1960s showed that 78 percent of urban schools practiced ability grouping in the elementary grades and that 91 percent used ability grouping in the secondary grades (National Education Association, 1965). Another nationwide survey, covering grades K—3 in both urban and nonurban districts, showed that about 20 percent of kindergarten students were in homogeneous ability classrooms while the figures for grades 1, 2, and 3 were 45 percent, 48 percent, and 49 percent, respectively (Gore and Koury, 1965).

The arguments for and against the clustering of students according to ability are well known. On the pro side, tracking supposedly makes it easier to meet students' individual needs because instructional objectives and methods can be tailored to the relatively narrow

Table 8–26. Expenditure per Pupil. [a]

	Input		Output			Direction of Effect [b]	Sample/Other Comments
Study	Measure	Level of Aggregation	Measure	Level of Aggregation			
B&K	School revenue per average daily attendance	District	Reading	District		POSITIVE (indirect through pupil-teacher ratio)	104 high school districts, Colorado
			Math	District		POSITIVE (indirect through pupil-teacher ratio)	
BFH2	Expenditure per pupil	School	Verbal	School		Nonsignificant (negative)	22 high schools, Atlanta
			Verbal residual	School		Nonsignificant (negative)	
BFH3	Expenditure per pupil	School	Verbal	School		Nonsignificant (positive)	181 small community schools of 12th graders
			Verbal residual	School		Nonsignificant (positive)	
C&M	Extracurricular expenditure per pupil	School	Verbal	School		POSITIVE under 2SLS	53 schools of 11th graders, Pennsylvania; 2SLS estimates in addition to OLS
			Verbal	School		Nonsignificant (positive) under OLS	
			Math	School		Nonsignificant (mixed)	
P	Expenditure per pupil	School	Verbal	Individual		POSITIVE	3,265 male 12th graders (Project Talent)
			Abstract reasoning	Individual		POSITIVE	

[a] The estimated effects reported in this table are partial effects. To ascertain the control variables used in a particular study, the reader is referred to Table 8–1, or to the appropriate section of the appendix.

[b] An effect is declared POSITIVE or NEGATIVE in this table if the null hypothesis can be rejected at the 95% confidence level (i.e., $p \leqslant .05$) in a two-tailed test. Nonsignificant effects are reported here only when the inputs have been retained in the analysis. In many instances, researchers will have dropped inputs whose coefficients are not significantly different from zero and, in such instances, the "noneffects" are not reported here.

range of students in any class, all of whom progress at approximately the same rate. In theory, this results in greater learning and hence higher achievement test scores. Moreover, survey evidence suggests that teachers prefer homogeneous groups. In one early survey, 60 percent of the elementary school teachers and 90 percent of the secondary school teachers endorsed homogeneous ability grouping (National Education Association, 1965).

On the con side of the argument, tracking may have undesirable consequences, especially for lower ability children in socially diverse schools. Ability grouping tends to increase segregation by social class and/or race, and this isolation may reduce the opportunities that lower class children have to acquire the attitudes, beliefs, social competencies, and acquaintances that facilitate social mobility. These qualities may be as important or even more important than academic achievement when it comes to lifelong success (Jencks et al., 1972). Even among socially similar students, ability grouping may be ill-advised because children in low-ability groups may be stigmatized and discouraged from working up to their full potential (Rosenthal and Jacobson, 1968; Thorndike, 1968). Besides, isolating children by ability levels places all students, irrespective of ability, in an artificial situation and retards their learning how to deal with the broad range of people that they will encounter later in life.

What do input-output studies say about the effects of ability grouping? The available results, summarized in Table 8—27, suggest that *on the average* tracking has a negative effect on the achievement of both blacks and whites. These results, while consistent, are based on just three samples, two of them subsamples of the EEO data set.

This apparent consistency is much less apparent when one considers a wider range of studies. In fact, the results appear to be quite mixed. If we look at the model tracking studies reviewed by the National Education Association (1968), we find that 35 percent report a positive effect of ability grouping on achievement test scores and, surprisingly, no one ability group appears to have gained more or suffered more than the others as a result of ability grouping. These studies led Jencks et al. to conclude (1972, p. 107) " . . . if tracking affects test scores at all, the effect is too small to be pedagogically significant."

But even if this were true of achievement test scores, the effect on noncognitive outcomes could be otherwise. A prototypic experiment on ability grouping (Goldberg, Passow, and Justman, 1966) provides some evidence. The study used an experimental design and five levels of ability (as defined by intelligence tests), and the results suggested that narrow-band ability grouping among middle-class children did

Table 8-27. Ability Tracking.[a]

	Input		Output			
Study	*Measure*	*Level of Aggregation*	*Measure*	*Level of Aggregation*	*Direction of Effect*[b]	*Sample/Other Comments*
B1	Tracking (1 = yes, 0 = no)	School	Verbal Math General academic ability	Individual Individual Individual	Nonsignificant (negative) NEGATIVE NEGATIVE	100 black male 12th graders (Project Talent)
MI1	Tracking (1 = yes, 0 = no)	School	Verbal Math	Individual Individual	NEGATIVE NEGATIVE	597 urban white 6th graders (EEO); 2SLS estimates in addition to OLS
MI2	Tracking (1 = yes, 0 = no)	School	Verbal	Individual	NEGATIVE	458 urban black 6th graders (EEO); 2SLS estimates in addition to OLS

[a] The estimated effects reported in this table are partial effects. To ascertain the control variables used in a particular study, the reader is referred to Table 8–1, or to the appropriate section of the appendix.

[b] An effect is declared POSITIVE or NEGATIVE in this table if the null hypothesis can be rejected at the 95% confidence level (i.e., $p \leq .05$) in a two-tailed test. Nonsignificant effects are reported here only when the inputs have been retained in the analysis. In many instances, researchers will have dropped inputs whose coefficients are not significantly different from zero and, in such instances, the "noneffects" are not reported here.

not affect academic interests or attitudes toward school. On the other hand, ability grouping had a significant impact on self-concept— " . . . the effects of narrowing the range or separating the extreme levels were to *raise* the self-assessment of the slow pupils, *lower* the initially high self-rating of the gifted, and leave the intermediate levels largely unaffected. The slow pupils also showed greater gains in their 'ideal image' when the gifted were absent than was true when they were present" (Goldberg, Passow, and Justman, 1966, p. 163).

The inconsistency among different tracking studies suggests that some critical variables are missing. More research is required before we can explain the seemingly contradictory results.

5.3 Enrollment

5.3.1 There seems to be no relationship between a student's achievement and the size of the school or district in which that student is enrolled.

As seen in Table 8–28, the regression coefficients on enrollment are not consistent in direction, nor are they statistically significant in most cases. This is interesting in light of other studies that show a relationship between enrollment and expenditure per pupil. For example, in a study of Wisconsin high schools (Riew, 1966), it was observed that per student cost declined significantly as school enrollment increased to 1,675 students, which was found to be the point of minimum cost per student. Further increases in school size were associated with higher levels of expenditure per student.

Presumably, the effect of enrollment on achievement is indirect with expenditure per pupil serving as the mediating variable. Riew's findings suggest that there are "economies of scale" at low levels of school enrollment, followed by "diseconomies of scale" at high levels of school enrollment. The effect of expenditure per pupil, as we surmised in the previous section, is probably mediated in turn through the quantity and quality of school inputs. With school inputs and/or expenditure per pupil included in the analysis, as is the case with each of the studies reported in Table 8–28, no effect of enrollment on achievement remains.

5.4 Nonteaching Staff

5.4.1 The effect of school administration on student achievement may depend on how this input is measured.

    (a) When the measure is the dollar expenditure on administrative personnel per pupil, the effect seems to be positive.

Table 8–28. Enrollment.[a]

	Input		Output			
Study	Measure	Level of Aggregation	Measure	Level of Aggregation	Direction of Effect[b]	Sample/Other Comments
BFH1	Average daily attendance	School	IQ & IQ residual	School	Nonsignificant (positive)	39 schools of 11th graders, Chicago
			Reading	School	Nonsignificant (positive)	
			Reading residual	School	Nonsignificant (negative)	
BFH2	Students registered	School	Verbal	School	NEGATIVE	22 high schools, Atlanta
			Verbal residual	School	Nonsignificant (negative)	
BFH3	12th grade enrollment	School	Reading and reading residual	School	Nonsignificant (positive)	181 small community schools of 12th graders
C	Average daily attendance	District	Verbal change	District	Nonsignificant (negative)	377 districts of 12th graders, Iowa
K	Enrollment	District	Verbal	District	Nonsignificant (positive)	56 elementary school districts, Boston
			Math	District	Nonsignificant (negative)	
P	Enrollment	School	Verbal	Individual	Nonsignificant (positive)	3,265 male 12th graders (Project Talent)
			Abstract reasoning	Individual	Nonsignificant (negative)	
	Enrollment squared	School	Verbal	Individual	Nonsignificant (positive)	
			Abstract reasoning	Individual	Nonsignificant (positive)	

[a] The estimated effects reported in this table are partial effects. To ascertain the control variables used in a particular study, the reader is referred to Table 8–1, or to the appropriate section of the appendix.

[b] An effect is declared POSITIVE or NEGATIVE in this table if the null hypothesis can be rejected at the 95% confidence level (i.e., $p \leq .05$) in a two-tailed test. Nonsignificant effects are reported here only when the inputs have been retained in the analysis. In many instances, researchers will have dropped inputs whose coefficients are not significantly different from zero and, in such instances, the "noneffects" are not reported here.

(b) When the measure is the ratio of administrators to pupils or administrators to teachers, the regression coefficient tends to be negative.

5.4.2 It has not been demonstrated that the ratio of professional staff to teachers is related to the achievement of students.

5.4.3 The amount of guidance services that students receive is positively related to achievement.

Common sense would tell us that the effect, if any, of additional school administrative services on student achievement is positive, other inputs remaining the same. Unfortunately, the results concerning school administration are not so unambiguous. Only in two of the studies reported in Table 8−29 do we find a significant relationship between administrative services and student achievement. In one of these the direction of the relationship is positive; in the other, however, it is negative.

To interpret the difference in results, we should note that the variable is measured quite differently in the two studies. In the one (KI1), the measure is the dollar amount spent per pupil on administrative staff. While this may be an indicator of administrative services, it is also in part a proxy for district wealth. In any event, these two factors would tend to affect achievement in the same direction. Hence the positive regression coefficient.

In the other study (B&K), the measure of administrative services is the ratio of administrators to teachers. While this may be an indicator of administrative services, it could just as well reflect the *need* for administrative services; that is, school districts with special problems of maintaining discipline are forced to hire relatively large numbers of administrators. Since discipline problems are associated with low achievement levels, we might, therefore, observe a negative relationship between achievement and the number of administrators. This seems to be the situation within the sample of districts studied by Bidwell and Kasarda. Whereas additional administrators may be associated with lower achievement levels, they should not be seen as the cause of lower achievement levels. Once again, this illustrates the need for more refined measures. We need to know what administrators actually *do*. What proportion of administrative time is spent in attending to delinquent students and what proportion in more constructive, achievement-enhancing activities?

Proposition 5.4.2 is based on two studies. In the one (B&K), Bidwell and Kasarda do not define precisely who are included among "professional staff," but we know that these are other than teachers and administrators since the numbers in each of these two categories are also included in the regression equations. In the other study (BFH1), Burkhead, Fox, and Holland state that "auxiliary man-years per student reflects librarians and library aides, ROTC instructors, driver education (in one school), and guidance counselors" (Burkhead, Fox, and Holland, 1967, p. 45).

Perhaps the nonsignificant results relating to "professional" or "auxiliary" staff are attributable to the "grab bag" nature of this input category. When Bowles assays a measure of guidance time per student, which is a quite narrowly defined aspect of professional services, he finds a positive relationship between this input and the achievement of black high school seniors.

5.5 Teacher Turnover
5.5.1 Teacher turnover is negatively related to both verbal and mathematics achievement.

There is consistent evidence (see Table 8−30) that the percentage turnover of teachers in a district or school is negatively related to the achievement of students. This is a predictable result since it takes time for a teacher to get used to a new situation and time for students to get used to a new teacher, and during this period of mutual adjustment students would tend to learn less than at other times. Moreover, the departure of a teacher may impair the morale of students in the class, and this too would tend to retard their rate of learning.

The relationship between teacher turnover and student achievement is, however, almost certainly more complicated than this. It seems very plausible that it is a two-directional relationship. Teachers in a district or school of low-achieving students may well become discouraged, and the most discouraged may choose to seek positions elsewhere. Certainly, we should expect that the percentage of teachers who quit owing to job dissatisfaction will be higher in a low-achieving student environment than in a high-achieving student environment.

5.6 Teachers' Salaries
5.6.1 Where it shows a statistically significant relationship, teachers' salaries are positively related to the achievement of students.

It would be naive to believe that teachers' salaries are based only on the effectiveness of teachers. In practice, teachers' salaries reflect primarily differences in teachers' education, experience, and (at least

Table 8–29.   Nonteaching Staff.[a]

Study	Input Measure	Input Level of Aggregation	Output Measure	Output Level of Aggregation	Direction of Effect[b]	Sample/Other Comments
B&K	Administrators per teacher	District	Reading	District	NEGATIVE	104 high school districts, Colorado
			Math	District	NEGATIVE	
	Professional staff per teacher	District	Reading	District	Nonsignificant (positive)	
			Math	District	Nonsignificant (positive)	
BFH1	Administrative man-years per pupil	School	IQ & IQ residual	School	Nonsignificant (positive)	39 schools of 11th graders, Chicago
			Reading and reading residual	School	Nonsignificant (negative)	
	Auxiliary man-years per pupil	School	IQ	School	Nonsignificant (positive)	
			IQ residual	School	Nonsignificant (negative)	
			Reading and reading residual	School	Nonsignificant (negative)	
B2	Average time in guidance per pupil	School	Verbal	Individual	POSITIVE	1,000 black male 12th graders (EEO)
C&M	Administrative man-hours per pupil	School	Verbal	School	POSITIVE under 2SLS	53 schools of 11th graders, Pennsylvania; 2SLS estimates in addition to OLS
			Verbal	School	Nonsignificant (positive) under OLS	
	Auxiliary man-hours per pupil	School	Verbal	School	Nonsignificant (negative)	
			Math	School	Nonsignificant (negative)	
	Hours worked per week by paraprofessional teacher aides	School	Math	School	Nonsignificant (negative)	

KI1	Expenditure per pupil on administrative staff	District	Composite achievement	District	Nonsignificant (positive)	97 districts of 6th graders, New York State
			Composite achievement change score	District	POSITIVE	
			Composite achievement (with prior score as independent variable)	District	POSITIVE	
			Math	District	Nonsignificant (positive)	
			Math (with prior score as independent variable)	District	Nonsignificant (positive)	
W1	Expenditure per pupil on administration and guidance	School	Verbal	Individual	Nonsignificant (negative)	388 black 8th graders, California; 1st grade IQ entered as independent variable
W2	Expenditure per pupil on administration and guidance	School	Verbal	Individual	Nonsignificant (positive)	385 white 8th graders, California; 1st grade IQ entered as independent variable

[a] The estimated effects reported in this table are partial effects. To ascertain the control variables used in a particular study, the reader is referred to Table 8–1, or to the appropriate section of the appendix.

[b] An effect is declared POSITIVE or NEGATIVE in this table if the null hypothesis can be rejected at the 95% confidence level (i.e., $p \leqslant .05$) in a two-tailed test. Nonsignificant effects are reported here only when the inputs have been retained in the analysis. In many instances, researchers will have dropped inputs whose coefficients are not significantly different from zero and, in such instances, the "noneffects" are not reported here.

Table 8–30. Teacher Turnover.[a]

	Input		Output			
Study	Measure	Level of Aggregation	Measure	Level of Aggregation	Direction of Effect[b]	Sample/Other Comments
BFH2	Teacher turnover per year	School	Verbal Verbal residual	School School	Nonsignificant (negative) NEGATIVE	22 high schools, Atlanta
K	Annual rate of teacher turnover	District	Verbal Math	District District	NEGATIVE NEGATIVE	56 elementary school districts, Boston
L	Percent of teachers who left in previous year	School	Verbal	Individual	Nonsignificant (negative)	597 urban white 6th graders (EEO); 2SLS estimates in addition to OLS

[a] The estimated effects reported in this table are partial effects. To ascertain the control variables used in a particular study, the reader is referred to Table 8–1, or to the appropriate section of the appendix.

[b] An effect is declared POSITIVE or NEGATIVE in this table if the null hypothesis can be rejected at the 95% confidence level (i.e., $p \leqslant .05$) in a two-tailed test. Nonsignificant effects are reported here only when the inputs have been retained in the analysis. In many instances, researchers will have dropped inputs whose coefficients are not significantly different from zero and, in such instances, the "noneffects" are not reported here.

until recently) sex, even though other characteristics may be more important in the educational production function.[7] When salary is included in a regression equation for achievement together with direct measures of a teacher's education, experience, and sex, the high degree of collinearity between salary and the other three variables should tend to inflate the standard errors of the regression coefficients, rendering them statistically nonsignificant.

Nevertheless, in several of the studies reported in Table 8–31, the positive effect of salary on student achievement remains statistically significant even when other measures of teacher performance are included in the equations. In all of these studies, however, salary is aggregated at the level of the school or district. In most cases, the measure is some average of salaries in the school or district. At this level of aggregation, a teacher's salary probably functions primarily as a proxy for the socioeconomic status of the school district.

5.7 Physical Plant
5.7.1 Where it shows a statistically significant relationship, physical plant is positively related to student achievement.

The various indicators that fall under the heading of "physical plant" (see Table 8–32) reflect a mixture of variables. Some of these variables we may be able to identify; others may well elude us. For example, the school facilities index, which Michelson finds to be positively related to achievement among white sixth graders, probably measures community wealth as well as the services of these facilities at the individual student level. School acreage, which he finds positively related to achievement as well, may be a proxy for population density. In other words, the larger the school site, the less likely it is that the school is an inner-city school in which achievement is generally lower than in suburban schools.

5.8 Age of Building
5.8.1 In general, there seems to be no relationship between the age of school buildings and the achievement of students.

It is not at all clear what building age is supposed to measure—the modernity of facilities, the establishment of the community, the size

---

7. See Section 4.0 of this chapter for a review of teacher characteristics and their effects on achievement scores. In addition, see Levin (1971) for an analysis of teachers' salaries and a discussion of how existing salary patterns should tend to influence the hiring practices of school administrators interested in raising the scores of disadvantaged school children.

Table 8–31. Teachers' Salaries. [a]

	Input		Output			
Study	Measure	Level of Aggregation	Measure	Level of Aggregation	Direction of Effect [b]	Sample/Other Comments
BFH2	Mean teacher's salary	School	Verbal Verbal residual	School School	Nonsignificant (positive) Nonsignificant (negative)	22 high schools, Atlanta
C	Teachers' salaries (enrollment held constant)	District	Verbal change score	District	POSITIVE	377 districts of 12th graders, Iowa
C&M	Mean teacher's salary	School	Verbal	School	Nonsignificant (mixed)	53 schools of 11th graders, Pennsylvania; 2SLS estimates in addition to OLS
KI1	Mean salary of teachers in top salary decile	District	Composite achievement	District	Nonsignificant (positive)	97 districts of 6th graders, New York State
			Composite achievement change score	District	Nonsignificant (positive)	
			Composite achievement (with prior score as independent variable)	District	Nonsignificant (positive)	
			Math change score	District	POSITIVE	
			Math (with prior score as independent variable)	District	POSITIVE	

P	Mean teacher's salary	School	Verbal Abstract reasoning	Individual Individual	POSITIVE[c] Nonsignificant (positive)	3,265 male 12th graders (Project Talent)
W1	Mean teacher's salary	School	Verbal	Individual	Nonsignificant (positive)	388 black 8th graders, California; 1st grade IQ entered as independent variable
W2	Mean teacher's salary	School	Verbal	Individual	POSITIVE	385 white 8th graders, California; 1st grade IQ entered as independent variable
BFH3	Beginning salary for male teachers	School	Verbal Verbal residual	School School	POSITIVE Nonsignificant (negative)	181 small community schools of 12th graders

[a] The estimated effects reported in this table are partial effects. To ascertain the control variables used in a particular study, the reader is referred to Table 8–1, or to the appropriate section of the appendix.

[b] An effect is declared POSITIVE or NEGATIVE in this table if the null hypothesis can be rejected at the 95% confidence level (i.e., $p \leqslant .05$) in a two-tailed test. Nonsignificant effects are reported here only when the inputs have been retained in the analysis. In many instances, researchers will have dropped inputs whose coefficients are not significantly different from zero and, in such instances, the "noneffects" are not reported here.

[c] Nonsignificant (positive) for high income children.

Table 8–32. Physical Plant.[a]

	Input		Output			
Study	Measure	Level of Aggregation	Measure	Level of Aggregation	Direction of Effect[b]	Sample/Other Comments
B2	Number of science labs	School	Verbal	Individual	Nonsignificant (positive)	1,000 black male 12th graders (EEO)
C	Building value per pupil	District	Verbal	District	Nonsignificant (positive)	377 districts of 12th graders, Iowa
KI1	Per pupil value of property	District	Composite achievement	District	Nonsignificant (negative)	97 districts of 6th graders, New York State
			Composite achievement change score	District	Nonsignificant (positive)	
			Composite achievement (with prior achievement as independent variable)	District	Nonsignificant (positive)	
			Math change score	District	Nonsignificant (negative)	
			Math (with prior achievement as independent variable)	District	Nonsignificant (negative)	

					597 urban white 6th graders (EEO); 2SLS estimates in addition to OLS
MI1	School facilities index	School	Verbal Math	Individual Individual	POSITIVE POSITIVE
	Acres of school site	School	Math	Individual	POSITIVE

[a] The estimated effects reported in this table are partial effects. To ascertain the control variables used in a particular study, the reader is referred to Table 8–1, or to the appropriate section of the appendix.

[b] An effect is declared POSITIVE or NEGATIVE in this table if the null hypothesis can be rejected at the 95% confidence level (i.e., $p \leqslant .05$) in a two-tailed test. Nonsignificant effects are reported here only when the inputs have been retained in the analysis. In many instances, researchers will have dropped inputs whose coefficients are not significantly different from zero and, in such instances, the "noneffects" are not reported here.

of the capital debt—or what the hypothesized relationship between building age and student achievement might be. Accordingly, only one of the nine coefficients reported in Table 8−33 is statistically significant at the 0.05 level in a two-tailed test, and this one rejection of the null hypothesis we may attribute to chance.

5.9 Library and Supplies

5.9.1 There seems to be no consistent relationship between achievement and the availability or current acquisition of library books and other teaching materials.

Although the relationship between achievement and library facilities (other school supplies) is not consistent, where a statistical relationship is observed it is most often positive in direction. Of course, for books in a library to yield benefits they must be read, and the mere presence of an extensive library in a school does not assure its frequent use. A better measure than the *number* of books in stock or books added to the library's stock would be the *circulation* of library books, but none of the authors whose studies are reported in Table 8−34 had access to or made use of the more sophisticated input measure.

Even if the library of a school is used heavily *on the average*, there may be considerable variation in the use of the library by individual students. In those studies (L, MI1, MI2, P) where output is measured at the individual level, a measure of schoolwide resource availability may be a very poor measure of any particular individual's exposure to the resource. Perl finds a positive effect of books in the library on the achievement of high-income students but none on the achievement of low-income students. This is not altogether surprising since if we were to look at individual participation rates, we would probably find that the high-income students use the library more frequently on the average than the low-income students.

5.10 Class Size

5.10.1 An additional student in class is sometimes found to have a positive effect, sometimes a negative effect, and sometimes no effect at all on the *average* achievement of students. Which of these three effects is observed is probably itself a function of class size; in other words, the true effect of class size may be curvilinear, and within the full range of possible class size values, the direction of the effect changes.

Table 8-33. Age of School Building.[a]

	Input		Output				
Study	Measure	Level of Aggre-gation	Measure	Level of Aggre-gation	Direction of Effect[b]	Sample/Other Comments
B1	Age of building	School	Math	Individual	Nonsignificant (negative)	100 black male 12th graders (Project Talent)
BFH1	Age of building	School	IQ & IQ residual	School	Nonsignificant (positive)	39 schools of 11th graders, Chicago
			Reading	School	Nonsignificant (positive)	
			Reading residual	School	Nonsignificant (negative)	
BFH2	Age of building	School	Verbal and verbal residual	School	Nonsignificant (positive)	22 high schools, Atlanta
BFH3	Age of building	School	Verbal	School	POSITIVE	181 small community schools of 12th graders
			Verbal residual	School	Nonsignificant (positive)	
P	Age of building	School	Verbal	Individual	Nonsignificant (positive)	3,265 12th graders (Project Talent)
			Abstract reasoning	Individual	Nonsignificant (positive)	

[a] The estimated effects reported in this table are partial effects. To ascertain the control variables used in a particular study, the reader is referred to Table 8-1, or to the appropriate section of the appendix.

[b] An effect is declared POSITIVE or NEGATIVE in this table if the null hypothesis can be rejected at the 95% confidence level (i.e., $p \le .05$) in a two-tailed test. Nonsignificant effects are reported here only when the inputs have been retained in the analysis. In many instances, researchers will have dropped inputs whose coefficients are not significantly different from zero and, in such instances, the "noneffects" are not reported here.

Table 8–34. Library and Supplies.[a]

Study	Input Measure	Input Level of Aggregation	Output Measure	Output Level of Aggregation	Direction of Effect[b]	Sample/Other Comments
BFH1	Textbook expenditure per pupil	School	IQ & IQ residual	School	Nonsignificant (negative)	39 schools of 11th graders, Chicago
			Reading	School	Nonsignificant (negative)	
			Reading residual	School	Nonsignificant (positive)	
	Expenditure on materials and supplies per pupil	School	IQ & IQ residual	School	Nonsignificant (positive)	
			Reading and reading residual	School	Nonsignificant (positive)	
BFH2	Library expenditure per pupil	School	Verbal	School	Nonsignificant (negative)	22 high schools, Atlanta
			Verbal residual	School	Nonsignificant (positive)	
BFH3	Books in library per pupil	School	Verbal	School	Nonsignificant (negative)	181 small community schools of 12th graders
			Verbal residual	School	POSITIVE	
KI1	Expenditure on books & supplies per pupil	District	Composite achievement	District	POSITIVE	97 districts of 6th graders, New York State
			Composite achievement change score	District	Nonsignificant (negative)	
			Composite achievement (with prior score as independent variable)	District	Nonsignificant (negative)	
			Math change score	District	Nonsignificant (negative)	
			Math (with prior score as independent variable)	District	Nonsignificant (negative)	

L	Books in library per student	School	Verbal	Individual	Nonsignificant (positive)	597 urban white 6th graders (EEO); 2SLS estimates in addition to OLS
MI1	Books in library	School	Verbal Math	Individual Individual	POSITIVE NEGATIVE	597 urban white 6th graders (EEO); 2SLS estimates in addition to OLS
MI2	Books in library	School	Verbal	Individual	Nonsignificant (positive)	458 urban black 6th graders (EEO); 2SLS estimates in addition to OLS
P	Books in library	School	Verbal Abstract reasoning	Individual Individual	POSITIVE[c] POSITIVE[c]	3,265 male 12th graders (Project Talent)

[a] The estimated effects reported in this table are partial effects. To ascertain the control variables used in a particular study, the reader is referred to Table 8–1, or to the appropriate section of the appendix.

[b] An effect is declared POSITIVE or NEGATIVE in this table if the null hypothesis can be rejected at the 95% confidence level (i.e., $p \leqslant .05$) in a two-tailed test. Nonsignificant effects are reported here only when the inputs have been retained in the analysis. In many instances, researchers will have dropped inputs whose coefficients are not significantly different from zero and, in such instances, the "noneffects" are not reported here.

[c] Nonsignificant (positive) for low income students.

Table 8—35 summarizes the results of over thirty tests of the hypothesis that class size has no effect on cognitive achievement. In five of these tests, class size appears to have a positive effect. In five, class size has a negative effect. In all of the rest, there is no significant effect of class size on achievement.

How are we to interpret these mixed results? Conceivably, the effect of class size on cognitive achievement is different for different populations of students. For example, the effect may be different for younger students than for older, for duller students than for brighter, or in some subject areas than in others, but no such pattern is apparent in an examination of Table 8—35. Far more likely is the possibility that the effect of class size is curvilinear. For example, as suggested in Chapter 5 in the introduction to quadratic production models, the effect may be positive over some range, but as size increases, it may become increasingly less positive until it eventually becomes zero and then negative. Given the absence of consistent results over a long history of class size studies (see the review of such studies by Blake, 1954), it is somewhat surprising that none of the recent studies reported here have tested parabolic or other nonlinear relationships between class size and achievement outcomes.

5.11 Calendar Questions
5.11.1 There is a positive relationship between the length of the school year and cognitive achievement.

Conceptually, differences in school exposure are twofold. There are between-school differences (different school calendars) and there are within-school differences (different rates of attendance). Attendance, properly measured, is an individual-level variable and was discussed in this chapter in the section on individual student characteristics.

In addition to being a determinant of cognitive achievement, individual attendance may in turn be influenced by cognitive achievement. Though not necessarily to the same extent, each one probably is an output of the educational process. On the other hand, the length of the school calendar may be considered a truly exogenous variable in any analysis of cognitive achievement at the individual student level. All else being equal, a longer school day or longer school year should result in more student learning.

Although the causal connection is impeccable from a theoretical point of view, we might anticipate statistically nonsignificant results owing to attenuated variance in this input. After all, in the United States today the school calendar within each state is relatively fixed

Table 8–35. Class Size.[a]

Study	Input		Output			Direction of Effect[b]	Sample/Other Comments
	Measure	Level of Aggregation	Measure		Level of Aggregation		
B&K	Pupil-teacher ratio	District	Reading Math		District District	NEGATIVE NEGATIVE	104 high school districts, Colorado
B1	Mean class size in science and math only	School	Reading Math General academic ability		Individual Individual Individual	NEGATIVE POSITIVE NEGATIVE	100 black male 12th graders (Project Talent)
BFH1	Pupils per teacher man-year[c]	School	IQ & IQ residual Reading and reading residual		School School	Nonsignificant (mixed) Nonsignificant (mixed)	39 schools of 11th graders, Chicago
BFH2	Enrollment per teacher	School	Verbal and verbal residual		School	Nonsignificant (mixed)	22 high schools, Atlanta
BFH3	Mean class size	School	Verbal and verbal residual		School	Nonsignificant (mixed)	181 small community schools of 12th graders
C	Mean class size	District	Verbal change		District	Nonsignificant (mixed depending on algebraic specification)	377 districts of 12th graders, Iowa
K	Percent of students in crowded (35+) classrooms[c]	District	Reading Math		District District	Nonsignificant (negative) Nonsignificant (positive)	56 elementary school districts, Boston

Table 8–35. continued

Study	Input Measure	Input Level of Aggregation	Output Measure	Output Level of Aggregation	Direction of Effect[b]	Sample/Other Comments
KI1	Pupil-teacher ratio[c]	District	Math change score	District	Nonsignificant (positive)	97 districts of 6th graders, New York State
			Math (with prior achievement as independent variable)	District	Nonsignificant (positive)	
			Composite achievement	District	POSITIVE	
			Composite achievement change score	District	Nonsignificant (positive)	
			Composite achievement (with prior score as independent variable)	District	POSITIVE	
MU1	Class size	Class	Reading	Individual	Nonsignificant (negative)	440 black 2nd graders, New Haven; fall score entered as independent variable
			Math	Individual	Nonsignificant (positive)	
MU2	Class size	Class	Reading	Individual	POSITIVE	440 black 3rd graders, New Haven; score from previous year entered as independent variable
			Math	Individual	Nonsignificant (positive)	
MU3	Class size	Class	Reading	Individual	Nonsignificant (positive)	440 black 3rd graders, New Haven; fall score entered as independent variable
			Math	Individual	Nonsignificant (negative)	
			Spelling	Individual	NEGATIVE	

P	Mean science class size	School	Verbal / Abstract reasoning	Individual / Individual	Nonsignificant (positive) / POSITIVE	3,265 male 12th graders (Project Talent)
	Mean nonscience class size	School	Verbal / Abstract reasoning	Individual / Individual	Nonsignificant (negative) / Nonsignificant (negative)	
W1	Pupil-teacher ratio	School	Verbal	Individual	Nonsignificant (negative)	388 black 8th graders, California; 1st grade IQ entered as independent variable
W2	Pupil-teacher ratio	School	Verbal	Individual	Nonsignificant (positive)	385 white 8th graders, California; 1st grade IQ entered as independent variable

[a] The estimated effects reported in this table are partial effects. To ascertain the control variables used in a particular study, the reader is referred to Table 8–1, or to the appropriate section of the appendix.

[b] An effect is declared POSITIVE or NEGATIVE in this table if the null hypothesis can be rejected at the 95% confidence level (i.e., $p \leq .05$) in a two-tailed test. Nonsignificant effects are reported here only when the inputs have been retained in the analysis. In many instances, researchers will have dropped inputs whose coefficients are not significantly different from zero and, in such instances, the "noneffects" are not reported here.

[c] For ease of reading and to maintain consistency in the presentation, the direction of this variable has been reversed from that in the original study.

by legislative mandate, and the variation in mandated school hours across states is small. Despite any pessimism stemming from inadequate data, the results found in Table 8–36 are rather supportive of the hypothesis. Though only one is significant at the 0.05 level in a two-tailed test, the regression coefficients are consistently positive. Although the variance in the input is small, Perl, using a subset of the nationwide Project Talent data set, gets a significant regression coefficient on number of days in the school year for one of his two output measures, abstract reasoning. Apparently, differences in the *quantity* of schooling that students receive *do make a difference.*

Table 8–36. The School Calendar.[a]

	Input		Output				
Study	Measure	Level of Aggregation	Measure	Level of Aggregation	Direction of Effect[b]		Sample/Other Comments
B2	Days in session	School	Verbal	Individual	Nonsignificant (positive)		1,000 black male 12th graders (EEO)
P	Days in school year	School	Verbal Abstract reasoning	Individual Individual	Nonsignificant (positive) POSITIVE		3,265 male 12th graders (Project Talent)

[a] The estimated effects reported in this table are partial effects. To ascertain the control variables used in a particular study, the reader is referred to Table 8–1, or to the appropriate section of the appendix.

[b] An effect is declared POSITIVE or NEGATIVE in this table if the null hypothesis can be rejected at the 95% confidence level (i.e., $p \leq .05$) in a two-tailed test. Nonsignificant effects are reported here only when the inputs have been retained in the analysis. In many instances, researchers will have dropped inputs whose coefficients are not significantly different from zero and, in such instances, the "noneffects" are not reported here.

✴ *Chapter 9*

The Future of Input-Output
Research in Education

Research on the production of educational outcomes has produced mixed results although patterns of consistent findings are beginning to emerge, as we saw in the last chapter. Past confusion has been due at least in part to the way input-output researchers have phrased their research questions and the methods they have used to address these questions. In asking whether or not schooling has an effect, researchers may be asking the wrong question. Of course schooling has an effect; this is self-evident "regardless of the results of simplistic data analyses and their even more simplistic interpretations," as Wiley (1976, p. 264) has argued. The problem can be illustrated by a simple analogy. Let us consider whether or not water has any effect on fish. To see the effect of water on fish, one would need to observe some fish in water and other fish completely out of water. The effects of small variations in water temperature or water salinity would tend to be small and difficult to measure, if indeed any effects existed.

Just as it could be misleading to test the effect of water on fish by concentrating on small differences in aquatic characteristics, it is difficult to say much about the effect of education on children when all of the children studied are in school. School children are exposed to many common experiences. For instance, nearly all teachers are college graduates, all students spend about the same number of hours in class, and class sizes fall within a very narrow range. The effect of a common experience is not statistically measurable. If all students are in school, we cannot hope to answer the question, "Does schooling make a difference?" We can only address the more restricted question, "Do the differences that exist between schools and within schools make a difference?" The difference in student achievement brought about by, say, a teacher with an M.A. as compared with a teacher with only a B.A. may be comparable to the effect of a tiny change in water temperature on the life of a fish—small or nonexistent.

We must move from the question, "Does schooling have an effect?" to the question, "What effects do specific school policies have on various educational outcomes?" In the previous chapter we saw that in fact some differences between and within schools do make a difference in achievement. Many characteristics of schools, teachers, and student bodies have been found consistently to affect educational outcomes. Admittedly, these inputs may have relatively smaller effects than do the characteristics of families and individuals; yet these inputs are subject to the control of policymakers and therefore deserve attention.

The input-output approach appears to hold some value as a method for understanding the effects of inputs on educational outcomes. But to be more useful to school decisionmakers and basic researchers, the input-output (I-O) approach must be applied more precisely. Fifteen recommendations to future researchers are presented below. These concern the following topics: (1) unit of analysis, (2) consistency in levels of aggregation, (3) nonrecursive models, (4) experimental designs, (5) time-series designs, (6) interactions between inputs, (7) proxy variables, (8) new input measures, (9) additional output measures, (10) achievement testing, (11) sampling, (12) sample attrition, (13) conclusion validity, (14) cost-effectiveness criteria, and (15) distribution of outcomes.

RECOMMENDATIONS

Unit of Analysis

Some studies have attempted to explain variation in outcomes at the level of the individual child while others have tried to explain variation at the level of some larger unit, such as the school or even the school district. Either of these approaches may be legitimate depending upon the researcher's objectives. However, often researchers have attempted to answer questions at one level with data that are inappropriate because they come from a different level. Inputs and outputs measured at the school or district level are averages that can tell us very little about how *individual* students learn.

Consistency in Levels of Aggregation

Because of the unavailability of data, researchers occasionally have related inputs and outputs at different levels of aggregation. In the EEO report, for example, individual outcomes were correlated with averaged teacher characteristics for a grade within a school. This was done because the size of the sample (over 640,000 students) made it difficult to match individual students with specific teachers. Inconsistent measurement of this kind underestimates the effect of any particular input. Future research should use consistent levels of aggregation across all inputs and outputs.

Nonrecursive Models

Most input-output studies to date have examined the effects of inputs on one output at a time without considering the possibility that variables may affect each other reciprocally. For example, affective inputs, such as locus of control beliefs, are both a cause of and a result of cognitive achievement. Educational researchers must be more sensitive to the possibility of reciprocal causation; technically, this means that nonrecursive models must be considered. Estimating techniques, such as two-stage least-squares, are available to test such bidirectional models.

Experimental Designs

Input-output studies have generated a number of hypotheses concerning the effects of inputs on educational outcomes. These studies have been limited by problems of multicollinearity (correlations among included inputs) and by problems of proxy variables (correlations between included inputs and unmeasured causes). In addition these studies are often constrained by limited natural variance in inputs. Experimental research eliminates these problems because inputs are manipulated independently and because pupils are randomly assigned to different combinations of inputs. While experimentation raises serious ethical questions and presents political problems (e.g., Campbell, 1969; Cook and Campbell, 1976; Riecken and Boruch, 1974), experimentation may be the only way to answer conclusively many questions about the effects of educational inputs.

Time-Series Designs

Most I-O researchers have measured inputs and outputs at just one point in time. While some causal inferences can be drawn from such data, inferences are more easily reached with longitudinal data. Both inputs and outputs should be assessed at multiple points during the child's schooling so that the causal effects of specific inputs can be inferred. This will necessitate some small changes in the way multiple regression analysis is applied (see Ostrom, 1978; Box and Jenkins, 1970; Nelson, 1973).

Interactions Between Inputs

Educational outcomes result from combinations of inputs, and it is important to identify how inputs combine and interact to determine outcomes. The effect of one input may be independent of all other inputs while the effect of another input may depend upon the presence or absence (or upon the particular level) of some other input(s). For example, we speculated that well-equipped school libraries may enhance the achievement of high-ability students but may have no effect on the achievement of low-ability students, which is to say that library facilities and student ability may interact to affect achievement. Other illustrations of interacting inputs were presented in Chapter 2. In the future, researchers should be more diligent in hypothesizing and testing theoretically relevant interactions among inputs.

Proxy Variables

Statistically significant effects may simply reflect the fact that the inputs included in a regression equation are correlated with the excluded, true causes of achievement. Finding statistically significant relationships between proxy variables and educational outcome measures does not indicate to policymakers which inputs to manipulate in order to enhance achievement. For example, knowing that ownership of a home vacuum cleaner is highly correlated with student achievement tells us very little about the educational process. To remedy this proxy problem, researchers should develop theories that specify causal variables, and all such variables should be included in their analyses. Experimental research, of course, obviates the problem of proxy variables because the random assignment of pupils to instructional "treatments" suggests that observed outcomes are indeed the result of the manipulated inputs.

New Input Measures

It seems that ease of measurement has been the major criterion for the selection of inputs in most input-output studies of education. Consequently, as noted in the preceding section, many of the inputs used to date have been crude proxies for unmeasured causal variables. We are now at the point where more refined and direct measures of immediate causes should be incorporated into the analysis of educational outcomes. In particular, attempts should be made to measure classroom process variables directly. Similarly, family processes need to be examined directly rather than by inference. For example, parents' educational background is known to be an important correlate of student achievement; a possible explanation is that differences in background reflect differences in how children spend their time (Liebowitz, 1974; Hill and Stafford, 1974).

Additional Output Measures

The vast majority of input-output studies in education have used standardized tests of verbal and reading achievement to measure output (see Chapter 3, especially Table 3–1). Input-output studies should broaden the range of cognitive measures used; for instance, more studies should examine the production of mathematics achievement, science achievement, and other skills emphasized in schools. Outcomes from the affective domain should also be included, for example, locus of control expectancies and self-concept. In addition, there are other variables that might be conceived of as educational outcomes. For instance, lifetime earnings seem to be positively related to school quality (Johnson and Stafford, 1973; Wachtel, 1975; Link and Ratledge, 1975). Research should explore the effects of school differences upon the economic and social indicators of "quality of life."

Achievement Testing

The 3Rs—reading, writing, and arithmetic—are the lowest common denominators of different groups' expectations for the schools and although the mix of output measures may be broadened in the future (as recommended in the preceding section), standardized achievement tests will probably continue to be the major dependent variable in input-output research. Reducing measurement error in test scores will make it possible to detect effects more precisely. More basic psychometric research is needed to determine how to measure achievement validly and reliably while minimizing the burden to pupils and school personnel. In the meantime, researchers may wish to consider these practical desiderata, which were introduced in Chapter 3:

a. Use an achievement test that has been recently normed on a well-documented national sample.
b. Avoid separate scoring media (i.e., separate test booklets and answer sheets).
c. Administer tests at the same time as the norming studies were conducted by the test manufacturer.

d. Whenever possible, match students and test administrators in race or ethnicity.
e. Try to minimize the number of children who "bottom out" on tests that are too hard for them or "top out" on tests that are too easy for them.
f. Avoid the deleterious effects of large group test administrations.

Sampling

Large-scale data collection is expensive and time-consuming, so there is a tendency to rely upon data from one school district or from a very few districts. The use of limited samples makes it difficult to generalize results. It is important that samples be representative of the population to which the researcher wishes to generalize.

Sample Attrition

Many studies have used samples that were diminished in size because of missing data. Sample attrition is particularly problematic if there is any reason to believe that the presence or absence of data is correlated with measures in the production model. For example, if lower ability teachers tend to drop out of the sample, the variance in teacher ability shrinks, and the true relationship between teacher ability and student achievement may be underestimated. Researchers must exert care to minimize missing data and to understand the effects of unavoidable attrition when it occurs.

Conclusion Validity [1]

Many effects of school and teacher inputs are small and yet are still of theoretical or policy importance. Input-output researchers must use samples large enough to ensure that small but important effects can be detected. In other words, the power of statistical tests should be sufficient to detect small effects (Cohen, 1971). This is particularly important when the unit of analysis is the school or classroom (Cronbach, 1976).

Cost-Effectiveness Criterion

Most input-output studies have sought to make policy recommendations, but with very few exceptions (e.g., Levin, 1971) the costs of alternative policies have been ignored. Given that schools must operate within constrained budgets, the criterion for assessing the impact of an educational input should be its cost-effectiveness relative to other inputs.

1. The term "conclusion validity" is borrowed from Cook and Campbell (1976).

Distribution of Outcomes

Each of the input-output studies examined in this book has attempted to measure the *average* impact of some set of inputs on some educational output or outputs, but averages seldom tell the whole story. It may be socially more desirable to raise the achievement levels of those students who are currently at the bottom of the achievement distribution than it is to raise the performance of pupils in the middle or at the top. An undifferentiated analysis that accepts a difference in the *mean* level of achievement as the measure of production may be inadequate (cf. Bloom, 1976; Brown and Saks, 1975; and Garner, 1978).

Admittedly, some studies have done subanalyses on partitioned samples, and others have allowed for interactions between a student's prior achievement level and other tractable inputs, such as teacher experience. Still, few such studies have addressed explicitly the "tradeoffs" in achievement between high- and low-ability students. Suppose, for example, that it costs more (in teacher time and other budgeted resources) to produce an achievement gain of a particular size among low-ability students than to produce the same size gain among high-ability students. Given that school resources are fixed, the decision to concentrate resources on low-ability students (in order to bring about a more equal distribution of achievement scores) implies a reduction in the mean level of achievement. More research needs to be done in order to understand how the achievement of low-ability students can be raised efficiently.

CONCLUDING COMMENTS

In addition to the methodological and analytical comments we have made in this chapter, we wish to recommend that educational production researchers be more explicit about their theoretical assumptions. Both *basic researchers*, who wish to understand the determinants of achievement, and *applied researchers*, who wish to manipulate resources to obtain practical objectives, need better theories. Most of the studies reviewed in this book have attempted to achieve both kinds of objectives; that is, they have tried to develop a theory of educational production *and* to derive policy recommendations. These objectives, while not mutually exclusive, usually cannot be accomplished successfully in the same study.

Basic and applied researchers have different concerns. The basic researcher may see great theoretical importance in small but statistically significant effects while the applied researcher, who wishes to engineer change, will be less impressed. Applied researchers are concerned with the cost-effectiveness of particular inputs, with *what* makes a difference and *how much* of a difference. Although what makes a difference is important to basic researchers as well, they are particularly interested in *why* differences occur. The psychological and social processes that mediate the effects of inputs are of crucial concern. Both types of research—basic theory building and applied problem solving—are essential. Each stimulates the other, and they are mutually instructive about where to look for effects and what to measure.

We believe that more attention should be given to understanding the determinants of educational outcomes from both the applied and theoretical perspectives. The input-output approach has been sufficiently productive, even in its early applications, to justify continued development. We have tried to identify methodological and conceptual improvements that should be incorporated into future research. Above all, researchers should be more explicit about their objectives and reflect critically on what samples, measures, and methods are most appropriate for meeting these objectives. Our conclusion, documented in Chapter 8, that differences within schools and classrooms are related to educational outcomes should encourage social scientists and educators to intensify their search for the variables that determine learning.

Study Abstracts

I. Bidwell and Kasarda (B & K)

Charles E. Bidwell and John D. Kasarda, "School District Organization and Student Achievement," *American Sociological Review*, 40 (1975): 55–70.

A. SAMPLE

The sample consists of 104 of the 178 public school districts in the state of Colorado. All data were gathered from the 1969–1970 annual reports of the individual school districts and from the 1971 summary report of the Colorado Department of Education. In addition, data from the 1970 Census were used to assess the socioeconomic characteristics of the population served by each school district. The unit of analysis is the school district.

B. VARIABLES

1. Inputs

    a. School district size: average daily attendance for the district.
    b. Fiscal resources: sum of all revenue received by the school district divided by the average daily attendance.
    c. Disadvantaged students: the percentage of all school-age children in the district who come from families with income below the nationally defined poverty level.
    d. Education of parents: the percentage of males 20–49 years old and females 15–44 years old in the district who have completed at least four years of high school.
    e. Percent nonwhite: The percentage of the district population classified as nonwhite by the U.S. Census.

f. Pupil-teacher ratio: average district daily attendance divided by the number of full-time teachers.

g. Administrative intensity: the ratio of administrators to teachers for each district.

h. Professional support component: the ratio of professional support staff to teachers for each district.

i. Certified staff qualifications: the percentage of the total district certified staff who hold at least an M.A.

2. Outputs

a. Reading achievement: median grade-standardized (nationally normed percentile) reading achievement level for high school students in each district.

b. Mathematics achievement: median grade-standardized mathematics achievement level for high school students in each district.

C.   METHODS OF ANALYSIS

A hierarchical regression analysis is used to assess the direct effects of inputs (a) through (e) upon achievement and the indirect effects through mediating organizational characteristics of the districts (inputs f through i). Standardized regression coefficients and their standard errors are reported.

D.   PRINCIPAL CONCLUSIONS

1. Fiscal resources (input *b*) have a strong positive indirect effect upon achievement, primarily through the organizational variables of professional support component (input *h*) and staff qualifications (input *i*). The direct effects upon achievement are negligible.

2. School district size (input *a*) has neither direct nor consistent indirect effects upon achievement. It tends to improve achievement by decreasing administrative intensity (input *g*), but this is counterbalanced by its negative indirect effects upon achievement through pupil-teacher ratio (input *f*).

3. Parental education has an indirect effect upon reading achievement through its positive effect upon staff qualifications (input *i*). For mathematics achievement, parental education has sizeable indirect effects.

4. Both direct and indirect effects of percentage disadvantaged (input *c*) are negligible.

5. Overall: the central hypothesis of the study that input variables *a* through *e* affect achievement primarily through their effects upon the district organization was supported, particularly for the verbal achievement measure.

E.   EVALUATION

This study is of interest from a number of points of view. Primarily, however, it points out that by assessing some of the indirect effects of variables upon achievement certain variables that may seem to have no effect upon achievement in other studies may in fact have significant effects.

While the findings of this study are provocative, they might be taken with caution because of the following problems:

1. All data are aggregated at the district level, thus ignoring school and classroom variance in achievement.

2. It might be argued that educational inputs are not adequately assessed. In this vein, there is no measure of initial ability or prior achievement.

3. It is unclear whether the organizational attribute variables are themselves seen as causally important or whether they serve primarily as proxies. What, for example, is the significance of administrative intensity and what does it represent?

II. Bowles (B1)

Samuel S. Bowles, "Educational Production Function: Final Report" (Washington, D.C.: U.S. Department of Health, Education, and Welfare, Office of Education, 1969).

A. SAMPLE

The sample consists of black male high school seniors in the Midwest who responded to a five-year follow-up conducted by Project Talent, an educational research study of the early 1960s. The original sample consisted of 207 students who were seniors in 1960. However, on the follow-up only 47 percent of the students responded.

Individual level data are available for outcome measures and background characteristics. School and teacher characteristics are aggregated at the school level.

B. VARIABLES

1. Inputs

a. Father's occupation: coded according to census occupational codes.

b. Mother's occupation: coded according to census occupational codes.

c. Father's education: years of schooling.

d. Mother's education: years of schooling.

e. Study facilities index: composite of whether student has his own room, a desk, and a typewriter.

f. A family index on the presence of appliances in the home.

g. A family index on the presence of TV, telephone, radio, and phonograph in the home.

    h. Dummy variable for real or surrogate parents.

    i. Mean school class size in science and math.

    j. Senior class size in high school.

    k. Starting salary of male teacher with a B.A. degree.

    l. Percentage of teachers in the school who were fully certified.

    m. Percentage of students in the school enrolled in a college preparatory program.

    n. Number of teachers in the school with graduate training divided by the number of classes in the school.

    o. Dummy variable for the presence of tracking in the school.

    p. Percent black students in the school.

    q. Age of school building.

    r. An educational innovation index, based on principal's responses to questions about school characteristics.

2. Outputs

    a. Raw score on a reading comprehension test.

    b. Raw scores on two mathematics achievement tests, made into an index.

    c. A composite index of general academic aptitude based on nine separate tests.

C. METHODS OF ANALYSIS

A linear additive regression model was used, regressing each of the three outcome measures upon the inputs. Regression coefficients, both raw and standardized, and their t-statistics are reported. In the reported regression equations not all of the inputs are present. It thus appears that Bowles deleted inputs whose effects did not attain statistical significance.

D. PRINCIPAL CONCLUSIONS

1. School characteristics (inputs j through r) appear to have a greater effect upon mathematics achievement than upon reading comprehension and general academic aptitude. The opposite seems to be true for individual background variables (inputs a through h).

2. Father's occupation and the index of consumer durables (TV, telephone, etc.) appear as positive determinants of achievement in all three equations. They do a better job in explaining the dependent measure than does parents' own education.

3. Teacher graduate training is related to all three measures of achievement. Class size has negative effects for reading comprehension and general achievement but a small positive effect for math achievement.

4. Percentage of students in a college preparatory curriculum shows no effect, but percentage of students who are black has negative effects on both mathematics and general achievement.

E. EVALUATION

Bowles acknowledges the major problems posed by these data and their analysis. In fact, the data are used primarily to illustrate the problems inherent in estimating educational production functions. These include:

1. Aggregation of school and teacher variables.
2. Nonresponse biases.
3. Lack of initial achievement inputs.
4. Independent variables as proxies for true causes.

Because of Bowles's lengthy discussion of the problems of production function analysis, this study has been very influential in determining analysis strategies for later studies.

III. Bowles (B2)

Samuel S. Bowles, "Towards an Educational Production Function," in W.L. Hansen, Ed., *Eduation, Income, and Human Capital* (New York: Columbia University Press, 1970).

A. SAMPLE

The sample consists of 1,000 black twelfth-grade students drawn from the 1965 Equality of Educational Opportunity data set (Coleman et al., 1966). For details on the EEO sample, see Chapter 7. As in the EEO study, outcomes and background variables are measured at the individual level while school and teacher characteristics are aggregated at the school level.

B. VARIABLES

1. Inputs

  a. Index measuring the presence of reading materials in the home.
  b. Number of siblings (inversely coded, i.e., positive = few).
  c. Parents' education level.
  d. Family stability index.
  e. Teachers' verbal ability test scores, school mean.
  f. Dummy variable for the presence of science labs in the school.
  g. Index of guidance counseling in school.
  h. Number of days school is in session.
  i. Size of senior class.
  j. Student's sense of environmental control.
  k. Index of student's self-concept.

2. Output

  a. Individual's raw score on a verbal achievement test.

C.   METHODS OF ANALYSIS

Bowles was quite critical of the analysis strategy adopted by Coleman et al. in the EEO report. Hence, his major purpose in this study was to reexamine those data through the interpretation of regression coefficients. He presents standardized and unstandardized regression coefficients for inputs that substantially affect the outcome. Inputs that have no effect are deleted from the final regression equation.

D.   PRINCIPAL CONCLUSIONS

The major conclusion from Bowles's analysis is that school and teacher variables seem to have an effect on achievement when regression coefficients are examined whereas they do not under the variance-partioning strategy adopted by Coleman et al.

E.   EVALUATION

Like B1, Bowles intended this study to illustrate the problems inherent in educational production function analysis rather than to arrive at conclusions about the determinants of achievement. The study succeeds in underlining the extent to which the original EEO data analysis may have led to erroneous conclusions because of the variance-partitioning strategy adopted.

The data are, of course, subject to the same problems of nonresponse, aggregation, and low reliability that plague the original EEO data base.

IV. Burkhead, Fox, and Holland (BFH1, BFH2, and BFH3)

Jesse Burkhead, Thomas G. Fox, and John W. Holland, *Input and Output in Large City High Schools.* (Syracuse, N.Y.: Syracuse University Press, 1967).

A.   SAMPLES

Three different samples are used in this study:

1.   Thirty-nine of the fifty-two public high schools in the city of Chicago, enrolling 55 percent of all high school students in that city. All of the thirty-nine schools included were comprehensive schools. Vocational schools and schools for the handicapped were left out. The sampled schools ranged in enrollment from 620 to 4,089. Data on these schools were gathered from school district records for the year 1961–1962, as well as from the 1960 Census.

2.   Twenty-two of the twenty-four schools in the city of Atlanta, enrolling 91 percent of all public high school students in the city. Two vocational high schools were left out of the analysis. Seventeen of the twenty-two schools were for white students and the remainder were for blacks, and

enrollment ranged from 535 to 2,668. Data were gathered from 1961 school district records and the 1960 Census.

3. One hundred and eighty-one public high schools in communities with populations between 2,500 and 25,000 and with only one high school, drawn from the Project Talent data bank. The data were originally gathered by Project Talent for the year 1960 from district school records and the 1960 Census.

Data in all three samples are aggregated at the school level.

B. VARIABLES

1. Chicago sample

a. Inputs

1. Median family income in school's attendance area, based on the 1960 Census.

2. Average daily attendance.

3. Age of school building.

4. Expenditures on textbooks per pupil.

5. Expenditures on materials and supplies per pupil.

6. Median years of teacher experience.

7. Percentage of teachers with an M.A. degree or higher.

8. Teacher man-years per pupil.

9. Administrator man-years per pupil.

10. Auxiliary man-years per pupil (e.g., librarians, guidance counselors, aides, etc.).

b. Outputs

1. Percentage of eleventh-grade students scoring above the city-normed 40th percentile on an IQ test, divided by 60. (This is an indication of IQ scores relative to the city as a whole.)

2. Identical index based upon the Davis Reading Test.

3. Percent dropouts in the eleventh grade.

4. Percentage of eleventh graders wanting to go to college.

5. Residual from regression of eleventh graders' IQ index on ninth graders' IQ index for same school during same year.

6. Identical residual index based on eleventh- and ninth-grade reading scores.

2. Atlanta sample

a. Inputs

1. Median family income for area, from 1960 Census.

2. Active registration of each school.

3. Age of school building.

4. Library expenditures per pupil.

5. Total expenditures per pupil.

6. Average teacher salary.

7. Enrollment per teacher.

8. Measure of teacher turnover.

b. Outputs

1. School median on tenth-grade verbal test.

2. Percent male dropouts in all grades.

3. Percentage of 1961 graduating class who were in post high school education in 1961–1962.

4. Residual from regression of tenth-graders' mean verbal score on eighth-graders' verbal score for same school during same year.

3. Small communities sample

a. Inputs

1. Median family income for area from 1960 Census.

2. Twelfth-grade enrollment.

3. Age of building.

4. Books in the library divided by number of twelfth-grade students.

5. Total expenditures per student.

6. Beginning salary, male teachers.

7. Median teacher's experience.

8. Mean class size.

b. Outputs

1. Mean twelfth-grade reading score.

2. Percent dropouts in all grades.

3. Percentage of graduates in 1960 class enrolled in college in 1961.

4. Residual from regression of mean twelfth-grade reading score on tenth-grade mean reading score for same school during same year.

C. METHODS OF ANALYSIS

Stepwise multiple regression (adding one independent variable at a time) is performed relating all independent variables to all dependent variables for each sample. Standardized regression coefficients, their significance levels, and the coefficients of multiple determination (R^2) are reported.

D. PRINCIPAL CONCLUSIONS

It is surprising how few of the inputs significantly predict outputs in the three samples.

For the Chicago sample only six regression coefficients are significantly different from zero in all six regression equations. Family income affects IQ, reading, and dropout rate outcomes. Dropout rates are also significantly affected by age of school building and expenditures on supplies and materials. Finally, on the reading residual outcome, teachers' experience has a significant effect.

In Atlanta, the story is much the same. The family income input has significant effects upon verbal scores and upon percent dropouts. Large schools are also associated with lower verbal scores and higher dropout rates. This finding is probably due, however, to the fact that the exclusively black schools tend to be much larger than the white schools. The various fiscal input measures also significantly affect dropout rates.

Much less output variance is explained in the small communities sample than in the other two samples. This is probably due to there being less between-school variation in this third sample. In spite of a fairly large sample size, there are no significant inputs for either dropout rates or college attendance rates. Reading scores are significantly predicted by median family income, building age, teachers' salaries, and teachers' experience. Number of library volumes significantly affects the reading residual outcome.

E. EVALUATION

The strength of this study is in its comparison of production processes in various locations and types of communities. However, its findings and implications are limited by the following problems:

1. Aggregation at the school level conceals significant within-school effects.

2. Small samples for Chicago and particularly Atlanta limit the possibility of significant findings.

3. It is unclear why variables were chosen and how to interpret their explanatory significance. For instance, why are library expenditures and per pupil expenditures *both* included in the analysis for Atlanta?

4. Variance in both dependent and independent variables may be relatively small, particularly in the small community sample.

V. Cohn (C)

Elchanan Cohn, "Economies of Scale in Iowa High School Operations," *Journal of Human Resources*, 3 (1968), 422–434.

A. SAMPLE

The sample consists of all 377 high school districts in the state of Iowa, of which 372 contain only one high school. The data on these schools were provided by the Iowa State Department of Public Instruction, and they are aggregated at the school level.

B. VARIABLES

1. Inputs

a. Average daily attendance.

b. Average number of teachers' college semester hours per teaching assignment.

c. Average number of different subject matter assignments per teacher.

d. Median teacher's salary.

e. Number of credit units offered by school (a unit is one course offered for a full school year).

f. Building value per pupil.

g. Bonded indebtedness per pupil.

h. Class size (number of pupils per teacher).

2. Outputs

a. Average composite scores for twelfth-graders in 1963 on the Iowa Tests of Educational Development minus the average composite score for tenth-graders in 1961 on the same tests.

b. Expenditure per pupil.

C. METHODS OF ANALYSIS

Three separate regression equations are computed for the first-outcome measure. First a linear model is presented, and then a multiplicative equation is computed. Finally, a regression is computed for the 87 of the 377 school districts where the 1960 population was greater than 5,000.

The second dependent measure, per pupil expenditure, is also regressed on the inputs and on the achievement outcome in order to estimate economies of scale.

D. PRINCIPAL CONCLUSIONS

For the linear regression model, only the following variables had significant regression coefficients: college hours per teaching assignment (negative); assignments per teacher (negative); and teachers' salary (positive). Only 0.05 percent of the variance in achievement change was accounted for in this regression.

When the multiplicative model was used, the same variables remain the only significant ones, but the R^2 increases to 0.06.

From the cost analysis regressions, the primary result of interest is that the effect of the achievement change score upon cost per pupil does not attain significance. From this analysis, it emerges that the most important variable in affecting cost per pupil is size of school, and this is a curvilinear relationship with economies of scale to a certain optimal size beyond which diseconomies of scale begin to appear.

Finally, when only the eighty-seven largest districts are included in the analysis the R^2 increases to 0.07, but the only significant regression coefficient occurs with assignments per teacher (negative).

E. EVALUATION

This study emphasizes the relationships in school between expenditure, size, and achievement variables. Its strength lies in the attempt to introduce cost analyses into production function research. It is, however, subject to many of the criticism that have been mentioned elsewhere, specifically:

1. Aggregation at the school level may hide significant within-school effects.

2. The measure of output does not control for changes in the school population between 1961 and 1963 (i.e., dropouts and new entrants).

3. Variance in dependent and independent variables may be restricted because of homogeneity in Iowa's high schools. This limits the probability of finding significant effects.

VI. Cohn and Millman (C & M)

Elchanan Cohn and S.D. Millman, *Input-Output Analysis in Public Education* (Cambridge, Mass.: Ballinger Publishing Company, 1975).

A. SAMPLE

The sample consists of fifty-three Pennsylvania schools on which data were collected in 1971. The outcome data are from tests administered to the eleventh-grade students in these schools; the exogenous variables generally assess schoolwide characteristics. Data were supplied by the Pennsylvania Department of Education as well as independently collected. In all analyses the data are aggregated at the school level.

B. VARIABLES

1. Exogenous

a. Teacher classroom practices.
b. Teacher's salary.
c. Teacher's experience.
d. Teacher's education.
e. Library books per pupil.
f. Library accessibility.
g. School innovations index.
h. Curriculum units offered per grade.
i. Index of teacher's teaching specialization.
j. Teacher's teaching load.
k. Class size.
l. Counselors per pupil.
m. Extracurricular expenditure per pupil.
n. Ratio of actual enrollment to building capacity.
o. Administrative man-hours per pupil.
p. Auxiliary man-hours per pupil.
q. Student-teacher ratio.
r. Paraprofessional support index.
s. *Four* socioeconomic status indices, constructed through factor analysis, measuring fourteen individual background characteristics.

2. Endogenous

    a. Self-concept index.
    b. Understanding others index.
    c. Test of verbal skills.
    d. Test of mathematics skills.
    e. Interest in school.
    f. Citizenship.
    g. Health habits.
    h. Creativity potential.
    i. Creativity output.
    j. Vocational development.
    k. Appreciation for human accomplishments.
    l. Preparation for change.

C. METHODS OF ANALYSIS

A simultaneous equation model is used in which the effects of subsets of the exogenous and endogenous variables are assessed upon each of the twelve endogenous measures in turn. The model is estimated via two-stage least-squares analysis. For each of the twelve outputs, both the structural and reduced form coefficients for each input are presented. In all equations, the four socioeconomic status indices are included as inputs although their effects are not reported. The choice of endogenous variables to be included as inputs in any structural equation is determined both by theory and by examination of correlations among outcomes. The choice of inputs included in any given structural equation is determined by a stepwise ordinary least-squares regression procedure.

D. PRINCIPAL CONCLUSIONS

It is exceedingly difficult to summarize succinctly the results of a simultaneous model involving twelve structural equations. Cohn and Millman present over 140 different structural and reduced form coefficients, many of which are statistically significant. No particular patterns in the results are observed, however, other than the general conclusion that a variety of teacher and school inputs have significant effects upon outcomes. Unfortunately, the structural coefficients of outcomes upon other outcomes are not presented.

When we focus upon the two measures of academic achievement (variables c and d), teacher's load seems to have a negative impact in both cases as does the number of curriculum units offered per grade. While the number of administrative man-hours per pupil affects positively the verbal skills measure, the number of auxiliary man-hours affects it negatively. The index of paraprofessional support is related negatively to mathematics achievement. These last findings are discussed at some length in the book by Cohn and Millman.

E. EVALUATION

This study is of particular interest because of the variety of outcomes examined and because of the complexity of the structural model assessed. Clearly, nonrecursive models are more appropriate than simple recursive ones for the analysis of educational production. This study represents a sophisticated attempt to construct such a model.

Its major problem, however, concerns the specification of the structural model, a fact acknowledged by the authors. Decisions about the presence or absence of any specific variable in a given structural equation are not made on theoretical grounds. Instead, correlations and ordinary least-squares regressions are used to help specify the model. In the absence of theory, the interpretation of structural coefficients is problematic.

In addition to the specification issue, the sample upon which the analyses are conducted is not large. This decreases the power of the model. It is probably also the case that there does not exist a great deal of variance between schools as compared with variance within schools. The aggregation makes interpretation difficult.

VII. Hanushek (H1a and H1b)

Eric A. Hanushek, *Education and Race: An Analysis of the Educational Production Process* (Lexington, Mass.: Lexington Books, 1972), Chapters 4 and 5.

A. SAMPLE

A subsample of the EEO data collected in 1965, is used. The subsample consists of all urban elementary schools for the Northeast and Great Lakes regions that had at least five white or black sixth graders (dependent on the analysis, which is stratified by race as explained below). There are 471 schools in the sample having five or more white sixth graders and 242 schools having at least five black sixth graders. All variables are taken directly from the EEO sample of individual students and then aggregated for the particular group of students (white or black) at the level of the school.

B. VARIABLES

1. Inputs[1]

a. Central city dummy variable: variable = 1 if school is in a standard metropolitan area, 0 otherwise.

---

1. Variables (b) through (h) use data only on white or black students depending upon the stratum being analyzed. For instance, in the analysis of black achievement scores, variable (e) is calculated as the percentage of *black* students who attended nursery school.

b. Goods index measuring family ownership of automobile, TV, refrigerator, and other appliances.

c. Father's education in years.

d. Family size.

e. Percentage of sixth graders who attended nursery school.

f. Percentage of sixth graders who expressed desire at least to finish high school.

g. Percentage of students who felt that people like themselves do not have much chance for success.

h. Percentage of sixth-grade students who had a nonwhite teacher during the previous year.

i. Percentage of school population that moved away during preceding year.

j. Teacher's verbal score.

k. Teacher's years of experience.

l. Percentage of students in the school who are black: dummy variable = 1 if 75 percent to 100 percent black.

m. Percentage of students in the school who are black: dummy variable = 1 if 45 percent to 75 percent black.

2. Outputs

a. Mean raw verbal ability score.

b. Mean raw math ability score.

C. METHODS OF ANALYSIS

A multiplicative model is used in the analysis. Regression coefficients and their t-statistics are reported. Apparently, the regressions were computed more than once, and those inputs with negligible effects were deleted.

D. PRINCIPAL CONCLUSIONS

1. In contrast to the findings of Coleman et al. (1966), teacher characteristics are important in both black and white achievement. The coefficients for teacher's experience are positive and significant in all four equations (white verbal, white math, black verbal, and black math), and those for teacher's verbal ability are positive and significant for all equations except in the case of black mathematics achievement.

2. The other teacher-related variable, percentage of students who had a nonwhite teacher during the previous year, has a significant negative effect in all equations except for black mathematics achievement.

3. Racial composition of the student body has effects upon both strata of students. For blacks, there is a negative effect if the student body is over 45 percent black. For whites, this negative effect shows up only above 75 percent black.

E. EVALUATION

The strength of this study lies in the use of more adequate regression models than those used in the original EEO report. This more complex analysis reveals teacher effects that were unobserved in the original analysis. The use of the multiplicative regression model may be preferable as well.

Because of the limitations of the EEO data, this study is subject to many of the shortcomings of that report:

1. The school aggregation of data conceals interschool differences and effects.

2. There is no historical or initial ability input measure, and therefore the effects of school inputs are probably underestimated.

3. It may be that the family background variables are inadequate, and thus the statistical effect of student body racial composition reflects unmeasured SES differences rather than any effect due to racial composition per se.

VIII. Hanushek (H2a and H2b)

Eric A. Hanushek, *Education and Race: An Analysis of the Educational Production Process* (Lexington, Mass.: Lexington Books, 1972), Chapter 3.

A. SAMPLE

The full sample consists of 1,061 third-grade students in a large school system in California during the year 1968—1969. This sample is stratified by race and socioeconomic status to form three separate samples: 515 Anglo children from blue-collar homes; 323 Anglo children from white-collar homes; and 140 Mexican-American children from blue-collar homes.

Data on individual students were gathered from school records and all kindergarten through third-grade teachers were surveyed. All variables are measured at the individual student level. Individual student data and teacher data have been matched, and longitudinal information is available on each student.

B. VARIABLES

1. Inputs[2]

    a. Race of student (Mexican-American or Anglo).

    b. Occupation of father.

    c. Sex dummy variable (= 1 if female).

    d. Repeat grade dummy variable (= 1 if grade was repeated).

    e. First-grade Stanford Achievement Test raw score.

    f. Percentage of time spent on discipline, estimated by third-grade teacher.

    g. Third-grade teacher's verbal ability.

    h. Years since most recent educational experience, third-grade teacher.

    i. Second-grade teacher's verbal ability.

    j. Years since most recent educational experience, second-grade teacher.

    k. Father's occupation dummy variable (= 1 if student's father has a clerical job).

    l. Third-grade teacher's years of experience with this socioeconomic level student.

    m. Second-grade teacher's years of experience with this socioeconomic level student.

    n. Teacher's college major dummy variable, academic vs. non-academic.

2. Output

    a. Third-grade Stanford Achievement Test raw score.

C. METHODS OF ANALYSIS

For each stratum as a first step, achievement is regressed on prior achievement and on a set of dummy variables representing the various third-grade teachers. This analysis determines whether or not there *are* teacher effects upon achievement regardless of the *particular* teacher inputs involved. In this analysis of covariance, teacher effects are found for the Anglo strata but not for the Mexican-American sample, which is analyzed no further.

Once the existence of teacher effects is shown for the two Anglo-American strata, regression equations are computed for these strata to essay the effects of particular teacher inputs. Prior achievement level is

---

2. Variables (a) and (b) are stratification variables and do not enter the regressions. Variables (k) through (m) apply only to students whose father had a white-collar occupation and thus enter the regressions only for that stratum. In addition to these inputs, Hanushek has computed student body or peer group variables from inputs (a), (b), and (c) based on all third graders enrolled in a particular school.

included as an input in all analyses. Regression coefficients and their *t*-statistics are reported.

D. PRINCIPAL CONCLUSIONS

1. As already stated, teacher effects upon achievement are found for the Anglo children but not for the Mexican-American children.

2. The recentness of a teacher's educational experience is related significantly to achievement for both Anglo strata.

3. Teacher's verbal ability exerts a significant effect on achievement only for the blue-collar Anglo stratum. Likewise, the percentage of time spent by a teacher on discipline affects achievement among blue-collar children.

4. The effects of teacher inputs that are usually rewarded by school systems—experience and graduate education—are examined. Neither of these affects achievement in Hanushek's study.

E. EVALUATION

Because of the richness of the data used, the matching of individual students and teachers, and the use of longitudinal data, this study seems to surmount many of the problems inherent in other studies that we review. The analyses are appropriate, and the conclusions seem justified. It is to be lamented that various interaction terms are not included and that models allowing for mutual or reciprocal causation are not tested.

IX. Katzman (K)

Martin T. Katzman, *The Political Economy of Urban Schools* (Cambridge, Mass.: Harvard University Press, 1971).

A. SAMPLE

The sample consists of all fifty-six elementary school districts in Boston, each district comprising several schools. Data on these schools were gathered for the school year 1964–1965 from district records and are aggregated at the district level in all cases.

B. VARIABLES

1. Inputs

a. Median number of students per class.

b. Percentage of students in crowded classrooms (in classes over thirty-five students).

c. Student-staff ratio.

d. District size: number of students in school district.

e. Percentage of teachers with permanent status (acquired by passing a certification exam).

f. Percentage of permanent teachers with M.A. degree.

g. Percentage of permanent teachers with one to ten years experience.

h. Percentage of annual teacher turnover (number of new teachers hired divided by the total number of teachers).

i. Percentage of school seating capacity used.

j. Cultural advantage: a composite index of socioeconomic status computed from 1960 Census data on each school district.

2. Outputs

a. Attendance rate: average daily attendance divided by the average daily membership for the district.

b. Membership rate: average daily membership divided by initial school enrollment.

c. Difference between the median district sixth-grade score on a battery of achievement tests in 1965 and median district second-grade score on same battery in 1965.

d. Percentage of all sixth graders who took the examination to get into the Boston Latin School in 1965.

e. Percentage of all sixth graders who passed the Boston Latin School examination in 1965.

f. Continuation rate: 100 minus the percentage of elementary school leavers in 1965 who did not enter high school in the fall.

C. METHODS OF ANALYSIS

Both linear and multiplicative regression models are estimated, regressing each of the six outcomes on all of the inputs. Interpretations are based in large part upon the linear model.

Regression coefficients and their associated significance levels are reported.

D. PRINCIPAL CONCLUSIONS

1. The most interesting conclusion from the analysis is that with the exception of socioeconomic status, none of the inputs has a significant effect on all of the outcomes. The effects of inputs are quite inconsistent across outcome measures.

2. For some outcomes there seem to be economies of scale. For instance, the size of district and the student-staff ratio have positive effects upon achievement.

E. EVALUATION

One of the important values of this study is that it was among the first to look at a variety of schooling outcomes. Its conclusion that no combination of inputs can maximize all outcomes is important. The findings of this study are, however, subject to certain problems.

1. The data are highly aggregated and thus ignore within-school variation.

2. Certain inputs may be poorly defined, and others are not present at all. Thus there are substantial proxy problems.

X. Kiesling (KI1)

Herbert J. Kiesling, *The Relationship of School Inputs to Public School Performance in New York State* (Santa Monica, Calif.: The Rand Corporation, 1969).

A. SAMPLE

The data used were gathered by the New York State Department of Education. Of the 1,400 school districts in New York State in the late 1950s, 97 were chosen for inclusion in the sample. Although the sample is not a probability sample, the districts included tend to be fairly representative of the state as a whole. The data were gathered both by the individual school districts and by the State Department of Education. The data are longitudinal in nature, consisting of all fourth-grade students in the chosen districts taking an achievement test in 1957, all fifth-grade students in 1958, and all sixth-grade students in 1959. All variables are aggregated at the level of the school district.

B. VARIABLES

1. Inputs

    a. Teacher-pupil ratio.

    b. Principals/supervisors to pupil ratio.

    c. Special staff personnel to pupil ratio.

    d. Expenditure per pupil on books and supplies.

    e. Median teacher's salary.

    f. Average salary of teachers in the top salary decline for elementary schools.

    g. Parental occupation index for fifth graders in district.

    h. Amount of school district debt per pupil.

    i. School district size: average daily attendance.

    j. School district yearly growth rate, 1950–1958.

    k. School property value per pupil.

    l. The salary of the district superintendent.

    m. Mean principal's salary.

    n. Expenditure per pupil on principals, assistant principals, and supervisors.

    o. School district value of buildings per classroom.

    p. School district value of furniture and equipment per classroom.

   q. Median years of teachers' experience.
   r. Urban or rural district.
   s. Tax rate of district.
   t. Tax base of district per pupil.

2. Outputs

   a. Composite score on the Iowa Test of Basic Skills.
   b. Arithmetic score on Iowa test.
   c. Language score on Iowa test.

C. METHODS OF ANALYSIS

For each of the three outcomes, three separate linear regression models are presented. First, the mean sixth-grade score of the district is regressed on inputs. Secondly, the mean change in a district's scores between the fourth grade and the sixth grade serves as the outcome. Thirdly, the mean sixth-grade score is used as the output in an equation with the mean fourth-grade score serving as an independent variable.

Separate regression equations are computed for each of five occupational strata as well as for the entire sample. For each subsample district mean outcomes for that subsample are computed as the dependent measures. Crossing the occupational stratification is an urban-rural stratification. Thus in total, there are 108 regression equations presented (9 outcomes $\times$ 6 occupational strata $\times$ 2 urban-rural strata).

Factor analysis is conducted in order to reduce the number of inputs to a manageable level. Three primary factors emerge: district property value, administrative resources in the schools, and miscellaneous school characteristics. Only a subset of inputs enters each regression.

Regression coefficients and their t-statistics are reported. Only 30 of the 108 regression equations are actually presented in the report.

D. PRINCIPAL CONCLUSIONS

1. Only the occupational index variable is significant in all fifty-four of the regressions run on rural school districts. None of the school variables has a significant effect in any of the equations. It is probable that the failure to find school effects is due primarily to the attenuated variance in the independent variables when aggregated at the district level.

2. For the urban school districts, the teacher to pupil ratio and the expenditure per pupil on books and supplies are negatively related to achievement, and this finding is consistent regardless of occupational stratum or dependent measure.

3. The variable with the most consistent effect upon achievement is expenditure per pupil on principals and supervisory staff. The positive effect is particularly strong for the extremes of the occupational stratification— that is, the higher or lower the stratum, the more positive this effect.

4. In contrast, the positive effects of teacher's salary and school property value are generally higher for the middle occupational strata than for the extremes.

E. EVALUATION

This study is of value from a number of points of view. First, it recognizes the threat posed by multicollinearity and seeks to increase the independence of inputs by reducing the number of inputs through factor analysis. Secondly, the data are longitudinal in nature in that achievement measures are available for students at both the fourth and sixth grade levels. This permits the analysis of achievement *gains*. Thirdly, the extensive stratification procedure makes it possible to examine whether inputs affect achievement differently for different groups of students. The major limitations of this study stem from the relatively small sample size and the district aggregation of data. Clearly, a great deal of within-district information is lost.

XI. Kiesling (K12)

Herbert J. Kiesling, *A Study of Cost and Quality of New York School Districts.* (Washington, D.C.: U.S. Office of Education, 1970).

A. SAMPLE

New York State school districts were selected for inclusion in the sample according to whether or not they used the Iowa Tests of Basic Skills in measuring the achievement of their fifth- and eighth-grade students. Roughly 15 percent of the 801 school districts in the state used these tests in 1964–1965. The final sample consists of 86 school districts; the remaining districts of the 15 percent using the Iowa tests are excluded owing to missing data. Data are aggregated at the district level and, for a very few analyses, at the school level. When the school is the unit of analysis, 273 schools in the 86 districts make up the sample.

Test scores and data concerning parents' education and occupation were obtained from school district records for the school year 1964–1965. Unlike Kiesling's earlier study the data are not longitudinal in nature. Fifth-grade and eighth-grade scores are based on different cohorts in the same year. The information on district and school characteristics were gathered from New York State's Basic Educational Data System, which was instituted in 1967. Thus, some inputs were assessed two years following the measurement of achievement and family background variables.

B. VARIABLES

1. Inputs

    a. Father's educational level.
    b. Father's occupational index.
    c. Urban vs. rural district, based on population density.
    d. Whether or not district was inside a Standard Metropolitan Statistical Area.
    e. Number of schools within district.
    f. Mother's educational level.
    g. Teacher's certification level.
    h. Teacher's degree level.
    i. Teacher's teaching experience.
    j. Teacher's salary.
    k. Percentage white students.
    l. Pupil-teacher ratio.
    m. Administrative expenditure per pupil.
    n. Pupils per classroom.
    o. Pupils per school.
    p. Teachers per classroom.
    q. Average daily attendance.
    r. State aid per pupil.
    s. Approved operating expenditure per pupil.
    t. Value of district-owned property per pupil.
    u. Mean salary of nonclassroom professionals.
    v. Principals and supervisors per pupil.
    w. Principal's experience.
    x. Principal's degree level.

2. Outputs

    a. Fifth-grade composite score on Iowa Test of Basic Skills.
    b. Fifth-grade verbal score on Iowa test.
    c. Fifth-grade arithmetic score on Iowa test.
    d. Eighth-grade composite score on Iowa Test of Basic Skills.
    e. Eighth-grade verbal score on Iowa test.
    f. Eighth-grade arithmetic score on Iowa test.

C. METHODS OF ANALYSIS

The analysis in this study parallels that of Kiesling's earlier study except that longitudinal data are not available. Based in part on factor analysis and in part on theory, each of the outcome measures is regressed on a subset of the inputs. Analyses are conducted for subsamples that are stratified by education of father and for subsamples that are stratified by occupation of father. For each of the seven occupational groups and each of the seven educational groups, separate district mean outcome measures are computed. In addition, the sample is divided into rural and urban subsamples.

All data are aggregated at the district level, although peripheral analysis is conducted at the school level as well.

D. PRINCIPAL CONCLUSIONS

1. Average teacher's salary is consistently unrelated to achievement. (In only 9 of the 127 regressions is its coefficient significant.) The same is true for pupil-teacher ratio and teacher's degree status.
2. Teacher's experience shows a positive relationship to achievement for students from higher socioeconomic backgrounds. For children from the lower end of the socioeconomic spectrum, the relationship is nearly always nonsignificant.
3. The value per pupil of district-owned property and the number of principals per pupil are essentially unrelated to achievement.
4. The number of students per classroom has a tendency (marginally significant in 60 percent of the regressions in which it was entered) to affect achievement positively.
5. The administrative expenditure per pupil is positively related to achievement, and this is particularly so for children from the middle of the socioeconomic spectrum.
6. Teacher's certification level has a significant positive effect on the achievement of fifth-grade students. For eighth-grade achievement, its effect is frequently negative and generally nonsignificant.

E. EVALUATION

This study offers the same strengths as Kiesling's earlier study with the exception that no longitudinal data are used. The complex stratification procedure allows the examination of different effects for different segments of the school population although it does make the presentation of results difficult to follow and summarize.

The major shortcomings of the data include the level of aggregation, the lack of longitudinal data, and the fact that school characteristics were measured in 1967 while student scores are for the school year 1964–1965.

XII. Levin (L)

Henry M. Levin, "A New Model of School Effectiveness," in *Do Teachers Make a Difference?* (Washington, D.C.: U.S. Department of Health, Education, and Welfare, Office of Education, 1970).

A. SAMPLE

The data used in this study are from a subsample of the 1965 EEO sample. The subsample consists of 597 white sixth-grade students enrolled in thirty-six schools in a large Eastern city, which the author has labeled

Eastmet. To avoid some of the problems of the EEO analysis, data were included on only those students who had never attended any schools other than that in which they were enrolled as sixth graders in 1965.

All variables are aggregated as they were in the EEO analysis. That is, background characteristics and achievement scores were gathered and measured at the individual student level while teacher and school characteristics are aggregated at the school level.

B. VARIABLES

1. Exogenous

    a. Sex of student.
    b. Age of student.
    c. Index of possessions in student's home.
    d. Student's family size.
    e. Person serving as mother of student.
    f. Person serving as father of student.
    g. Student's father's education.
    h. Student's mother's employment status.
    i. Student's kindergarten attendance.
    j. Teacher's verbal score.
    k. Teacher's parents' income.
    l. Teacher's teaching experience.
    m. Teacher's undergraduate college type.
    n. Teacher's satisfaction with present school.
    o. Racial composition of student body.
    p. Teacher turnover.
    q. Volumes per student in school library.

2. Endogenous

    a. Raw verbal achievement score.
    b. Student's attitude of personal efficacy (locus of control).
    c. Student's grade aspiration.
    d. Parents' educational expectations for student as reported by the student.

C. METHODS OF ANALYSIS

Ordinary least-squares regression equations are presented for each of the four endogenous variables on subsets of the exogenous variables. The inclusion or exclusion of any given exogenous variable in any given equation is not justified. With the exception of the fourth (parents' educational expectations), all endogenous variables are used as independent variables in the equations where another endogenous variable is the dependent variable. Regression coefficients and their *t*-statistics are reported.

Levin also estimates a simultaneous model using two-stage least-squares. For the first three outcomes (achievement, efficacy attitude, and

grade aspiration), reciprocal causation is allowed (see Figure 8–1). Both reduced form and structural coefficients are presented. Again, the selection
of exogenous variables for any given structural equation is not well justified.

D. PRINCIPAL CONCLUSIONS

1. The two-stage least-squares model is presented for purposes of
comparison with the ordinary least-squares model, and therefore the
reader may assess the extent to which ordinary least-squares estimates are
biased in educational production research. In this vein it is interesting to
compare the structural coefficients for particular inputs in the two models.
For instance, family size exerts a significant effect upon achievement in
the OLS model, whereas its direct effect upon achievement in the 2SLS
model is not large. Its effects upon achievement seem therefore to be indirect. Likewise, the direct effect of students' sex upon achievement is substantially altered in the 2SLS model.

2. Very few inputs have significant direct effects upon achievement
in the 2SLS model. While neither locus of control nor grade aspiration significantly affects achievement, achievement does, however, affect these
outputs.

E. EVALUATION

The major contribution of this study lies in its use of the two-stage
regression model and its comparison of that model with the ordinary least-
squares model. Such a comparison indicates that the presence of mutually
causative variables may be biasing studies that make use of the ordinary
least-squares model. While the conclusions reached from Levin's analysis
are only tentative, the reliance upon a different econometric model is
intriguing.

There are of course a number of severe limitations in the data used by
Levin. These limitations are imposed by the nature of the EEO data and
include the following:

1. The lack of longitudinal achievement measures.
2. Aggregation of school and teacher characteristics.
3. Nonresponse bias.

XIII. Michelson (MI1 and MI2)

Stephan Michelson, "The Association of Teacher Resourceness with Children's Characteristics," in *Do Teachers Make a Difference?* (Washington,
D.C.: U.S. Department of Health, Education, and Welfare, Office of Education, 1970).

A. SAMPLE

The data used in this study are from two subsamples of the 1965 EEO sample. The first subsample is identical to the subsample examined by Levin (1970)—597 white sixth-grade students from a large Eastern city. The second subsample consists of 458 black sixth graders from the same city. Sixth graders who had not attended the same school since the first grade are not included in the samples.

Data are aggregated as in the original EEO analysis—outcomes and individual backgrounds at the individual level and school and teacher characteristics at the school level.

B. VARIABLES

1. Exogenous

    a. Sex of student.
    b. Age of student.
    c. Index of possessions in student's home.
    d. Student's family size.
    e. Student's father's education.
    f. Student's father's occupation.
    g. Student's mother's education.
    h. Real or surrogate mother.
    i. Student's kindergarten attendance.
    j. Teacher's verbal ability score.
    k. Teacher's teaching experience.
    l. Proportion of teachers with tenure.
    m. Teacher's parents' education.
    n. Teacher's race.
    o. Teacher's years of schooling.
    p. Teacher's college major.
    q. Teacher's race preference: percent white students desired by teacher.
    r. Race discrepancy: difference between teacher's race preference and reported percentage of students who are white in the school.
    s. School tracking.
    t. Number of volumes in library.
    u. Age of school building.
    v. Adequate texts (definition unclear).
    w. Assignment (definition unclear).
    x. School facilities index: presence of cafeteria, gym, auditorium, etc.
    y. Acres of school site.
    z. Percentage of students in school (sixth grade) who score in upper quartile (national norm) on verbal ability test.
    aa. Teacher turnover rate.

bb. Four three-way interaction terms between various levels of (1) student's socioeconomic background; (2) student body socioeconomic background; and (3) composite of teacher's verbal ability and experience. (The formation and values of these interaction terms are unclear.)

  2. **Endogenous**

     a. Verbal achievement test raw score.
     b. Mathematics achievement test raw score.
     c. Reading ability test raw score.
     d. Index of student's attitudes (self-concept, control of environment).
     e. Student's grade aspiration.

C. METHODS OF ANALYSIS

Ordinary least-squares regression equations are computed separately for the white and black students, using the three achievement measures as the dependent variables. More than one equation is computed for each of the dependent variables, using different sets of independent variables. It is unclear, however, what the criteria are for the inclusion of independent variables. Results are reported in terms of regression coefficients and their *t*-statistics.

Following these ordinary least-squares regressions, a simultaneous model like Levin's (1970) is estimated using two-stage least-squares. The three endogenous variables in the simultaneous model are verbal achievement, student's attitudes, and student's grade aspiration. The two-stage equations are computed for both blacks and whites although significance levels are reported for the white subsample only.

D. PRINCIPAL CONCLUSIONS

1. For the white subsample, a total of seven different OLS regressions are presented for the three achievement outcomes. Only a very few of the exogenous variables enter all seven equations, and all those that do are individual and background characteristics. The effects of other variables are, therefore, somewhat hard to summarize.

2. For the black subsample, a total of five OLS regression equations are presented for the three achievement outcomes. It is interesting to compare the OLS results for the white and black subsamples. First the regression equations do a much better job in accounting for variance in white achievement than in black achievement. Secondly, parents' education seems to be more important for blacks than for whites. Finally, teacher characteristics show different relationships. Experience has an effect for whites but not for blacks, verbal ability likewise, and college major is associated negatively with black reading achievement but positively with white mathematics achievement.

3. The results from the simultaneous model estimated by two-stage least-squares are roughly consistent with Levin's analysis (1970). Together, these studies suggest that many of the effects found in OLS analysis may be indirect effects. For instance, consistent with Levin, Michelson finds that the number of people at home affects achievement indirectly, through its effect upon attitudes, rather than directly.

E. EVALUATION

Like Levin's work, this study is important for its use of a simultaneous model and for its comparison of 2SLS and OLS results. It is also of interest in its discussion of discrepancies between the production functions for black and white students.

The results are subject to the criticisms that apply to all results using EEO data: aggregation issues, nonresponse bias, and errors in measurement. In addition, however, the study is unclear at many points, leaving the reader uncertain about the definition of variables and the reasons underlying the formation of alternative regression equations.

XIV. Murnane (MU1, MU2, and MU3)

Richard J. Murnane, *The Impact of School Resources on the Learning of Inner City Children* (Cambridge, Mass.: Ballinger Publishing Company, 1975).

A. SAMPLE

Two cohorts of elementary school children in New Haven, Connecticut, are used in this study. One cohort was assessed at the beginning and end of both the second and third grades, and separate analyses are reported for the two grades. The second cohort was followed for one school year only, from the beginning to the end of the third grade. Sample size is about 440 students in each group. Data are for the years 1970–1972. They are taken from school records and from 1970 Census track records. The latter are used to identify average family characteristics in the block where a particular student lived. As indicated above, longitudinal data are available on all students.

To the extent possible all data concern individual students. The characteristics of individual teachers and classrooms were matched to individual students.

B. VARIABLES

1. Inputs

   a. Rating of teacher's performance by principal.
   b. Teacher's undergraduate major.

    c. Highest degree obtained by teacher.

    d. Teacher's undergraduate grade point average.

    e. Teacher's teaching experience.

    f. Teacher's race.

    g. Teacher's sex.

    h. Teacher's marital status.

    i. Student turnover within classroom.

    j. Class size.

    k. Teacher's tenure status.

    l. Mean achievement of students in classroom, measured at beginning of the year on Metropolitan Achievement Test.

    m. Standard deviation of achievement scores in classroom, measured at beginning of the year.

    n. Student's verbal achievement at beginning of year, Metropolitan Achievement Test.

    o. Student's mathematics achievement at beginning of year, Metropolitan Achievement Test.

    p. Number of days student attended school during academic year.

    q. Family living environment: dummy variable = 1 if family lives in a publicly subsidized housing project, 0 otherwise.

    r. Percentage of children in block who live in households headed by females.

    s. Percentage of rental units in block renting at less than $60 per month.

    t. Student's sex.

2. Outputs

    a. Student's verbal achievement score at end of year, Metropolitan Achievement Test.

    b. Student's mathematics achievement score at end of year, Metropolitan Achievement Test.

C. METHODS OF ANALYSIS

Murnane's first step is to analyze whether teachers make a difference in achievement. As in Hanushek's analysis (1970), for each of the three samples he tests a regression model using a series of dummy variables to represent individual teachers. All three samples reveal teacher-related differences in student achievement.

Following this, both achievement measures are regressed for each sample on prior achievement and on inputs (a), (i), (j), (l), (m), and (p) through (t). Some interactions are also tested in these regressions.

Having found effects for input (a), which is the rating of teacher by principal, new regressions are computed substituting teacher characteristics for (a). Again the contributions of some interactions are assessed.

Regression coefficients and their *t*-statistics are presented.

D. PRINCIPAL CONCLUSIONS

1. The preliminary analyses reveal achievement variations both between and within schools. Substantial variation was found between individual classrooms, especially for mathematics achievement. This analysis controls for prior achievement.

2. The following results emerge from subsequent equations:

a. When prior achievement is controlled, student background characteristics show no consistent effects.

b. The principal's evaluation of a teacher's performance relates to the teacher's actual performance, especially for mathematics achievement. Specific teacher characteristics showed little effect, however, with the exception of sex and teaching experience. The effect of teaching experience is positive over the first two years of experience, and then it diminishes.

c. Class size has no consistent effect, nor does the mean achievement of peers in the classroom.

d. Only a few of the interactions between teacher characteristics and student characteristics affect achievement significantly.

E. EVALUATION

There is very little to criticize in this study. Its use of individual data, interaction terms, longitudinal achievement measures, and nonlinear terms is to be admired. In addition, the care of analysis and presentation could well serve as a model.

XV. New York State

Bureau of School Program Evaluation, New York State Education Department;

a. *Performance Indicators in Education, Local District Results—1972* (Albany, September 1972).

b. *Performance Indicators in Education: Manual for Interpreting Local District Results for the School Years 1971—72 and 1972—73* (Albany, Spring 1974).

c. *Accounting for the Urban Factor: Inclusion of 31 New York City School Districts in 1974 Performance Indicators in Education Report* (Albany, July 1974).

d. *Does Attendance Rate Make a Difference on Reading and Arithmetic Achievement?* (Albany, August 1974).

e. *District Wealth and Student Achievement: Does a Relationship Exist?* (Albany, November 1974).

f. *Does Student Mobility Affect School District Results on Reading and Math Achievement?* (Albany, January 1975).

g. *Identifying Expenditure Variables Which Relate to Student Performance at the District Level* (Albany, January 1975).

h. *The Relationship Between Per Cent of Certified Teachers and Student Achievement in New York School Districts* (Albany, March 1975).

i. *Personal and Professional Teacher Characteristics and Student Achievement in New York State* (Albany, April 1975).

j. *Teacher Salaries and Student Achievement in New York State* (Albany, April 1975).

A. SAMPLE

The data used throughout these papers are from school districts in the state of New York. The exact number of districts used in the analysis differs from report to report. For instance, the 1972 report (a) uses data on 628 school districts, omitting the 31 districts of New York City and 5 other districts that were largest in the state. Generally, it is correct to assume that the results reported are for the 628 districts used in that first study. There are, however, exceptions to this rule. For instance, the July 1974 report (c) explicitly includes the New York City districts in the analysis.

Most data were collected from state and district records by solicitation from the State Education Department. In addition, some of the socioeconomic data are 1970 Census results, broken down by school districts. As will be apparent, data on many of the variables were gathered for more than one year. Thus, the achievement scores used in the analyses range in time from 1966 to 1973.

It should be mentioned that this research is unique in the literature reviewed in this volume. Its purpose was to provide school districts in New York with comparative information that could be used to evaluate the districts' performance. Only secondarily are these papers concerned with the theoretical questions of educational production.

B. VARIABLES

1. Inputs

a. Full tax valuation, 1968: the tax valuation of the district per enrolled pupil in 1968.

b. Pupil ethnicity, 1970: proportion of minority pupils in the third grade in 1970.

c. Enrollment, grades one to twelve, 1968.

d. Enrollment growth, 1970.

e. Enrollment stability, 1970.

f. Enrollment density, 1968: square miles of district per pupil.

g. Total district population, 1970: U.S. Census.

h. Percentage of district population that is rural, 1970: U.S. Census.

i. Percentage of children under 18 in district living in two-parent families, 1970: U.S. Census.

j. Percentage of district's dwelling units that are owner-occupied, 1970: U.S. Census.

k. Percentage of district population living 1.01 persons per room or more, 1970: U.S. Census.

l. Percentage of district population living in units lacking some plumbing, 1970: U.S. Census.

m. State aid to district education: a ratio of state aid to total district expenditure.

n. Ratio of district average daily attendance to district total enrollment, 1971.

o. Student mobility, 1972; percentage of students transferring.

p. Total district expenditure per pupil, 1970.

q. Expenditure on "regular day instruction" per pupil, 1970.

r. Expenditure on teachers per pupil, 1970.

s. Expenditure on central administration per pupil, 1970.

t. Expenditure on principals per pupil, 1970.

u. Expenditure on supervisors per pupil, 1970.

v. Percentage of teachers certified, 1970.

w. Median teacher's age, 1971.

x. Median teacher's teaching experience, 1971.

y. Percentage of teachers married, 1971.

z. Percentage of teachers male, 1971.

aa. Percentage of teachers having graduate training, 1971.

bb. Median teacher's salary, 1971.

cc. Mean first-grade readiness score, tests of New York State Pupil Evaluation Program (PEP).

dd. Standard deviation of first-grade readiness scores, PEP tests.

ee. Mean of third-grade reading and arithmetic scores, PEP tests.

ff. Standard deviations of third-grade reading and arithmetic scores, PEP tests.

gg. Mean change, grades 1 to 3, reading and arithmetic scores, PEP tests.

2. Outputs

a. Mean third-grade reading score, PEP tests; and subtests on (1) word knowledge and (2) reading comprehension.

b. Mean sixth-grade reading score, PEP tests; and same two subtests.

c. Mean third-grade arithmetic score, PEP tests; and subtests on (1) arithmetic concepts, (2) arithmetic computation, and (3) arithmetic problem solving.

d. Mean sixth-grade arithmetic score, PEP tests; and same three subtests.

e. Mean gain in reading, grades 3 to 6, PEP tests.

f. Mean gain in arithmetic, grades 3 to 6, PEP tests.

Given the goals of this set of reports and the variety of variables used, a simple description of the methods employed in the analysis is difficult. It is perhaps easiest to discuss the methods of the 1972 report (a) first and then to deal with the remaining nine reports as a group, for these employ similar techniques.

The 1972 report (a) assesses the relationship between socioeconomic indicators of the districts (inputs a through f) and the outcomes when prior achievement levels (inputs cc through gg) are controlled. No teacher or school characteristics are examined in the regression model. Regression coefficients are presented without significance levels.

The later reports assess the variance explained in achievement by teacher characteristics, fiscal resources, and student mobility and attendance rates when socioeconomic indicators are controlled. Prior achievement levels are generally not controlled. Results are reported in terms of the unique variance explained by (contribution to R^2 of) each of the inputs.

D. PRINCIPAL CONCLUSIONS

The 1972 report explores the relationships between socioeconomic indicators and achievement, controlling for prior achievement. District tax value and pupil ethnicity show consistent relationships to achievement across outcomes; the other socioeconomic indicators do not.

The following conclusions emerge from the later reports:

1. District attendance rates do not uniquely explain variance in achievement when socioeconomic indicators are controlled.

2. Student mobility rates explain unique variance in achievement only for mathematics achievement.

3. The expenditure inputs (p through u) explain some unique variance in mathematics achievement but not in other areas of achievement. Comparative contributions among these inputs cannot be made since regression coefficients are not presented.

4. Some teacher inputs (v through bb) uniquely explain variance. Again, however, meaningful comparisons within this set of inputs cannot be made because of the analytic procedure.

E. EVALUATION

The primary strength of these reports lies in their evaluative utility for New York school districts. As an evaluative tool, the research is quite commendable. As research toward the goal of understanding education production, these reports are rather uneven.

The major shortcoming of this research lies in its attempts to look at the effects of teacher and school characteristics (fiscal policy especially) upon achievement. Here, because of multicollinearity among variables, the addition to R^2 criterion is inadequate. Other problems include the inconsistent use of prior achievement measures and the exclusive reliance upon data at the district level.

XVI. Perl (P)

Lewis J. Perl, "Family Background, Secondary School Expenditures, and Student Ability," *Journal of Human Resources*, 8 (1973), 156–180.

A. SAMPLE

The sample used in this study is drawn from male high school students who participated in the 1960 Project Talent Survey, a national survey of high school seniors. All males in the original 1960 sample were sent follow-up questionnaires one and five years after their graduation in 1960. A total of 26,000 male students responded to these follow-up questionnaires. From this sample, Perl used a systematic sampling procedure to select every fifth student for inclusion in his subsample. Because of missing data, the sample size was further reduced to 3,265 students.

Achievement measures and family background variables are measured at the individual level. Teacher and school characteristics, which were gathered from principals' questionnaire responses, are all aggregated at the level of the school.

B. VARIABLES

1. Inputs

 a. Student's family income.
 b. Student's father's education.
 c. School mean family income.
 d. Standard deviation of family income for school.
 e. Number of days in school year.
 f. Average class size in science courses.
 g. Average class size in nonscience courses.
 h. Starting salary for teacher with B.A. degree.
 i. Percentage of teachers who are male.
 j. Percentage of teaching time spent by teacher outside of his/her area of specialization.
 k. Average teacher's teaching experience.
 l. Percentage of teachers with M.A.
 m. Percentage of teachers with Ph.D.
 n. Percentage of teachers certified.
 o. Age of school building.
 p. Number of volumes in school library.
 q. School enrollment.
 r. Expenditure per pupil.

2. Outputs

 a. Composite achievement index of abstract reasoning.
 b. Composite achievement index of general information and verbal ability.

C. METHODS OF ANALYSIS

Project Talent administered a large number of achievement tests to its sample of high school seniors. Because of the generally high correlations between these tests, Perl undertakes a factor analysis of output measures. Two primary factors emerge from this analysis. Students' scores on these factors are employed as the dependent variables.

Regression equations are computed for both outcome variables, regressed on all eighteen inputs plus enrollment (input q) squared. Equations are computed for the entire sample and for two family income strata. Regression coefficients and their significance levels are reported.

D. PRINCIPAL CONCLUSIONS

1. Father's education is consistently related to achievement scores, whereas family income seems to affect low income students only and on the second achievement measure only.

2. Mean family income of the student body is consistently related to achievement. The size of the relationship seems to be larger for higher income students.

3. The effects of class size are contradictory though generally it seems to exert a larger impact on the achievement of low income students. Total enrollment (and its square) is consistently unrelated to outcomes.

4. The only teacher variable consistently related to achievement is the percentage of time that teachers spend in their specialty, and this is found for high income students only. Teacher's sex seems to have an impact for low income students on the first output measure.

5. The school facilities proxy, number of library volumes, is positively related to achievement only for high income students.

6. Even when many expenditure items (e.g., teachers' salaries, experience, and degree level) and student's socioeconomic background are controlled for, expenditure per pupil shows a highly significant relationship to student achievement.

E. EVALUATION

This study is well designed and executed. However, the following potential problems do exist:

1. The Project Talent data base is particularly susceptible to criticism because of high nonresponse rates. Lower achieving students are substantially underrepresented.

2. There are no longitudinal achievement inputs included.

3. The school measures are possibly inadequate—there are only two of them. Furthermore, the reliability of some measures might be questioned as they are all gathered from questionnaires to principals.

4. The school level aggregation minimizes the estimates of school and teacher effects by masking within-school variance.

XVII. Summers and Wolfe (S&W1, S&W2, and S&W3)

Anita A. Summers, and Barbara L. Wolfe, (a) "Equality of Educational Opportunity Quantified: A Production Function Approach." Paper presented at the winter meetings of the Econometric Society, December 1974; (b) "Do Schools Make a Difference?" *American Economic Review*, 67 (1977), 639–652.

A. SAMPLE

The samples consist of 627 sixth-grade students from 103 elementary schools in Philadelphia, 553 eighth-grade students from 42 junior high schools in Philadelphia, and 716 twelfth-grade students from five senior high schools in Philadelphia. The elementary and junior high schools were randomly selected from the population of Philadelphia schools; the senior high schools were not. Within schools, students at all three levels were randomly selected for inclusion in the samples. All data date from the school year 1971–1972 and from the immediately preceding years.

From school and district files, data were gathered on the educational history of individual students. Achievement was measured at the level of the individual student, and students were matched with their individual teachers. Student background variables are measured using block estimates from the 1970 Census. School facility variables are assessed at the individual school level.

B. VARIABLES

1. Inputs

    a. Student's race.

    b. Mean income for block in which student resides.

    c. Student's sex.

    d. Student's prior achievement: grade equivalent scores.

        1. First-grade score on Philadelphia Verbal Ability Test.

        2. Third-grade score on Iowa Test of Basic Skills.

        3. Sixth-grade score on Iowa Test of Basic Skills.

        4. Seventh-grade score on Iowa Test of Basic Skills.

        5. Ninth-grade percentile score on Cooperative School and College Abilities Test.

    e. Student's average number of unexcused absences per year over three years.

    f. Student's average number of latenesses per year over three years.

    g. Student's average number of days present during school year over three years.

    h. Total number of residential moves by student over three years.

i. Native-born American: dummy variable = 1 if student born in United States, 0 otherwise.

j. Mean class size: consists of two dummy variables.

1. Class ≥ 34; dummy variable = 1 if size ≥ 34, 0 otherwise.

2. Class 28–33; dummy variable = 1 if size ≥ 28 but ≤ 33, 0 otherwise.

k. Size of school: number of pupils enrolled.

l. Headstart participation: dummy variable = 1 if participated (for sixth-grade students only).

m. Number of pupils per science laboratory (for twelfth-grade students only).

n. Playground footage per pupil (for sixth-grade students only).

o. Rating of general physical condition of school building.

p. Age of school building.

q. Library books per pupil.

r. Total expenditure per pupil.

s. Total expenditure on counseling.

t. Total expenditure on remedial education.

u. Principal's experience (number of years).

v. Principal's education credits beyond M.A.

w. Principal's degree status.

x. Teacher's experience.

y. Teacher's score on National Teacher's exam.

z. Teacher's score on test in area of specialty.

aa. Rating of teacher's undergraduate college.

bb. Teacher's extra education credits beyond B.A.

cc. Teacher's race.

dd. Percentage of teachers in school who are black.

ee. Percentage of students in school who are black.

ff. Percentage of students in school who scored above 84th national percentile on achievement test.

gg. Percentage of students in school who scored below 16th national percentile on achievement test.

hh. Average high school dropout rate (twelfth grade only).

ii. Average income, school feeder area (1970).

jj. Number of disruptive incidents in school per year.

2. Outputs

For each sample, the difference between current achievement and prior achievement on a composite achievement test was used as the outcome measure. For the sixth-grade sample, the difference score was the sixth-grade Iowa Test grade equivalent score minus the third-grade score. For the eighth-grade sample, the difference between the eighth-grade and sixth-grade Iowa scores was used. For the twelfth-grade sample, the difference was between the twelfth-grade national percentile score on the California Aptitude Test and the ninth-grade national percentile score on the Cooperative School and College Abilities Test.

C. METHODS OF ANALYSIS

The three dependent change score measures were regressed upon various independent variables. The reasons for the inclusion or exclusion of independent variables in the various equations are not made explicit. Presumably, variables were eliminated if their regression coefficients were not significant, and then the equations were recomputed. However, this presumption is not borne out in full because the final equations include some variables whose regression coefficients do not attain significance levels.

Even though change scores are used as the dependent measures, prior achievement measures are included as inputs. Thus, the sixth- minus third-grade equation uses first- and third-grade achievement as inputs; the eighth- minus sixth-grade equation uses third- and sixth-grade achievement as inputs; and the twelfth- minus ninth-grade equation uses seventh- and ninth-grade achievement as inputs.

Numerous interaction terms are tested in the equations. These are usually interactions between students' prior achievement, race, and income, on the one hand, and teacher and school characteristics, on the other. Some nonlinear relationships are also assessed; for instance, the percentage of students in the school who are black is entered as a two-piece linear variable in the eighth-grade equation and as a three-piece linear variable in the sixth-grade equation.

Regression coefficients and their t-statistics are reported.

D. PRINCIPAL CONCLUSIONS

Given the complexity of the data and the number of inputs tested in the regression models, it is difficult to summarize succinctly the conclusions reached by Summers and Wolfe.

One conclusion that is important is that many of the interaction terms between student characteristics and teacher or school variables have significant regression coefficients. Thus, the study demonstrates that various school and teacher inputs have different effects upon different segments of the student population.

E. EVALUATION

The analysis by Summers and Wolfe is praiseworthy on a number of grounds. First, rich data are available on individual students. A host of constructs are measured, and individual students are matched with teachers and schools. Secondly, the data are longitudinal in nature, thus permitting extensive use of prior achievement controls. Thirdly, many student by school or teacher interactions are assessed.

Unfortunately, it is difficult to conclude a great deal from the interesting analysis and rich data for two reasons. First, the theoretical rationale for the regression models constructed is not presented. As we have indicated, the inclusion or exclusion of specific inputs is not justified. Secondly, certain discrepancies have been found to exist between the regression statistics presented and the discussion of findings by the authors, particularly in the earlier presentation of the data.

XVIII. Wiley (WY)

David E. Wiley, "Another Hour, Another Day: Quantity of Schooling, a Potent Path for Policy," in W.H. Sewell, R.M. Hauser, and D.L. Featherman, Eds., *Schooling and Achievement in American Society* (New York: Academic Press, 1976).

A. SAMPLE

The sample consists of sixth-grade children in the Detroit Metropolitan Area who participated in the EEO survey. The EEO data were collected in 1965.

Individual student data are available for outcome measures and family background characteristics. School characteristics are aggregated at the school level.

B. VARIABLES

1. Inputs

a. Average daily attendance of school attended by student, as a proportion of enrollment.
b. Number of hours in the school day.
c. Number of days in the school year.
d. Student's race.
e. Number of children in student's family.
f. Number of possessions in student's home.

2. Outputs

a. Verbal ability raw score.
b. Reading comprehension raw score.
c. Mathematics achievement raw score.

C. METHODS OF ANALYSIS

Wiley is primarily interested in the effect of quantity of schooling, for which he derives an index from the product of the first three inputs. This index is a school level variable while achievement is measured at the individual level. Through analyses of variance and covariance, Wiley examines both within- and between-school variance in achievement. He then derives a predicted outcome measure for each student based upon the family background characteristics (inputs d through f). Finally, he regresses each of the three outcome measures upon his effective quantity of schooling index (transformed into natural logarithmic values) and upon the predicted outcome measure.

Details of the analyses of variance and covariance are presented, as are regression coefficients and their standard errors from the last analysis.

D. PRINCIPAL CONCLUSIONS

1. Quantity of schooling emerges as a substantial determinant of achievement for all three outcome measures.

2. The aggregation inconsistencies in much of the literature on educational production make the traditional analyses problematic.

E. EVALUATION

Given the limited objectives, this is a remarkably well-conducted study. The analysis is relatively complex, but then so are the analytic issues with which it attempts to deal. The conclusions are both well documented and justified.

XIX. Winkler (W1 and W2)

Donald R. Winkler, "Education Achievement and School Peer Group Composition," *Journal of Human Resources*, 10 (1975), 189–205.

A. SAMPLE

The two samples consist of 388 black students and 385 white students chosen from the secondary schools of a large urban school district in California during 1964–1965. Extensive longitudinal achievement records were available on each student from district records. Additional longitudinal data relating to teacher characteristics, school characteristics, and student body variables are also used. Student family background variables are measured by a questionnaire completed by the student.

The various student achievement and family background measures are all available on individual students. Student body, school, and teacher variables all represent school aggregates.

B. VARIABLES

1. Inputs

a. Initial achievement level: student's first-grade percentile score on the California Mental Maturity Test.

b. Number of cultural items in student's home: index based upon student's indication of presence/absence in home of musical instrument, map of United States, daily newspaper, news weekly, encyclopedia, books.

c. Number of siblings in student's home.

d. Home ownership: dummy variable = 1 if student's parents own home.

e. Aggregate expenditure per pupil on administrators and guidance counselors, for schools attended grades 1 to 8.

f. Aggregate monthly expenditure on teachers' salaries, for schools attended grades 1 to 8.

g. Aggregate student-teacher ratio, for schools attended grades 1 to 8.

h. Proportion of teachers encountered by student in grades 7 and 8 from "prestigious colleges" (mainly Stanford and University of California, Berkeley).

i. Proportion of school peers of low socioeconomic backgrounds, for schools attended grades 1 to 8.

j. Change in socioeconomic status of school peers: proportion low status students in junior high school minus proportion low status students in elementary school.

k. Proportion of school peers who are black, for schools attended grades 1 to 6.

l. Change in racial composition of school peers: proportion black in junior high school minus proportion black in elementary school.

2. Outputs

a. Student's sixth-grade percentile score on the Stanford Reading Test.

b. Student's eighth-grade percentile score on the Stanford Reading Test.

C. METHODS OF ANALYSIS

Separate regression equations are presented for each dependent measure for the black and white students. With the exception of independent variables (j) through (l), all variables are included in all regressions; these last are added to various regressions to observe the effects of their inclusion on other variables.

Following the calculation of these regressions, a further regression equation is presented for blacks to determine whether the effect found for change in racial composition of peer group (input l) was due to students going to more integrated or less integrated schools.

Regression coefficients and their standard errors are reported.

D. PRINCIPAL CONCLUSIONS

1. Teacher's salary is consistently related to achievement for both samples, though the relationship is stronger in the case of white students.

2. Teacher's attendance at a prestigious college is consistently related to achievement for both samples.

3. Socioeconomic composition of peer group and racial composition of peer group are related to white achievement (the former is negative in direction, the latter positive), but they are not consistently related to black achievement.

4. The change in socioeconomic composition of peers from elementary to junior high schools is unrelated to differences in achievement.

5. The change in racial composition of peers from elementary to junior high schools is related to achievement for blacks but not for whites. The coefficients here indicate that the transfer of a black student from a segregated elementary school to a more integrated junior high school has an adverse effect upon his or her achievement.[3]

E. EVALUATION

Winkler's analysis is valuable for its detailed treatment of student body effects upon achievement. The length of longitudinal information on each student, permitting the assessment of changes in peer group composition, is unique in the educational production function literature.

The shortcomings of the study are few in number. First, it is unfortunate that more teacher and school characteristics were not included in the analysis. Secondly, the aggregation procedure for teacher characteristics is rather confusing and does not permit the assessment of within-school differences in teachers.

3. Note our discussion of this effect in Chapter 8.

References

Anastasi, A. 1976. *Psychological Testing, 4th ed.* New York: Macmillan.

Armor, D.J. 1972. "The Evidence on Busing." *The Public Interest* 28: 90–126.

Averch, H.A., Carroll, S.J., Donaldson, T.S., Kiesling, H.J., and Pincus, J. 1974. *How Effective Is Schooling? A Critical Review and Synthesis of Research Findings.* Englewood Cliffs, N.J.: Educational Technology Publications.

Battle, E., and Rotter, J.B. 1963. "Children's Feelings of Personal Control as Related to Social Class and Ethnic Groups." *Journal of Personality* 31: 482–490.

Bidwell, C.E., and Kasarda, J.D. 1975. "School District Organization and Student Achievement." *American Sociological Review* 40: 55–70.

Blake, H.E. 1954. *Class Size: A Summary of Selected Studies in Elementary and Secondary Public Schools.* New York: Teachers College, 1954.

Bloom, B.S. 1976. *Human Characteristics and School Learning.* New York: McGraw-Hill.

Bloom, B.S. 1974. "Time and Learning." *American Psychologist* 29: 682–288.

Bloom, B.S., Hastings, T.S., and Madaus, G.F. 1971. *Handbook of Formative and Summative Evaluation of Student Learning.* New York: McGraw-Hill.

Bowlby, J. 1969. *Attachment and Loss, vol. 1; Attachment.* New York: Basic Books.

Bowles, S.S. 1970. "Towards an Educational Production Function." In *Education, Income, and Human Capital*, edited by W.L. Hansen. New York: Columbia University Press.

Bowles, S.S. 1969. *Educational Production Function: Final Report.* Washington, D.C.: U.S. Department of Health, Education, and Welfare, Office of Education.

Bowles, S.S., and Levin, H.M. 1968. "The Determinants of Scholastic Achievement—An Appraisal of Some Recent Evidence." *Journal of Human Resources* 3: 393—400.

Box, G.E.P., and Jenkins, G.M. 1970. *Time Series Analysis Forecasting and Control.* San Francisco: Holden-Day.

Bridge, R.G. 1974. *Nonresponse Bias in Mail Surveys.* Santa Monica, Calif.: Rand Corporation.

Bridge, R.G. 1971. "Internal-External Control and Seat Belt Use." Paper presented at the meetings of the Western Psychological Association, San Francisco, Calif., April.

Bridge, R.G., and Blackman, J. 1978. *A Study of Alternatives in American Education: Family Choice in Schooling.* Santa Monica, Calif.: Rand Corporation.

Bronfenbrenner, U. 1974. "Is Early Intervention Effective?" *Teachers College Record* 76: 279—303.

Brown, B.W., and Saks, D.H. 1978. *Production Technologies and Resource Allocations within Classroom and Schools: Theory and Measurement.* Chicago: Educational Finance and Productivity Center, Department of Education, University of Chicago.

Brown, B.W., and Saks, D.H. 1975. "The Production and Distribution of Cognitive Skills within Schools." *Journal of Political Economy* 83: 571—593.

Burkhead, J., Fox, T.G., and Holland, J.W. 1967. *Input and Output in Large-City High Schools.* Syracuse, N.Y.: Syracuse University Press.

Cain, G.G., and Watts, H.W. 1970. "Problems in Making Policy Inferences from the Coleman Report." *American Sociological Review* 35: 228—242.

Campbell, D.T. 1969. "Reforms as Experiments." *American Psychologist* 24: 409—429.

Campbell, D.T., and Fiske, D.W. 1959 "Convergent and Discriminant Validation by the Multitrait-Multimethod Matrix." *Psychological Bulletin* 56: 81—105.

Campbell, D.T., and Stanley, J.C. 1966. *Experimental and Quasi-experimental Designs for Research.* Chicago: Rand-McNally.

Carroll, J.B. 1963. "A Model for School Learning." *Teachers College Record* 64: 723—733.

Cochran, W.G. 1963. *Sampling Techniques, 2nd ed.* New York: John Wiley.

Cohen, J. 1970. *Statistical Power Analysis for the Behavioral Sciences.* New York: Academic Press.

Cohen J. 1968. "Multiple Regression as a General Data Analytic System." *Psychological Bulletin* 70: 426—443.

Cohen, J., and Cohen, P. 1975. *Applied Multiple Regression: Correlation Analysis for the Behavioral Sciences.* New York: Halsted Press.

Cohn, E. 1968. "Economies of Scale in Iowa High School Operations." *Journal of Human Resources* 4: 422—434.

Cohn, E., and Millman, S.D. 1975. *Input-Output Analysis in Public Education.* Cambridge, Mass.: Ballinger Publishing Company.

Coleman, J.S. 1970. "Reply to Cain and Watts." *American Sociological Review* 35: 228—242.

Coleman, J.S., Campbell, E.Q., Hobson, C.F., McPartland, J., Mood, A.M., Weinfeld, F.D., and York, R.L. 1966. *Equality of Educational Opportunity.* Washington, D.C.: U.S. Department of Health, Education, and Welfare, Office of Education, U.S. Government Printing Office.

Collins, B.E. 1974. "Four Separate Components of the Rotter I-E Scale: Belief in a Difficult World, a Just World, a Predictable World, and a Politically Responsive World." *Journal of Personality and Social Psychology* 29: 381–391.

Cook, T.D., ed. 1978. *Evaluation Studies Review Annual, vol. 3.* Beverly Hills, Calif.: Sage Publications.

Cook, T.D., and Campbell, D.T. 1976. "The Design and Conduct of Quasi-experiments and True Experiments in Field Settings." In the *Handbook of Industrial and Organizational Psychology*, edited by M. Dunnette, pp. 223–326. Chicago: Rand-McNally.

Crain, R.L., and Mahard, R.E. 1977. "Desegregation and Black Achievement." Paper presented at the conference on Social Science and Law in Desegregation, Amelia Island, Florida, October.

Crandall, V.C., Katkovsky, W., and Crandall, V.J. 1965. "Children's Beliefs in Their Control of Reinforcements in Intellectual Academic Achievement Behaviors." *Child Development* 36: 91–109.

Cremin, L.A. 1977. *Traditions of American Education.* New York: Basic Books.

Cronbach, L.J. 1976. *Research on Classrooms and Schools: Formulation of Questions, Design, and Analysis.* Stanford, Calif.: Occasional Paper of the Stanford Evaluation Consortium, School of Education, Stanford University.

Cronbach, L.J. 1970. *Essentials of Psychological Testing, 3rd ed.* New York: Harper and Row.

Cronbach, L.J., and Snow, R.E. 1977. *Aptitudes and Instructional Methods: A Handbook for Research on Interactions.* New York: Irvington Publishers.

Davies, D. 1976. "Harnessing the Testing Machine." In *Citizen Action in Education.* Boston: Institute for Responsive Education.

Duncan, O.D. 1975. *Introduction to Structural Equation Models.* New York: Academic Press.

Duncan, O.D. 1961. "A Socioeconomic Index for All Occupations." In *Occupations and Social Status*, edited by A.J. Reiss et al., pp. 109–138. New York: Free Press.

Durost, W.N., Bixler, H.H., Wrightstone, J.W., Prescott, G.A., and Balow, I.H. 1971. *Teachers Handbook, Metropolitan Achievement Tests.* New York: Harcourt, Brace, Jovanovich.

Edwards, A.J. 1972. *Individual Mental Testing: Part II: Measurement.* Scranton, Penn.: Intext Educational Publishers.

Erikson, E.H. 1963. *Childhood and Society, 2nd ed.* New York: W.W. Norton.

Farrar, D.E., and Glauber, R.R. 1967. "Multicollinearity in Regression Analysis: The Problem Revisited." *Review of Economics and Statistics* 49: 92–107.

Friedman, M. 1953. "The Methodology of Positive Economics." In *Essays in Positive Economics*, edited by M. Friedman. Chicago: Chicago University Press.

Furth, H,G. 1970. *Piaget for Teachers.* Englewood Cliffs, N.J.: Prentice-Hall.

Galton, F. 1869. *Hereditary Genius: An Inquiry into Its Laws and Consequences.* New York: D. Appleton and Co.

Garner, W.T. 1978. "The Public Economics of Mastery Learning." *Educational Technology* 18: 12–17.

Garner, W.T. 1973. "The Identification of an Educational Production Function by Experimental Means." Ph.D. dissertation. University of Chicago.

Goldberg, M., Passow, A.H., and Justman, J. 1966. *The Effects of Ability Grouping.* New York: Teachers College Press.

Gore, P.S., and Rotter, J.B. 1963. "A Personality Correlate of Social Action." *Journal of Personality* 31: 58–64.

Gray, P.H. 1958. "Theory and Evidence of Imprinting in Human Infants." *Journal of Psychology* 46: 155–166.

Gurin, P., Gurin, G., Lao, R.C., and Beattie, M. 1969. "Internal-External Control in the Motivational Dynamics of Negro Youth." *Journal of Social Issues* 25: 29–53.

Guttentag, M., ed. 1977. *Evaluation Studies Review Annual, vol. 2.* Beverly Hills, Calif.: Sage Publications.

Guttentag, M., ed. 1976. *Evaluation Studies Review Annual, vol. 1.* Beverly Hills, Calif.: Sage Publications.

Hanushek, E.A. 1972. *Education and Race: An Analysis of the Educational Production Process.* Lexington, Mass.: Lexington Books.

Hanushek, E.A., and Kain, J.F. 1972. "On the Value of *Equality of Educational Opportunity* as a Guide for Public Policy." In *On Equality of Educational Opportunity*, edited by F. Mosteller and D.P. Moynihan. New York: Vintage Books.

Harcourt, Brace, Jovanovich. 1973. *The Effect of Separate Answer Document Use on Achievement Test Performance of Grade 3 and 4 Pupils.* New York: Harcourt, Brace, Jovanovich, Test Department, Report No. 24.

Harvey, O.J., Hunt, D.E., and Schroder, H.M. 1961. *Conceptual Systems and Personality Organization.* New York: John Wiley.

Heise, D.R. 1975. *Causal Analysis.* New York: John Wiley.

Herrnstein, R.J. 1973. *IQ in the Meritocracy.* Boston: Little, Brown and Company.

Hess, E.H. 1973. *Imprinting: Early Experience and the Developmental Psychobiology of Attachment.* New York: D. Van Nostrand.

Hill, R.C., and Stafford, F.P. 1974. "Time Inputs to Children." In *5000 American Families: Patterns of Economic Progress, vol. 2,* edited by J.N. Morgan, pp. 319–344. Ann Arbor, Mich.: Institute for Social Research.

Hinde, R.A. 1970. *Animal Behavior: A Synthesis of Ethology and Comparative Psychology, 2nd ed.* New York: McGraw-Hill.

Hunt, D.E. 1971. *Matching Models in Education.* Toronto: The Ontario Institute for Education, Monograph Series 10.

Hunt, D.E. 1975. "Person-Environment Interactions: A Challenge Found Wanting Before It Was Tried." *Review of Educational Research* 45: 209–230.

Hunt, D.E., and Sullivan, E.V. 1974. *Between Psychology and Education.* Hinsdale, Ill.: Dryden.

James, W.H. 1957. "Internal versus External Control of Reinforcement as a Basic Variable in Learning Theory." Ph.D. dissertation, Ohio State University.

Jamison, D.T., Suppes, P.C., and Wells, S.J. 1974. "The Effectiveness of Alternative Instructional Media: A Survey." *Review of Educational Research* 44: 1–67.

Jencks, C.S., Smith, M., Acland, H., Bane, M.J., Cohen, D.K., Gintis, H., Heyns, B., and Michelson, S. 1972. *Inequality: A Reassessment of the Effect of Family and Schooling in America.* New York: Basic Books.

Jensen, A. 1969. "How Much Can We Boost IQ and Scholastic Achievement?" *Harvard Educational Review* 39: 1–123.

Jessen, R. 1978. *Statistical Survey Techniques.* New York: John Wiley.

Jinks, J.L., and Fulker, D.W. 1970. "Comparison of Biometrical Genetical, MAVA, and Classical Approaches to the Analysis of Human Behavior." *Psychological Bulletin* 73: 311–349.

Johnson, G.E., and Stafford, F.P. 1973. "Social Returns to Quantity and Quality of Schooling." *Journal of Human Resources* 8, 139–155.

Johnston, J. 1972. *Econometric Methods*, 2nd ed. New York: McGraw-Hill.

Jones, E.E. 1964. *Ingratiation: A Social Psychological Analysis.* New York: Irvington.

Kamii, C., and DeVries, R. 1976. *Piaget, Children and Number.* National Association for Child Education.

Kamin, L. 1974. *The Science and Politics of I.Q.* Potomac, Maryland: Lawrence Erlbaum Associates (Wiley).

Kane, E.J. 1968. *Economic Statistics and Econometrics: An Introduction to Quantitative Economics.* New York: Harper and Row.

Karweit, N. 1976. "A Reanalysis of the Effect of Quantity of Schooling on Achievement." *Sociology of Education* 49: 236–246.

Katz, I. 1964. "Review of Evidence Relating to Effects of Desegregation on the Intellectual Performance of Negroes." *American Psychologist* 19: 381–399.

Katz, I., Henchy, T., and Allen, H. 1968. "Effects of Race of Tester, Approval-Disapproval, and Need on Negro Children's Learning." *Journal of Personality and Social Psychology* 8: 38–42.

Katzman, M.T. 1971. *The Political Economy of Urban Schools.* Cambridge, Mass.: Harvard University Press.

Kenny, D. 1979. *Correlation and Causation.* New York: Wiley-Interscience.

Kerlinger, F.N., and Pedhazur, E.J. 1973. *Multiple Regression in Behavioral Research.* New York: Holt, Rinehart and Winston.

Kiesling, H.J. 1970. *The Study of Cost and Quality of New York School Districts: Final Report.* Washington, D.C.: U.S. Department of Health, Education, and Welfare, Office of Education.

Kiesling, H.J. 1969. *The Relationship of School Inputs to Public School Performance in New York State.* Washington, D.C.: U.S. Department of Health, Education, and Welfare, Office of Education.

Kish, L. 1965. *Survey Sampling.* New York: John Wiley.

Kmenta, J. 1971. *Elements of Econometrics.* New York: Macmillan.

Kohn, M. 1969. *Class and Conformity.* Homewood, Ill.: Dorsey-Irwin.

Koran, M.L. 1969. "The Effects of Individual Differences in Observational Learning in the Acquisition of a Teaching Skill." Ph.D. dissertation, Stanford University.

Lane, R.E., and Sears, D.O. 1964. *Public Opinion.* Englewood Cliffs, N.J.: Prentice-Hall.

Lefcourt, H.M. 1966. "Internal-External Control of Reinforcement: A Review." *Psychological Bulletin* 65: 206–220.

Lefcourt, H.M., and Ladwig, G.W. 1966. "Alienation in Negro and White Reformatory Inmates." *Journal of Social Psychology* 68: 152–157.

Lefcourt, H.M., and Ladwig, G.W. 1965. "The American Negro: A Problem in Expectancies." *Journal of Personality and Social Psychology* 1: 377–380.

Leibowitz, A. 1974. "Education and Home Production." *American Economic Review* 64: 243–250.

Lessing, E.E. 1969. "Racial Differences in Indices of Ego Function Relevant to Academic Achievement." *Journal of Genetic Psychology* 115: 153–167.

Levin, H.M. 1971. "A Cost-Effectiveness Analysis of Teacher Selection." In *Economics and Education: Principles and Applications*, edited by D.C. Rogers and H.S. Ruchlin, pp. 134–140. New York: The Free Press.

Levin, H.M. 1970. "A New Model of School Effectiveness." In *Do Teachers Make a Difference? A Report on Recent Research on Pupil Achievement.* Washington, D.C.: U.S. Department of Health, Education, and Welfare, Office of Education, Bureau of Educational Personnel Development.

Lewis, M. 1976. "What Do We Mean When We Say 'Infant Intelligence Scores'?: A Sociopolitical Question." In *Origins of Intelligence*, edited by M. Lewis, pp. 1–17. New York: Plenum Press.

Linden, K.W., and Linden, J.D. 1968. *Modern Mental Measurement: A Historical Perspective.* Boston: Houghton-Mifflin.

Link, C.R., and Ratledge, E.C. 1975. "Social Returns to Quantity and Quality of Education: A Further Statement." *Journal of Human Resources* 10: 78–89.

Loehlin, J.C., Lindzey, G., and Spuhler, J.N. 1975. *Race Differences in Intelligence.* San Francisco: W.H. Freeman.

Lundy, J.R. 1972. "Some Correlates of Contraceptive Use." *Journal of Psychology* 80: 9–14.

McCall, R.B. 1974. "Toward an Epigenetic Conception of Mental Development in the First Three Years of Life." In *Origins of Intelligence*, edited by M. Lewis, pp. 97–122. New York: Plenum Press.

MacDonald, A.P. 1970. "Internal-External Locus of Control and the Practice of Birth Control." *Psychological Reports* 27: 206.

McGuire, W.J. 1969. "The Nature of Attitudes and Attitude Change." In *Handbook of Social Psychology*, vol. 2, edited by G. Lindzey and E. Aronson, pp. 136–314. Reading, Ma.: Addison-Wesley.

McKenna, B. 1977. "What Is Wrong with Standardized Testing?" *Today's Education* March/April: 36.

Maracek, J. and Mettee, D.R. 1972. "Avoidance of Continued Success as a Function of Self-esteem Certainty, and Responsibility for Success." *Journal of Personality and Social Psychology* 22: 98–107.

Mayeske, G.W., Cohen, W.M., Wisler, C.E., Okada, T., Beaton, A.E., Jr., Proshek, J.M., Weinfeld, F.D., and Tabler, K.A. 1972. *A Study of our Nation's Schools.* Washington, D.C.: U.S. Department of Health, Education, and Welfare, Office of Education, DHEW OE–72–142.

Mayeske, G.W., and Beaton, A.E., Jr. 1975. *Special Studies of Our Nation's Students.* Washington, D.C.: U.S. Department of Health, Education, and Welfare, Office of Education.

Mayeske, G.W., Okada, T., Beaton, A.E., Jr., Cohen, W.M., and Wisler, C.E. 1973a. *A Study of the Achievement of Our Nation's Students.* Washington, D.C.: U.S. Department of Health, Education, and Welfare, Office of Education, DHEW OE–72–131.

Mayeske, G.W., Okada, T., and Beaton, A.E., Jr. 1973b. *A Study of the Attitude Toward Life of Our Nation's Students.* Washington, D.C.: U.S. Department of Health, Education, and Welfare, Office of Education, DHEW OE–73–01700.

Michelson, S. 1970. "The Association of Teacher Resourceness with Children's Characteristics." In *Do Teachers Make a Difference? A Report on Recent Research on Pupil Achievement.* Washington, D.C.: U.S. Department of Health, Education, and Welfare, Office of Education, Bureau of Educational Personnel Development.

Mischel, W., Zeiss, R., and Zeiss, A. 1974. "Internal-External Control and Persistence: Validation and Implications of the Stanford Preschool Internal-External Scale." *Journal of Personality and Social Psychology* 29: 265–278.

Mollenkopf, Wm. G., and Melville, S.D. 1956. *A Study of Secondary School Characteristics as Related to Test Scores.* Research Bulletin RB–56–6. Princeton: Educational Testing Service.

Mood, A. 1972. Foreward. *A Study of Our Nation's Schools,* edited by G.W. Mayeske et al., pp. iii–v. Washington, D.C.: U.S. Department of Health, Education, and Welfare, Office of Education, DHEW OE–72–142.

Murnane, R.J. 1975. *The Impact of School Resources on the Learning of Inner City Children.* Cambridge, Mass.: Ballinger Publishing Company.

National Education Association. 1968. *Ability Grouping.* Washington, D.C.: NEA Research Division, Research Summary 1968–53.

National Education Association. 1965. *Elementary School Classroom Organization.* Washington, D.C.: NEA Research Division, Research Memo 1965–23.

Nelson, C.R. 1973. *Applied Time Series Analysis.* San Francisco: Holden-Day.

New York State Department of Education, Bureau of School Program Evaluation. 1975. *Identifying Expenditure Variables Which Relate to Student Performance at the District Level.* Albany.

_____. 1975. *Personal and Professional Teacher Characteristics and Student Achievement in New York State.* Albany.

_____. 1975. *The Relationship Between Per Cent of Certified Teachers and Student Achievement in New York School Districts.* Albany.

_____. 1975. *Teacher Salaries and Student Achievement in New York State.* Albany.

_____. 1974. *Accounting for the Urban Factor: Inclusion of 31 New York City School Districts in 1974 Performance Indicators in Education Report.* Albany.

_____. 1974. *District Wealth and Student Achievement: Does a Relationship Exist?* Albany.

_____. 1974. *Does Attendance Rate Make a Difference on Reading and Arithmetic Achievement?* Albany.

_____. 1974. *Does Student Mobility Affect School District Results on Reading and Math Achievement?* Albany.

_____. 1974. *Performance Indicators in Education: Manual for Interpreting Local District Results for the School Years 1971–72 and 1972–73.* Albany.

_____. 1972. *Performance Indicators in Education, Local District Results—1972.* Albany.

Ostrom, C.W., Jr. 1978. *Time Series Analysis: Regression Techniques.* Beverly Hills, Calif.: Sage Publications.

Pearson, K. 1904. "On the Laws on Inheritance in Man, II: On the Inheritance of the Mental and Moral Characters in Man: Its Comparison with the Inheritance of Physical Characters." *Biometrika* 3: 131–160.

Pedhazur, E.J. 1975. "Analytic Methods in Studies of Educational Effects. In *Review of Research in Education, Vol. 3,* edited by F.N. Kerlinger, pp. 243–286. Itasca, Ill.: R.E. Peacock Publishers.

Perl, L.J. 1973. "Family Background, Secondary School Expenditure, and Student Ability." *Journal of Human Resources* 8: 156–180.

Perrone, V. 1977. *The Abuses of Standardized Testing.* Bloomington, Ind.: Phi Delta Kappa Educational Foundation.

Pettigrew, T.F., and Green, R.L. 1976. "School Desegregation in Large Cities: A Critique of the Coleman 'White Flight' Thesis." *Harvard Educational Review* 46: 1–53.

Phares, E.J. 1957. "Expectancy Shifts in Skill and Chance Situations." *Journal of Abnormal and Social Psychology* 54: 339–342.

Piaget, J. 1970. "Piaget Theory." In *Carmichael's Manual of Child Psychology,* edited by P.H. Mussen. New York: John Wiley.

Piaget, J., and Inhelder, B. 1969. *The Psychology of The Child.* New York: Basic Books.

Pincus, J. 1977. "The Serrano Case: Policy for Education or for Public Finance." *Phi Delta Kappa* 59: 173–179.

Reid, D.W., and Ware, E.E. 1973. "Two-dimensions of Internal-External Locus of Control: Their Differential Validity and Importance for a Multidimensional Interpretation of I-E." Paper presented at the meeting of the American Psychological Association, Montreal, August.

Riecken, H.W., and Boruch, R.F., eds. 1974. *Social Experimentation: A Method for Planning and Evaluating Social Interventions.* New York: Academic Press.

Riew, John. 1966. "Economies of Scale in High School Operations." *Review of Economics and Statistics* 48: 280–287.

Rokeach, M. 1973. *The Nature of Human Values.* New York: Free Press.

Rosenthal, R., and Jacobson, L. 1968. *Pygmalion in the Classroom.* New York: Holt, Reinhart, and Winston.

Rotter, J.B. 1966. "Generalized Expectancies for Internal vs. External Control of Reinforcements." *Psychological Monographs* 80, Whole No. 609.

Rotter, J.B., and Mulray, R.C. 1965. "Internal versus External Control of Reinforcements and Decision Time." *Journal of Personality and Social Psychology* 2: 598–604.

Russell, G.W., Bullock, J.L., and Corenblum, B.S. 1977. "Personality Correlates of Concrete and Symbolic Precautionary Behaviours." *International Review of Applied Psychology* 26: 51–58.

Rudman, H.C. 1977. "The Standardized Test Flap." *Phi Delta Kappa* 59: 179–185.

Scott, J.P. 1967. "The Development of Social Motivation." In the *Nebraska Symposium on Motivation, 1967,* edited by D. Levine, pp. 11–132. Lincoln: University of Nebraska Press.

Scott, J.P. 1963. "The Process of Primary Socialization in Canine and Human Infants." *Monographs of the Society for Research on Child Development* 28: 1–47.

Seeman, M. 1972. "Alienation and Knowledge-Seeking: A Note on Attitude and Action. *Social Problems* 20: 3–17.

Shavelson, R.J., Hubner, J.J., and Stanton, G.C. 1976. "Self-Concept: Validation of Construct Interpretations." *Reivew of Educational Research* 46: 407–441.

Shaw, R.L., and Uhl, N.P. 1969. "Relationship between Locus of Control Scores and Reading Achievement of Black and White Second Grade Children from Two Socioeconomic Levels." Paper presented at the meetings of the Southeastern Psychological Association Convention, New Orleans.

Simmons, J. and Alexander, L. 1975. "The Determinants of School Achievement in Developing Countries: A Review of the Research." Paper presented at the annual meeting of the American Educational Research Association, Washington, D.C., April.

Smith, M.S. 1972. "Equality of Educational Opportunity: The Basic Findings Reconsidered." In *On Equality of Educational Opportunity,* edited by F. Mosteller and D.P. Moynihan. New York: Vintage Books.

Strickland, B.R. 1972. "Delay of Gratification as a Function of Race of the Experimenter." *Journal of Personality and Social Psychology* 22: 108–112.

Strodtbeck, F.L. 1958. "Family Interaction, Values and Achievement." In *Talent and Society,* edited by D.C. McClelland, pp. 135–194. New York: Van Nostrand.

Sudman, S. 1976. *Applied Sampling.* New York: Academic Press.

Suits, D.B. 1957. "Use of Dummy Variables in Regression Equations." *Journal of the American Statistical Association* 52: 548–551.

Summers, A.A., and Wolfe, B.L. 1977. "Do Schools Make a Difference?" *American Economic Review* 67: 639–652.

Summers, A.A., and Wolfe, B.L. 1974. "Equality of Educational Opportunity Quantified: A Production Function Approach." Paper presented at the meetings of the Econometric Society, San Francisco, Calif., December.

Terman, L.M. 1916. *Measurement of Intelligence: An Explanation of and a Complete Guide for the Use of the Stanford Revision and Extension of the Binet-Simon Intelligence Scale.* Boston: Houghton Mifflin.

Thorndike, R.L. 1968. "Review of Pygmalion in the Classroom." *American Educational Research Journal* 5: 708–711.

Thorndike, R.L., and Hagen, E.P. 1977. *Measurement and Evaluation in Psychology and Education, 4th ed.* New York: John Wiley.

Treiman, D.J. 1977. *Occupational Prestige in Comparative Perspective.* New York: Academic Press.

UCLA Center for the Study of Evaluation. 1972. *Test Evaluations: Tests of Higher-Order Cognitive, Affective, and Interpersonal Skills.* Los Angeles: CSE–RBS.

White, R.W. 1960. "Competence and the Psychosexual Stages of Development." In the *Nebraska Symposium on Motivation*, edited by M.R. Jones, pp. 97–141. Lincoln: University of Nebraska Press.

Wiley, D.E. 1976. "Another Hour, Another Day: Quantity of Schooling, a Potent Path for Policy." In *Schooling and Achievement in American Society*, edited by W.H. Sewell, R.M. Hauser, and D.L. Featherman, eds. New York: Academic Press.

Wiley, D.E., and Harnischfeger, A. 1974. "Explosion of a Myth: Quantity of Schooling and Exposure to Instruction, Major Educational Vehicles." *Educational Researcher* 3: 7–12.

Winkler, D.R. 1975. "Educational Achievement and School Peer Group Composition." *Journal of Human Resources* 10: 189–205.

Wolf, R. 1977. *Achievement in America.* New York: Teachers College Press.

Wonnacott, R.S., and Wonnacott, T.H. 1970. *Econometrics.* New York: John Wiley.

Zytkoskee, A., Strickland, B.R., and Watson, J. 1971. "Delay of Gratification and Internal versus External Control among Adolescents of Low Socioeconomic Status." *Developmental Psychology* 4: 93–98.

Index

Ability, of students, 47, 202, 205, 288, 291
  and IQ tests, 46, 54-56
  and norm-referenced tests, 47, 49-50, 66
Ability composition, of peers, 227, 234
Abstract reasoning, 229, 251
Academic motivation, 174, 184-86, 203, 205-12
Achievement, 1-3, 6, 10, 163, 189, 191. *See also* Math achievement; Outputs; Verbal achievement
  vs. ability of students, 47, 202, 205, 288, 291
  and class size and teacher's verbal ability in school performance model, 94-97, 102-107, 111-20, 124-32, 134, 138-42
  in EEO study, 150-53, 161-80, 189-90
  and expenditure in school performance model, 73-74, 90-95, 109
  and expenditure per pupil, 10, 16, 20, 172-74, 179-80, 257-58, 262
  and family inputs, 151-53, 213-27, 288-89
  in IEA study, 162, 187-90
  and interactions between inputs, 16-18, 31, 288
  in Mayeske study, 153, 162, 180-86, 189-90
  and norm-referenced tests, 46-52
  with partial regression coefficients, 154-55

  and peer group inputs, 2, 6, 227-34
  and proxy variables, 27, 205
  and school inputs, 2, 6-7, 153, 256-82
  and student inputs, 202-13
  and substitution of inputs, 14, 25-26, 31
  and teacher inputs, 6, 235-56
  with 2SLS technique, 157-60
Achievement in America, 162, 187
Achievement test scores, 3, 6-7, 10, 146, 191, 201-202. *See also* Outputs
  and EEO study, 12, 163, 172
  vs. IQ tests, 11, 52, 54-57, 66-67
  problems with, 46-52
  and tracking, 260
Administration, 1, 3, 262-65
Affective outcomes, 5, 10, 15, 33, 59-67, 212, 289
  vs. cognitive outcomes, 59-60, 67, 208-12, 287
  as input for achievement, 203 205-12
  and internal-external control expectancies, 15, 60-63, 67, 212
  in Mayeske study, 184-86
  and self-concept and self-esteem, 15, 63-64, 67, 212
  and state-trait problem, 65
Age, of physical plant, 257, 269-74
Age, of student, 3, 10, 205, 212, 217, 231-34, 235-39
  in EEO study, 167-69, 171-75, 179
  and I-E beliefs, 62

About the Authors

R. Gary Bridge is associate professor of psychology and
education at Teachers College, Columbia University, and
a resident consultant at the Rand Corporation. His degrees
include a B.A. in economics and an M.A. and Ph.D. in social psychology, all from the University of California, Los Angeles.

Charles M. Judd is an assistant professor in the Department of
Psychology and Social Relations at Harvard University. He has a B.A.
from Yale University, and an M.Div. from Union Theological Seminary; his M.A. and Ph.D. degrees in social psychology are from
Teachers College, Columbia University.

Peter R. Moock is associate professor of economics and education at Teachers College, Columbia University. He has a B.A. from
Williams College, a diploma in education from Makerere University
in Uganda, and a Ph.D. in economics and education from Teachers
College, Columbia University.

Dl.